PENGUIN SHAKESPEARE LIBRARY

PSL2

SHAKESPEARE'S COMEDIES

Laurence Lerner was born in 1925 of one Jewish and one English parent, in Cape Town, where he went to school and university, and also worked as an insurance clerk and later as a teacher. In 1947 he went to Pembroke College, Cambridge, and graduated again in 1949. Since then his vocation has been poetry, his profession teaching. He has taught in Ghana, Belfast, France, and America: and is at present at the University of Sussex. His nomadic temperament is now restrained by the existence of his four children, but fortunately he finds in their company ample compensation.

His book *Shakespeare's Tragedies* is available in Penguins as a companion volume. His first collection of poems, *Domestic Interior*, came out in 1959; the second, *The Directions of Memory*, in 1964. He has also published a novel about South Africa (*The Englishmen*) and two books of literary criticism: *The Truest Poetry*, an essay on the question What is Literature, and *The Truthtellers* (on Jane Austen, George Eliot and D. H. Lawrence).

SHAKESPEARE'S COMEDIES

An Anthology of Modern Criticism

EDITED BY
LAURENCE LERNER

*

PENGUIN BOOKS

Penguin Books Ltd, Harmondsworth, Middlesex, England
Penguin Books Inc., 3300 Clipper Mill Road, Baltimore 11, Md, U.S.A.
Penguin Books Australia Ltd, Ringwood, Victoria, Australia

—

First published 1967

—

This selection copyright © Laurence Lerner, 1967

—

Made and printed in Great Britain
by Cox & Wyman Ltd, London, Fakenham and Reading
Set in Monotype Fournier

CONTENTS

CONTENTS

CONTENTS

ON COMEDY: AND ON SHAKESPEARIAN COMEDY

ACKNOWLEDGEMENTS

THANKS are due to the following for permission to reprint the contents of this anthology:

Mrs G. R. Elliott and the University of Toronto Press, for 'Weirdness in *The Comedy of Errors*' by G. R. Elliott.

Francis Fergusson, Esq., for 'Two Comedies (*The Comedy of Errors* and *Much Ado*)'.

Chatto & Windus Ltd, for the extracts from *Shakespeare and the Idea of the Play* by Anne Righter; and for the extract from *Seven Types of Ambiguity* by William Empson.

The Society of Authors, for the discussion of *The Taming of the Shrew* by George Bernard Shaw.

Holt, Rinehart & Winston, Inc., for '*The Taming of the Shrew*' from *Shakespeare* by Mark Van Doren.

Mrs T. C. Kemp, for the discussion of the staging of *The Taming of the Shrew* by T. C. Kemp.

Field Roscoe & Co., and Princeton University Press, for the extract from Harley Granville-Barker's Preface to *Love's Labour's Lost*.

MacGibbon & Kee Ltd, for the extract from *Shakespeare and the Popular Dramatic Tradition* by S. L. Bethell.

Alfred A. Knopf, Inc., for 'Navarre and His Bookmen' from *The Hyacinth Room: An Investigation into the Nature of Comedy, Tragedy and Tragicomedy* by Cyrus Hoy.

Ernest Benn Ltd, and Curtis Brown Ltd, for the extract from *Shakespeare's Workmanship* by Sir Arthur Quiller-Couch.

Cambridge University Press, for the extract from *The Court Masque* by Enid Welsford.

The Johns Hopkins Press, for '*A Midsummer Night's Dream* and the Meaning of Court Marriage' by Paul A. Olson, and for the extract from '*The Merchant of Venice*: The Gentle Bond' by Sigurd Burckhardt.

Ernest Benn Ltd, Sigmund Freud Copyrights Ltd, Mr James Strachey and The Hogarth Press Ltd, for the extract from *Introductory Lectures on Psycho-Analysis* (Volume XV of the Standard Edition of the Complete Psychological Works of Sigmund Freud).

Mrs J. Middleton Murry, for 'Money and *The Merchant*' by Max Plowman.

Macmillan & Co. Ltd, St Martin's Press, Inc., and The Macmillan Company of Canada, for the extract from *Comic Characters of Shakespeare* by John Palmer.

Faber & Faber Ltd, and Random House, Inc., for the extract from 'Brothers and Others' and the extract from 'Music in Shakespeare', both by W. H. Auden.

ACKNOWLEDGEMENTS

Michael MacLiammóir, Esq., for his discussion of the staging of *The Merchant of Venice*.

J. R. Brown, Esq., for his discussion of the staging of *The Merchant of Venice*.

Longmans Green & Co. Ltd, and Theatre Arts Books, for the extract from *Angel With Horns* by A. P. Rossiter.

The Clarendon Press, for the chapter from *Shakespeare's Comedies* by Bertrand Evans.

Elek Books Ltd, for the extract from *A Play Tonight* by J. C. Trewin.

Princeton University Press, for the extract from *Shakespeare's Festive Comedy* by C. L. Barber.

Longmans Green & Co. Ltd, for Helen Gardner's essay on *As You Like It* from *More Talking of Shakespeare*.

Jonathan Cape Ltd, and the executors of the J. M. Murry Estate, for the extract from *Shakespeare* by J. Middleton Murry.

The Bodley Head, for the passage by L. A. G. Strong from *Talking of Shakespeare*.

Tulane Drama Review, for the extract from 'Directions for *Twelfth Night*, or What You Will' by J. R. Brown.

Columbia University Press, for 'The Argument of Comedy' by Northrop Frye.

The Beacon Press, for the extract from *Fiction and the Unconscious* by Simon O. Lesser.

Methuen & Co. Ltd, for the extract from *Shakespearian Comedy* by H. B. Charlton.

INTRODUCTION

FOR better or worse, it is impossible to stop the flood of Shakespeare criticism. 'For worse', some will say, contemplating the squat bound volumes of *Shakespeare Survey*, *Shakespeare Quarterly*, *Shakespeare Jahrbuch*, the books, the editions, the scattered articles that stream from the press almost as thickly in 1966 as they did in the jubilee year 1964. Of course there is too much Shakespeare criticism: but then in a world of three thousand million people there is too much of everything. If we feel bad because the world is so full, there is no need to project our feelings on to one harmless human activity. To be sure, most criticism is indifferent and much of it is bad, just as most poetry is indifferent and most people are ordinary. This does not prevent poems and people being the most precious things on earth.

Shakespeare criticism is not as valuable as poems or people, but it is useful and inevitable: inevitable because as two spectators come out of a play they will talk about it; and if they have seen other plays and reflected on drama, their talk will be better informed, more penetrating and more valuable. When such talk is written down it becomes criticism. There is something to be said for muzzling – well, not muzzling but muffling – such discussion, for reminding ourselves that the most precious response to a masterpiece is silence. But after we have been silent for a while we shall talk again, and talk all the better for it. And when we do talk, we want to do so as well as we can, and listen to others who talk better.

This is the justification for this book. It is for the theatregoer, the student, the poetry lover, the casual reader -- for anyone who sees or reads a Shakespeare play, who is silent and reflects for a while, and then wants to talk about it or hear what others have to say. He cannot work his way through the *Shakespeare Jahrbuch*, *Shakespeare Quarterly*, *Shakespeare's Imagery*, *Shakespeare's Bawdy*, *Shakespeare's Pronunciation* to see if they have anything to say to him. No one can work his way through them all, but I have done my best: I have looked through all the critics I admire, and many that I don't, to find if they have anything useful to say about the comedies.

As with the tragedies, I have looked for essays that illuminate particular plays. The aim of this book is primarily to enrich the reader's experience of the nine comedies that it deals with. But to understand the particular is necessarily to set it against the general, by comparing it with other plays, or finding in it a principle of organization. There are many such comparisons and principles, and which one the critic favours will depend on his conception of what a play is. Thus Bertrand Evans and Granville-Barker see a Shakespeare comedy mainly as an example of technical skill, controlling the reactions of the audience, producing the response desired by the craftsman-author. Freud and Empson see it as an expression of the author's own desires and conflicts or – these are hard to keep apart – his knowledge that people have such conflicts. Enid Welsford and Helen Gardner are concerned largely with dramatic tradition, and see the play as a supreme example of a long series – or, in the case of *A Midsummer Night's Dream* and the masque – as replacements of the tradition by something finer. Paul A. Olson also writes about tradition, this time non-dramatic: he sees Shakespeare as putting into drama certain Renaissance ideas on love and marriage, and his essay takes to an extreme the view of Shakespeare as intellectual and even learned. The other extreme is perhaps found in Shaw, who turns into modern form the old view of Shakespeare wanting art – warbling his native woodnotes with no sophistication and only intermittent skill. C. L. Barber and Northrop Frye are concerned with drama as it answers a larger social need, and examine the comedies in terms of their emotional patterns of release and responsibility. This seems to me the most exciting approach to Shakespeare's comedies that we now have, and Barber's book the best that has ever been written on the subject.

None of these critics, however profound, however illuminating, has found the one right way to discuss Shakespeare. A play is a complex thing; it can express its author's neurosis, and also entertain; embody a carefully planned allegory, and also give the feel of human behaviour; follow tradition, and speak with a personal voice. The only just view of what a play is must be a pluralist view; an anthology like this one is a statement of belief in pluralism; and the preface is no doubt the place to point this out. Yet it need not distress us that so many critics – and so many of the best critics – have been monists. A touch of monomania can light up a literary experience; and perhaps only the most drearily systematic of critics will constantly remember the other ways he could be talking about what he so vividly and assertively feels. A limited view of what a play is seems a small price to pay for retaining the feel of its original impression among your opinions.

When *Shakespeare's Tragedies* appeared, it received more attention from reviewers than I had expected. This is always a mixed pleasure for the anthologist: delighted that the book is noticed, he reflects humbly that its success is due to others, not himself. I read the reviews eagerly, hoping that the second volume would be able to profit from their suggestions, but the profit has been small: they contradicted one another with uncanny thoroughness. Two useful criticisms did, however, emerge. The first was that I had included too much that was readily available, and not rescued enough good essays from inaccessible journals, or books now out of print. I feel sympathetic to this view, but I have had to decide not to act on it. In the first place, a good anthology should have an inner, not an outer, *raison d'être*: choosing the best, and then modifying one's choice so that the pieces should complement one another, is difficult enough, without introducing another, purely external, criterion. And furthermore, so much is widely available, and (since publishers are not fools) so much of the best, that to follow this rule strictly would have led to including the over-learned, the precious and the otherwise second-rate. So though I have done a little disinterring (usually of short pieces) I have not hesitated to draw freely on the best-known critics.

The second criticism was that I had neglected the theatre, and this one too I have pondered at length. I do believe that

Shakespeare's plays are really plays, and take on their best life in performance: I have produced a few, and I go to see them constantly. But it was hard to know how to act on this belief. To see the plays is invaluable; how great is the value of talking about seeing them? There are two main kinds of theatre-centred criticism. There are the attempts by scholars to write about the great actors of the past: these are often fascinating, but I have never found that they tell us anything about Shakespeare. There is even something ghostly about a discussion of the acting of Garrick or Kean or Booth, dead before the critic ever went to a theatre. Then there are press notices of plays: but are these not too ineluctably fixed in the here and now – or rather the there and then? Do we care what Miss Spinks was like as Hermia, or Mr Binks as Theseus, in a performance we barely remember or never saw? In the end, I have compromised, and introduced just one or two such notices (they take up very little space, after all). Once in a while, you can find a critic who uses a performance to say something interesting about the play; this is especially true of the annual contributions to *Shakespeare Survey*, written by the very literate, and not written hot for the press. I have trimmed all these notices to leave out as much as possible of the merely topical. I have also trimmed the learned articles by removing footnotes: those which contain points of substance have been incorporated into the text, others have been dropped.

Nine plays are treated in this volume, which excludes the last plays and the so-called problem comedies. There is no elaborate theory of Shakespearian comedy behind this decision, merely the wish to have plenty of space, and so represent a range of opinions on all the important plays. The omitted comedies are being saved for a later volume, as are the histories and poems.

A few of the articles have been abridged, and I will say outright what I hope is obvious, that such abridging does not imply any opinion of mine that the author has been long-winded. I hope that any reader whose interest is caught will turn up the full article, or the book it is taken from, or other works by the same critic: anthologies should invite, not discourage, further reading.

Though, of course, the further reading that really matters is to look again at the plays themselves. The best criticism should always die slightly when it has been read – die into the work it was criticizing.

1966   LAURENCE LERNER

THE COMEDY OF ERRORS

ONE

Weirdness in *The Comedy of Errors*

THE 'The' in the title of this play may be taken in a generic sense –
that is, as the author's characteristically modest intimation that he
has provided merely one more species of a well-recognized genus.
'Here,' says he, 'are the Twins of Plautus again; here is the age-old
comedy of resemblances.' But time has made the 'The' distinctive:
here is indeed *the* comedy of errors. It is hard to see how the hoary
sport of mistaken identities could be better worked up as the central
theme of a drama.

I think the underlying reason for its success is the fact that
Shakespeare was thoroughly penetrated by the comic horror, so to
call it, implicit in the subject. Real horror attaches to the notion of
the *complete* identity of two human beings; as in Poe's ghastly tale
of a girl who turned out to be the re-embodiment of the mother
who died in giving birth to her; and as in certain ancient legends of
various lands, notably China. All normal persons (and especially
Shakespeare) set so much store by human individuality that they
shrink from the thought of its being submerged. And since the
amusing, when intense, is nigh to the serious, there is something
shuddery in the close resemblance of persons just when this appears
to us intensely entertaining. I recall a school-teacher many years ago
who found in her class at the beginning of the term two little girls
who were remarkably, even weirdly, 'identical' twins; the very
freckles on their noses seemed to correspond; and of course their
proud mother attired them precisely alike. At the end of the first
week the teacher exclaimed to us all with comic horror: 'These two
are the same – how can I tell them apart?' After a moment of dead
silence a small boy (not I) piped out, 'Mary's temper's better'n
Martha's.' The general laughter which ensued had in it a note of
relief that was not exclusively comic. And *The Comedy of Errors*
has a note of real weirdness just when its mirth is keenest.

Another and related feature of this play that has also, I think, not been sufficiently appreciated is its structural excellence. Critics have regarded the piece as uninspired because of its comparatively conventional style. But whole form, no less than style, may be the vehicle of inspiration. And the intensity with which Shakespeare gave himself here to the limited but uncanny fun of twinship impelled him to weave his strands into a very close and telling pattern; which, moreover, is often subserved, as I shall point out in a striking instance below, by the very conventionality of the style. I think that in sheer composition this drama surpasses most of his early works and some of his mature ones. It testifies that this poet, who was later to achieve the most expressive of styles, set his heart at the outset upon achieving wholeness of form. How much he was *directly* influenced in this matter by the Latin classics (not to speak of the Greek) cannot be known and is not very important. His friend to be, Ben Jonson, who was notoriously more intimate with those classics than he, was capable in maturity of producing such a work as *Bartholomew Fair*, rich in humour and humanity but hopelessly flimsy in architecture; no doubt it made Plautus turn in his grave. Compared with it *The Comedy of Errors*, by a young and 'non-classical' writer, is a beautifully carved gem.

Perhaps it was written, as Professor Adams supposes, during or just after a schoolmastering interval before Shakespeare's migration to London. But in this case how did he attain the warm grasp of theatric art that appears in the play? Maybe his histrionic activity began in early years in the country; a discovery of new but dubious evidence pointing in this direction has recently been announced. Maybe, as Professor Adams and others maintain, he rewrote the play after he had attained a mastery of theatric art in London. In any case it is clear that the budding dramatist, more or less influenced by the ancient classical sense of form, was reacting from the slipshod construction of contemporary romantic comedy. And indeed if he had not early been sharply critical of that mode at its lowest – that 'most lamentable comedy', in Quince's phrase – he could not have learned how to carry it to its height, as in *Twelfth Night* and *As You Like It*. In this later period he vented through the mouth of Polonius a feeling which must have been at work in him all along, a kindly but critical sense of the amazing variety and confusion of forms in contemporary drama. He desired for his own work the variety without the confusion. From the first he aimed at the sort of drama so tellingly described by Hamlet soon after Polonius's outburst: 'an excellent play, well digested in the scenes, set down with as much modesty as cunning'. Accordingly in his first play (as I take the one under discussion to be) he preferred the 'scene individable', the unity of place, to the 'poem unlimited'; he followed the 'law of writ' rather than 'the liberty'.

> Why, headstrong liberty is lashed with woe.
> There's nothing situate under heaven's eye
> But hath his bound, in earth, in sea, in sky. . . .
> *The Comedy of Errors*, II. I. 15

This thought, uttered by the gentle Luciana, is reiterated in Shakespeare's subsequent works. Of course it expresses the ancient doctrine of temperance which the writers of the Renaissance so much admired – often only verbally, but deeply at their best. Hamlet's praise of temperance to the Players and then to Horatio (III. 2. 1–74) voices Shakespeare's very real love of it in art and in personality. For him well-temperedness, as it may better be termed, was a quality both moral and artistic. His writings and the records of his character, taken together, show this quality preponderant in him as man and as author. Often enough his work is poorly tempered, ill shaped. But one sees him continually striving for excellence of form even more than for variety of form. Thus it was natural for him in his earliest comedy to have recourse to the aid of unity of time and place.

Obviously he was free from the pedantic notion that this device is an essential principle of drama. But he saw that the outward sort of unity, observed strictly or approximately, could be an aid to inward form. And he saw that a strict observance of it was demanded by the material and mood of *The Comedy of Errors*. Therefore he confined the action to a single day in a single city, Ephesus, summarizing the antecedent events in Aegeon's narrative in the first scene. No doubt a skipping series of scenes displaying some of those adventures on the stage would have pleased the average audience of the time. But that display would not have fitted the whole emotional pattern at which the author, consciously or not, was aiming and which may be described as follows. An initial mood of swift and strange, almost weird, romance is saturated, as the play proceeds, with fun that is swift, strange, weird. Thus the romance and the fun are congruent. And they are humanized by pathos at the first and last, and, in the central phase of the action, by touches of high comedy (comedy of character) involving pathos.

Such is the ideal mood-and-mode, so to speak, of this drama. It was fulfilled to a remarkable extent by the dramatist, but, of course, not perfectly. The opening scene is too heavy – especially when its long speeches are not rendered by the actors 'trippingly on the tongue'. Aegeon's sorrowfulness is immense. The dramatist hints, unconvincingly, that it is not merely the fruit of circumstance: it is constitutional. The old man tells us that he 'would gladly have embraced' death (line 69) on a certain occasion when he was still young, rich, and blessed with a happy household! We don't see why; but we see that this stroke is intended to intensify his air of sadness. To be sure that air is convincing and satisfying in such verses as the following (lines 132 ff.):

> Five summers have I spent in furthest Greece,
> Roaming clean through the bounds of Asia,
> And, coasting homeward, came to Ephesus,
> Hopeless to find – yet loath to leave unsought
> Or that or any place that harbours men.

This has the very rhythm and movement of seeking, yearning love; in contrast with the 'hopeless and helpless' rhetoric of the closing lines of the scene:

> Hopeless and helpless doth Aegeon wend,
> But to procrastinate his lifeless end.

On the whole, his story takes hold of us. His emotion helps to float the strange episode of the mast that served as a 'helpful ship' (line 103) to save the lives of six, and then to divide them nicely into the two triads required by the plot. But the author fails to bring out unmistakably the sole aspect of the tale that could render it fully plausible, namely its weirdness or uncanniness. Certainly this note is present, but not explicitly enough. In other words, the opening scene, from the standpoint of the play's whole mood, is not well tempered. Relatively too much stress is placed on the pathos of the romance, and too little on its weirdness. This error is not made in the final scene of the play. There the pathetic joy of the recognition and reunion of the members of Aegeon's household is skilfully intermixed with the characteristic comedy of this drama. But though the last scene of a play is important, the first scene is more so. And it is clear that in the present instance, as not in any later comedy, Shakespeare yielded to the temptation of capturing his audience at the outset by means of a heavy dose of heart-appeal.

The second scene, however, is finely turned: it provides exactly the right transition from the initial scene to the main body of the piece. The old despairing Aegeon is immediately succeeded by a young man who demeans himself very gravely. We are artfully informed at once that he too hails from Syracuse. His name, Antipholus, is here withheld from mention on the stage; but in good time we learn that he is in search of 'a mother and a brother' (line 39) and we recall his father's reference to him towards the end of the preceding scene (lines 124 ff.). The fine point, however, is that his very air is felt to be *fathered* by Aegeon's, though quite different. The old man's voluble gloom gives place to the son's sober sadness. And this 'humour' (mood) is susceptible of lightening. Antipholus, smiling slightly (not laughing, I think), at his Dromio's joke, remarks that the latter is

> A trusty villain, sir, that very oft,
> When I am dull with care and melancholy,
> Lightens my humour with his merry jests.

Thus the mood of the play is modulated in the direction of mirth; and the way is actively opened by Antipholus's determination to relieve his lonely sorrow by wandering up and down in this foreign city, viewing its sights. Note the comic irony of his 'I will go lose myself' (line 30), repeated (line 40) just as Dromio of Ephesus enters to take him for his brother. Superb is the sudden but carefully prepared plunge, here, into the comedy of errors. The fact that Antipholus is 'not in a sportive mood' is, of course, the soul of the sport. Incidentally the new Dromio is seen by the audience to be brother in soul, even more than in body, to his jestful twin. The closing speech of the scene and act is notable. Antipholus soliloquizes:

> Upon my life, by some device or other
> The villain is o'er-raught of all my money.
> They say this town is full of cozenage;
> As, nimble jugglers that deceive the eye,
> Dark-working sorcerers that change the mind,
> Soul-killing witches that deform the body,
> Disguised cheaters, prating mountebanks,
> And many such-like liberties of sin. . . .

This sounds the note of weirdness; which, however, is not fully brought out till the close of the second act.

Meanwhile (II. 1) high comedy, centred in Adriana, comes upon the scene. From now on, it gleams through the pattern of the play like a thin gold thread, appearing and disappearing. It is closely intertwined with the dominant comedy of action. We cannot imagine Rosalind or Beatrice exclaiming to a servant, 'Back, slave, or I will break thy pate across'. But it is quite natural for their forerunner, Adriana, to speak thus to Dromio of Ephesus (line 78). Her sister Luciana's rebuke of her – 'Fie, how impatience loureth in your face!' – is histrionically revealing; such was the look that Shakespeare intended the boy-actor who 'created' this part to employ continually. That look goes along with conduct, potentially at least, violent. And certainly the heroine of this drama has her full share in its mad doings. Yet louring impatience is merely on the surface of her; deep beneath is a devoted, yearning love for her husband. And the conflict of those two emotions in her is high-comic.

There is pathos, too, in her case, but the dramatist carefully subordinates it. When her sister urges her to be patient with her careless husband, Adriana exclaims (II. 1. 34 ff.):

> A wretched soul, bruised with adversity,
> We bid be silent when we hear it cry;
> But were we burdened with like weight of pain,
> As much, or more, we would ourselves complain. . . .

True enough. But our sympathy with the speaker is overtopped by amusement at her mood of angry exaggeration. She is far from being a 'wretched soul bruised with adversity'. Her only real woe, here, is that her husband is very late for dinner. To be sure, she hints that he may be with another woman (line 30). But this suspicion, entirely unfounded so far as the audience knows, is very faint and transient. All the more comical, therefore, is her great blaze of jealousy (lines 87 ff.) when the strange demeanour of Antipholus of Syracuse, mistaken for her husband, has been reported to her. At this juncture the device of mistaken identity is superbly used for comedy of character. Antipholus of Syracuse, unlike his jaunty brother, is gravely moral. When finally he enters Adriana's presence and she regards him as Antipholus of Ephesus, he is exactly the man to 'look strange and frown' (II. 2. 119). No wonder his bearing turns Adriana's suspicion into a settled conviction. But now comes the finest stroke of all. Confronted with real trouble, with a real evil, as she believes, in her husband's life, her better nature comes to the fore. She drops her initial notion (II. 1. 10) that her own way of life should, by rights, be as free as her husband's. She maintains indeed that there should be (in modern parlance) a single standard for both sexes but she urges passionately that it should be pure and high (II. 2. 133):

> Ah! do not tear thyself away from me,
> For know, my love, as easy mayst thou fall
> A drop of water in the breaking gulf
> And take unmingled thence that drop again,
> Without addition or diminishing,
> As take from me thyself and not me too.
> How dearly would it touch thee to the quick
> Shouldst thou but hear I were licentious
> And that this body, consecrate to thee,
> By ruffian lust should be contaminate! . . .
> I *am* possessed with an adulterate blot;

> My blood is mingled with the crime of lust:
> For if we two be one and thou play false
> I do digest the poison of thy flesh,
> Being strumpeted by thy contagion. . . .

How direct and powerful is the style here over against the neat, conventional rhetoric of the preceding quotation! This is one of many instances in the course of the play where Shakespeare's good luck or good revision, or both, enables him to sharpen the style in accordance with the emotion. Here the pathos, by itself, would be too keen for comedy. But it is checked for us, even as Adriana speaks, by the amazed looks of her two Syracusan listeners, wondering what it is all about; and it is submerged by the mirth, madder than ever, that ensues; to which I shall return presently.

In the next scene (III. 1) the audience is kept outdoors with Antipholus of Ephesus to watch his obtrusive cheeriness give place to rage, which in turn yields to merry vengefulness, while his double dines with his wife inside. Thus the love and pathos of Adriana are literally kept *within door* at the crucial stage of the plot. Instead we are allowed to witness (III. 2) the slighter episode, couched in conventional rhymed verse, of the Syracusan Antipholus's love for Luciana. And just when that highly moral man has attempted to seize the hand of the gentle girl who believes him to be her sister's husband, Dromio of Syracuse dashes in, escaping the embraces of the spherical Nell: 'Marry, sir, she's the kitchen-wench and all grease; and I know not what use to put her to but to make a lamp of her and run from her by her own light. . . .' This sudden explosion of fun from below stairs is a superb burlesque of the goings-on of the principal personages. Nell's mistaking the foreign Dromio for his brother at the end of the third act is the sequel of her mistress Adriana's similar error at the end of the second act. But the parallelism is not forced and obvious, as it so often is in Shakespeare's early work. The two episodes are at once vitally related and vitally different: they are at opposite poles in method and tone. Hence they beautifully complement each other.

More significantly, in each case the hyperbolical tone rises to eeriness. In the close of Act II, Dromio of Syracuse, dazed by the staid Luciana's seconding of her tense sister in taking him and his master for two other persons, cries out (II. 2. 197 ff.):

> Oh for my beads! I cross me for a sinner.
> This is the fairy land; oh, spite of spites,
> We talk with goblins, owls, and elvish sprites!
> If we obey them not, this will ensue,
> They'll suck our breath or pinch us black and blue.

He and his Antipholus are overcome by a dreamlike sense of transformation, romantic in the master, grotesque ("Tis so, I am an ass . . .') in the man. This 'complex' occurs again in the finale of Act III, but with overwhelming emphasis on the weird grotesquerie of the situation. Here the mounting hyperbole of Dromio's account of Nell renders dramatically plausible even the premiss that both he and his twin had a similar mark on the shoulder, a mole in the neck, and a great wart on the left arm! These twins are so 'identical' that they approach identity. And the vast wench's vast powers of divination cause Dromio, astounded, to run from her 'as a witch', in fear of being transformed by her into a bobtail dog at work in the treadmill of her turnspit (III. 2. 151 ff.). Significantly Shakespeare refrains from bringing Nell on to the stage in person. The temptation to do so must have been great; the scene would have rejoiced the hearts of ninety per cent of his audience. But he sacrificed the physical fun of that scene to what we may call the metaphysical fun of Dromio's inspired narrative, culminating in his bizarre picture of the globular wench as a witch. Moreover, Nell's absence from the scene enables the audience to concentrate upon the all-important effect that the tale has on Dromio's master.

'There's none but witches do inhabit here', Antipholus concludes (III. 2. 168). The artfully general and vague premonition that Shakespeare made him utter in the final speech of Act I, quoted earlier, wherein he mentioned 'sorcerers' and 'witches' among other kinds of cozeners, has been fulfilled with a vengeance. Dromio's story of Nell is the last straw for Antipholus. The fun of the thing impresses this earnest gentleman far less than its weirdness. If the wench who claims his man for her betrothed is a sorceress, all the more so is 'She that doth call me husband'; and he abhors

Adriana 'for a wife' as utterly as Dromio does Nell, though on higher grounds. These comparisons between his own and Dromio's case are not stated explicitly; Shakespeare's art is here too fine for that; but they are clearly implied in his speech. And the climactic implication is that even the sensible and normal Luciana is infected by the prevalent atmosphere of sorcery in which she lives. She,

> Possessed with such a gentle sovereign grace,
> Of such *enchanting* presence and discourse,
> Hath almost made me traitor to myself. . . .

The last line recalls the comic irony of his desire to lose himself, at the first, in this strange city (I. 2. 30, 40). And the word that I have italicized in the second line is deliciously ambiguous. By way of developing the equivoque we may say that the *bewitching* Luciana, as Antipholus now sees the matter in retrospect, put him almost *beside himself.* The more he made love to her, the more she insisted he was not himself; he was another man, well known to her, her brother-in-law unfortunately, making immoral advances to her. And he, so the implication runs, had been almost ready to lose his own identity if only thus he could win her interest. But now, 'lest myself be guilty of self-wrong', he is determined to fly from the girl who a little while ago feared and fled from him; she is doubly an enchantress: 'I'll stop my ears against the mermaid's song'.

He must speedily get away from this city, which he had felt at the first to be 'full of cozenage' when it seemed that some 'cheater' had made away with 'all my money' (I. 2. 97 ff.). But now an event of exactly opposite nature occurs as he is hastily moving off. A cheerful and trustful citizen enters, hands him a fine gold chain, refuses present payment, and terms him, what he least is, 'a merry man, sir'. It takes a good actor to represent Antipholus's state of mind in this masterly finale of the third act. He is so stunned that at first he can only ask weakly, 'What is your will that I shall do with this?' In the upshot, despite his scrupulous nature, he retains the chain. Why? Because one feature of this illusive city is, apparently, the giving of 'such golden gifts' to strangers in the streets. Because, in short, Antipholus's mood, together with the mood of the play, has now become thoroughly fey.

That mood may be traced by the reader in many passages that cannot be treated here. It is worked up more and more during the course of the first three acts and dominates the remainder of the piece. In Act IV the arrest of Antipholus of Ephesus, prominent and wealthy citizen, for the supposed theft of the gold chain brings this personage fully into the atmosphere of enchantment. Hitherto he had moved only in the outskirts of it; his healthy gaiety kept him aloof. At the end of Act III, Scene 1, he had determined to meet his domestic complexities with level head and mirthful heart. But now the increasing complications are too much for him. Soon he is wearing 'pale and deadly looks' (IV. 4. 94), or at least something approximating thereto sufficiently for Pinch and others to imagine him insane. A similar look, we may assume, is on the face of Antipholus of Syracuse when he comes on at the close of this act with drawn sword, resolved finally to escape those whom he calls 'these witches'. Thus the two male principals cooperate, now, to intensify the note of bewitchment.

This note might easily have been overdone by Shakespeare. Of course he offsets the serious desperation of the two masters by the humorous desperation of the two servants, especially Dromio of Syracuse with his persistent nightmare of Nell: 'but for the mountain of mad flesh that claims marriage of me, I could find it in my heart to stay here still, and turn witch' (IV. 4. 155 ff.). A further offset to the two Antipholuses is needed, however, and it is provided by Pinch, the conjuring schoolmaster of 'saffron face' (IV. 4. 62). Later his complete appearance is given retrospectively by Antipholus of Ephesus (V. 1. 238 ff.):

> ... a hungry lean-faced villain,
> A mere anatomy, a mountebank,
> A threadbare juggler, and a fortune-teller,
> A needy, hollow-eyed, sharp-looking wretch,
> A living dead man. ...

In passing, notice that these words echo the tone-setting speech of Antipholus of Syracuse, at the end of the first act, upon jugglers, sorcerers, and so forth. Pinch is a tonal masterpiece. His pedantic gravity parodies and relieves the increasing angry seriousness of the two Antipholuses. But, above all, he bodies forth concretely the play's spirit of weird fun.

Adriana, again, contributes to that mood. Convinced that her husband has tried to make love to her sister, she vents her rage in a monstrous picturization of him (IV. 2. 19ff.).

> He is deformed, crooked, old and sere,
> Ill-faced, worse bodied, shapeless everywhere;
> Vicious, ungentle, foolish, blunt, unkind,
> Stigmatical in making, worse in mind.

Her wrathful, hyperbolic fancy is a better conjurer than Pinch. But the pathos and high comedy of her, though kept subordinate, come out in frequent touches. She closes the present episode with this simple cry: 'My heart prays for him, though my tongue do curse'. (The subjunctive 'do' is nicely suggestive.) Thus we are prepared for the effective dialogue of Adriana and the Abbess early in the last act. Religiously beguiled by the older woman into confessing her fault, Adriana hugely exaggerates her scoldings of her husband (v. 1. 62 ff.) and is rebuked by the Abbess, with proportional severity, as the sole cause of his supposed madness. She makes no reply – to the utter astonishment of her sister, who, reversing her customary role as critic of Adriana's impatience, has now to exclaim, 'Why bear you these rebukes and answer not?' The other says simply, 'She did betray me to my own reproof'. Her difficult silence is Adriana's self-imposed penance. Recalling her earlier line, quoted above, we may say that her heart is now praying so entirely for her husband that her tongue, so far from cursing, has no word even of proper self-defence.

That serious touch, together with the ensuing speech of the Second Merchant concerning 'the melancholy vale' (v. 1. 120), leads up to the re-entrance of the hapless and gloomy Aegeon. But, as remarked earlier, his pathos is not allowed anything like free rein here. He stands in the background during the long climax of the story of Antipholus of Ephesus. This episode opens with Adriana's line, 'A most outrageous fit of madness took him' (line 139), and terminates with the Duke's 'I think you are *all* mated or stark mad' (line 282, italics mine). The note of witchery is explicitly given by Adriana's fear that her husband 'is borne about invisible' (line 187) and the Duke's fancy that 'you all have drunk of Circe's cup' (line 271). Upon the close of this episode Aegeon is allowed the centre of the stage for fifty lines. The pathos of his appeal to him whom he takes to be 'my only son' is very moving, but, of course, it is checked by his mistaking Antipholus of Ephesus for him of Syracuse. Thus Aegeon is drawn into the atmosphere of illusion; so is even the stiff-backed Duke a little later (line 366). The tearful joys of the reunion of the old man's family are finely interwoven with enchanting mistakes (lines 322–416), and parodied at the close by the conference of the two Dromios. When Dromio of Syracuse declares to his new-found brother (italics mine):

> There is a fat *friend* at your master's house
> That kitchened me for you today at dinner:
> She now shall be my *sister*, *not* my wife . . .

the speaker's sense of relief is as vast as the girth of Nell. This speech brings us back towards everyday reality. Yet it reminds us, surely, of this Dromio's dread of Nell as a 'diviner' and a 'witch' (III. 2. 150 ff.). Thus at the close there is a faint, last flicker of the ray of weird light, romantic and comic, that plays upon *the* 'Comedy of Errors'.

'Weirdness in *The Comedy of Errors*' by G. R. Elliott, *University of Toronto Quarterly*, 1939

Two Comedies (*The Comedy of Errors* and *Much Ado*)

SHAKESPEARE'S comedy, both the plays called comedies and the comic passages in the rest of his work, is even harder to understand than his tragedy. The comic in general defies analysis: is there a definition of the laughable, even Bergson's, in which one can have much confidence? Some shrewd observations have been made on particular comedies or writers of comedy, but usually the critics merely prove that every real sense of humour, and even every comic effect, is unique. Molière comes as close as any master of comedy to having a stable point of view, an intelligible convention, and an infallible touch; but it is impossible to reduce all this to a formula. As for Shakespeare, his point of view shifts continually, he employs various conventions in his comedy, and there are many who find his touch far from infallible. Broadway reviewers, who think they know what makes the readers of *The New Yorker* laugh, and antiquarians, who think they know what made the Elizabethans laugh, tend to agree that Shakespeare's comedy is comic no more: here again they clasp hands, with a sophisticated wink, over the safely dead body of our heritage.

If one nevertheless does enjoy Shakespeare's humour, what is the best way to explore its range, learn its habits, assure oneself that one is really getting the point which Shakespeare intended? One method is to keep in mind the fact that Shakespeare wrote to be acted before an audience. One then reflects that laughter in the theatre depends upon so many factors – the mood of the audience, what the author has led the audience, in advance, to expect; the rhythm of the performance as a whole; subtleties of timing, attitude, and the like – that it is to be understood and controlled only empirically. Directors and actors know this. Comedians, however talented, have to learn by trial and error how to make audiences laugh at them. Directors often have to experiment with a comic scene, cutting it, changing its timing or business, before they can see how it works. There is every reason to believe that Shakespeare, a practical theatre man, worked that way. Starting with an old play or an old story, having in mind a certain company of actors, he wrote his plays in such a way as to control all the elements, and from their combination, before an audience, to get the intended effect of humour or pathos. Each of his comic effects is unique; emerging from the context of the whole acted play, it reflects his sure grasp of the action of *that* play, its comic as well as its pathetic aspects. His sense of humour apparently never sleeps; he reveals it, at will, by manipulating the theatrically perceptible elements which his story provides.

The most ambitious way to learn about Shakespeare's comedy would be to try to produce it. But the opportunity to do that is rare, and an actual production tests many things besides Shakespeare's dramaturgy, notably the skill and talent of the actors, and the moral and physical stamina of the hopeful director. It is an ordeal not to be lightly undertaken. A more practicable (as well as self-indulgent) method is to imagine the ideal performance as one reads the play – not, of course, in all its material details, but as a musician might 'hear' a symphony as he read the score. Such a reading of Shakespeare's comedy would, I suppose, turn up much that is obvious; but it might have the value of a prolegomenon: a pedestrian preparation for understanding Shakespeare's comic genius.

The Comedy of Errors and *Much Ado About Nothing* are far from exhausting Shakespeare's comic resources. But they are very different from each other, and by thinking them over together, with an eye to their theatrical point, one may begin to sense the variety and scope of his comic repertoire.

I

Shakespeare took the main story of *The Comedy of Errors* from Plautus's *The Two Menaechmuses*. The basic situation is that of two brothers, identical twins, who were separated in childhood and find themselves by chance in the same city when they are grown; they are so identical that no one can tell them apart. It is very improbable that twins could be so similar that even the wife of one of them couldn't distinguish between them, but Plautus, and Shakespeare after him, calmly assume that identity, and they are right, for this initial absurdity sets the key of the farce to follow. The audience must accept the silly postulate at once; so it is warned to expect, not a fable purporting 'truth', but a joke and a tall story.

I do not know why two people who are identical are laughable, but they are, and if they are not only the same height and age and weight, but walk and sit in the same way at the same time, the comic effect is stronger. And if there are more than two, we are still more pleased with them. This principle is well used in the Kaufman–Hart comedy, *Once in a Lifetime*, when twelve movie magnates, the identical Glogauer brothers, march on to the stage in a double-quick procession just before the second act curtain.

Shakespeare must have counted on this property of human identity, for when he devised *The Comedy of Errors* he provided Plautus's identical twins with servants who were also identical twins. He thus exaggerates Plautus's farcical exaggeration, and is enabled thereby to play many more variations than Plautus could on the plot which may be derived from the basic situation. This situation is the childishly simple one of mistaken identity: every scene in the play is an instance of it; every character in the play is always and only trying to straighten out such a mistake, which the audience always perfectly understands in advance. The most striking quality of this comedy – unique among Shakespeare's plays – is its perfect unity of action, plot and tone. As it quickly unrolls before us it gives the superficial impression of ceaseless movement, variety, and surprise. But that is a matter of great, but essentially mechanical, ingenuity: the play is built like a round, which delights a group of light-hearted singers by piling up and overlapping a single pattern.

It is true that the first scene, in which we see the twins' long-suffering father in trouble, and the last scene, in which father, mother, and the boys are reunited with happy tears, are different in tone from the body of the play: sentimental rather than farcical. But the first scene is a prologue, and the last scene not only brings the intrigue to its happy end, but also serves the essential purpose of changing the mood. Writers of farce have usually some trouble with the end of their fun. There is no inherent reason for halting the perpetual-motion machine of a good farcical plot; the arabesques of absurdity in *The Comedy of Errors* might continue indefinitely, or at least to the limits of the author's ingenuity and the audience's complacency. The plot is wound up neatly and naturally enough by the simple expedient of bringing both sets of twins together, but that is not enough: the postulate – or call it the attitude, or frame of mind – of farce must be broken through; the audience must be relaxed and dismissed in another mood. This may be accomplished in countless ways, but all who successfully devise farce for the theatre feel the need of this final change of mood. I used to notice that the old burlesque shows at Minsky's recognized it instinctively. The travelling salesmen would be guffawing all evening at slapstick, broad jokes, and chorines with but three crucial rhinestones; but at the end the lights would soften, the music would slide from the hot, through the blue, to the frankly old-timy, and a grey-haired mamma or 'mom' would take the centre of the stage to gaze thoughtfully into the electric moonlight. So the patrons received the whole treatment, gently eased at last out of their farcical mood into something warmer, damper and homier.

There is one strand running through the whole *Comedy of Errors* which might seem, on a first reading, to break the mood of farce: the troubled adventures of Antipholus of Ephesus's long-suffering wife. She is so disturbed when the other Antipholus treats her strangely that one might think Shakespeare wanted us to share her tears and frustrations. She and her sister and her maid, and eventually her real husband's mistress, form a dreary female procession through the quick twists of the plot. But I believe that Shakespeare expected us to laugh at them also, and that, in performance, would be largely a matter of tempo. The film of a funeral, even, may be made laughable if it is run off at twice the proper speed, and if we saw the bewildered women running and dripping at the same time we should understand how they fit into the whole farcical scheme.

When Shakespeare wrote *The Comedy of Errors* he was aiming, with great accuracy, at the perennial popular theatre. He demanded, therefore, very little of his audience. He does not expect us to be interested in the subtleties of character: the figures in this farce are labelled (as servant, man-about-town, wife or courtesan) just accurately enough to enable us to tell them apart. We are not called upon for much sympathy or imagination: in fact we must not try to see through these characters' eyes, or feel what they feel. It would ruin everything to take the wife's troubles, or Dromio's many beatings, at all seriously. All we have to do is grasp the broadly absurd situation, and follow the ingenious fugue of the plot. To get the point, nothing beyond mental alertness of an easy kind is required. The foolishness presented in this play is that of the incredible and arbitrary basic situation, not the ineluctable folly of mankind.

The play belongs in the stream of popular comedy, from Menander to Minsky; but it also shows an intelligence and control, on the part of the author, which is rare in any kind of play. It is much lighter and funnier than *The Two Menaechmuses*. This mastery is revealed, not so much in the language, though that is perfectly adequate to its modest purposes, as in the consistency with which its farcical limitations are accepted, and in the ingenuity of the plot. This plot really is built like the proverbial 'Swiss watch': it is as absurdly neat as Leibniz's pre-established harmony. Comedy of this type, or taste – rationalistic, built on a Latin base – was to be more fully explored in the succeeding age of the Enlightenment, in the innumerable comedies which lighted the theatres of Europe from Molière through Mozart. But Shakespeare was developing in a different direction, not toward the univocal perfection of the geometric diagram, but toward the harmonizing of complementary perspectives; not toward further ingenuity, but toward deeper insight.

The Comedy of Errors, like other comedies of that taste, is so clear that it *ought* to be reducible to a formula. Molière's comedies often strike us in the same way. Certainly one can find in them many standard and publicly available devices, whether of plotting, attitude, or conventional characterization. Without that heritage I do not suppose Shakespeare could, at so early an age, have written

36

anything so easy and assured. Yet he uses it for his own purposes, like a good cook who first learns and then forgets the basic recipes, or a dress designer who assumes the clichés of fashion only to go beyond them to something not quite predictable. Only Shakespeare could derive *The Comedy of Errors* from Plautus, and only he could proceed from that simple fun to the enigmatic humour of his maturity.

2

When Shakespeare wrote *Much Ado About Nothing* he had lost none of his skill as a maker of plots; on the contrary, he had attained further mastery in the ten years or more since the writing of *The Comedy of Errors*. There are three main narrative-lines: that of Claudio, Hero, and the wicked Don John; the connected story of Dogberry and the Watch; and the contrasting story of Beatrice and Benedick, all interwoven with clarity and apparent ease. But in this play Shakespeare uses the plot for a further and deeper end. Each of the three narrative-lines has its own humour, and by the interplay of the three a more general vision of man as laughable is suggested: a vision which is at once comic and poetic.

The story of young Claudio and Hero caught in Don John's wicked schemes was Shakespeare's starting point, and the somewhat casual framework of the plot of the whole play. He had read this story in Bandello's version, *Timbreo di Cardona*, the story of a girl unjustly accused of adultery. This tale, though it ends happily, is not very funny in itself, and Shakespeare does not so much avoid its painful and pathetic aspects as absorb them in his more detached comic vision. The scene in the church, when poor Hero is wrongly accused and her father Leonato loudly laments, may be played for a 'tragic' effect, but that I think would not be quite right. The audience knows that it is all a mistake, and it is by that time accustomed to smile at Claudio, an absurdly solemn victim of young love's egoism. When he first appears he tries to tell the Duke what the Duke knew already: his all-important love for Hero. He glumly decides that the Duke, wooing Hero in his behalf, has stolen her, and so is wrong again. Beatrice labels him for us: 'glum

37

as an orange, and something of that jealous complexion'. His false accusation is his third mistake: we must sympathize, but at the same time smile, at this final instance of his foolishness. The whole Claudio–Hero story is comic in itself and in its own way, but to understand what Shakespeare meant by it it is necessary to think of it in relation to the two other stories which unfold in alternation with it.

Dogberry and the Watch are closely connected with the Claudio story, which requires someone to uncover Don John's plot, but Shakespeare developed this element into a farcical sequence with its own tone and interest. At the same time he uses it to lighten the catastrophe at Hero's wedding, and the character of Don John: we cannot take a villain seriously who can be apprehended by Dogberry. Dogberry is not suffering the delusions of young love, like Claudio, but those of vanity and uncontrollable verbosity. His efforts to find his way, with lanterns, through the darkness of the night and the more impenetrable darkness of his wits, forms an ironic parallel to the groping of the young lovers through their mists of feeling. Dogberry also has his version of the underlying mood of the play – that of a leisurely and joyful ease, such as we attribute to Eden or the Golden Age. In Dogberry this infatuated leisureliness, this delusion that nothing terrible can really happen, takes the form of interminable verbalizing while the evil plot hatches and the villains lurk uncaught.

The story of Beatrice and Benedick's self-tormented love affair is entirely Shakespeare's creation. He seems to have felt the need of that pair's intelligence and agility to ventilate Claudio and Hero. We should tire quickly of Claudio's total submersion in love if Benedick were not there, pretending to be too intelligent for that. Hero, who can only sigh and blush, would be too soggy without Beatrice, who can only make sharp remarks, pull pigtails, and stick her tongue out at the boys. But the two contrasting stories together suggest a vision of early infatuation – provided we don't take Shakespeare's characters more seriously than he intended – which is both deeper and more comic than the victims themselves can know.

Beatrice and Benedick are notoriously hard to act on the modern stage, especially in the first two acts, where they indulge in so many quibbles and conceits in the taste of their times. There is no use trying to make the verbal jokes funny; but I am not sure that Shakespeare himself took them seriously as jokes. I once had the pleasure of seeing John Gielgud and Pamela Brown act several of the Beatrice–Benedick scenes. They 'threw away' the words, or even, at moments, made fun of their far-fetched elaboration, and by this means focused their audience's attention on the noble, silly, intelligent and bewildered *relation* of the two – a relation as agile, musical, and deeply comic as that of Congreve's reluctant lovers, Mirabel and Millamant. I feel sure that this approach to the play is right: its surfaces, its literal words, characters and events, are not to be taken seriously: the point is in the music of unseen motivation, in the fact that it *is* unseen by the characters themselves – and that all the fun and folly plays against a background of mystery.

The main Claudio–Hero–Don John intrigue is also not to be taken too seriously, as though it were the point of the play: Shakespeare gets it under way casually, after the underlying mood of the play as a whole, and its 'action' of elaborate play, or leisurely enjoyment, has been firmly established. The opening scene, in which Leonato's household prepares to celebrate the return of the Duke, Benedick and Claudio from their comic-opera war, tells us what the play is really about: it is a festive occasion, a celebration of a certain evanescent but recurrent human experience. The experience is real in its way, all may recognize it, but under its spell everything the characters do is much ado about nothing. The progress of the underlying action of the play as a whole is therefore marked by a series of somewhat dreamy and deluded festive occasions. The first of these is Leonato's masked ball, in Act II, a visible and musical image of the action. Then comes Dogberry's nocturnal and incomprehensible charge to the Watch: a farcical version of the theme. The fourth act consists chiefly of the marriage which turns out to be no marriage at all, but a bad dream. In the fifth act there is Claudio's funeral tribute to Hero, by night, at her supposed tomb; but this is a funeral which is no funeral, corresponding to the marriage which was no marriage. After that pathetic and comic expiatory rite, daylight returns, the torches are put out, and we are ready for the real and double marriage, in daylight, with the ladies unmasked at last, which ends the play in dance and song.

We are just beginning to understand the technical value of the 'ceremonious occasion' as an element of plot, though it has been used in countless ways from Aristophanes to Henry James. When people assemble for a ceremonious occasion (whether it be the festival of Dionysos or one of James's thorny tea parties) they must abate, or conceal, their purely individual purposes, and recognize the common concern which brings them together. A dramatist may use the festive occasion, therefore, to shift his audience's attention from the detail of the literal intrigue to some general plight which all more or less unwittingly share. All are social and political animals; all must suffer spring, mating, and death. Ceremonious occasions are especially useful to dramatists who are seeking poetry, which, as Aristotle remarked, is concerned with something more general than the particular facts, the unique events, of human life. The point – the comic point – of *Much Ado* is poetic in that sense, and hence it is the festive ensemble scenes which most clearly adumbrate the basic vision of the play. In this respect the plot of *Much Ado* contrasts sharply with that of *The Comedy of Errors*. The point of that play lies precisely in the unique situation of mistaken identity, and in the strings of absurd events which quickly follow from it. An 'occasion' of any kind would break the tight concatenation of *contretemps*; and that Shakespeare is careful to avoid doing until he is ready to end the whole play.

One might say that *Much Ado* presents a comic vision of mankind which is also poetic, while the purpose of *The Comedy of Errors* is closer to that of the professional vaudevillian, who gauges his success by clocking the laughs: the provoking of thoughtless mirth, an almost reflex response. The difference between the two plays is clearest, perhaps, when one reflects that both are concerned with mistaken identity, but in *The Comedy of Errors* the mistake is simply a mistake in fact, while in *Much Ado* it is a failure of insight, or rather many failures of different kinds by the different characters.

Shakespeare accomplishes the denouement of *The Comedy of*

Errors in one swift scene. It is not difficult to correct an error in fact: it may be done instantly by providing the right fact: and as soon as both pairs of twins are on stage together, the error is gone. But correcting a failure of insight is a most delicate and mysterious process, which Shakespeare suggests, in *Much Ado*, in countless ways: through the symbolism of masks, night, and verbal ambiguities, and in peripeteias of his three variously comic subplots.

The farcical efforts of Dogberry and Verges never deviate into enlightenment. They learn as little as the characters in *The Comedy of Errors*: but, like them, they do stumble eventually upon the right fact: they manage to apprehend the villains and convey that fact to Leonato.

Claudio, with his dark fumes of love, has a long way to go before he can see anything real. After his false wedding Shakespeare puts him through a false and painful challenge from his best friend, Benedick, and then the mocking (but touching) mummery of his visit to Hero's empty tomb. Even then the audience learns more from Claudio's masquerade-like progress through the maze than he does himself.

Beatrice and Benedick come the closest, of all the characters, to grasping the whole scope of the comic vision which the play slowly unfolds. But even after their friends have tried to kid them out of their frightened vanity during the first three acts, it takes most of the fourth and fifth acts, where all the painful things occur, to bring them to conscious acceptance of their absurd selves, each other, and their love. It is the fiasco of Claudio's first attempt at marriage which marks the crucial turn in their relationship:

BENEDICK Lady Beatrice, have you wept all this while?
BEATRICE Yea, and I will weep a while longer.

> *Much Ado About Nothing*, IV. 1. 255–6

and a little later:

BENEDICK I do love nothing in the world so well as you. Is not that strange?
BEATRICE As strange as the thing I know not. It were as possible for me to say I love nothing so well as you; but believe me not; and yet I lie not; I confess nothing. . . .   IV. 1. 266–70

In this exchange the love-warmed final scene of the play is fore-shadowed, but the misfortunes of Claudio and Hero, which here bring Beatrice and Benedick near together, immediately carry them apart again. Benedick has to challenge Claudio, and that boy's delusions have to be repented and dispelled, before Beatrice and Benedick can trust their intuition of love, or accept it fully and in good conscience. I do not attempt to follow the subtle shifts in their relationship which Shakespeare suggests, in a few quick, sure strokes during the fifth Act. But it is Beatrice and Benedick who dominate the final scene:

BENEDICK Soft and fair, Friar. Which is Beatrice?
BEATRICE (*unmasking*) I answer to that name. What is your will?
BENEDICK Do not you love me?
BEATRICE Why no, no more than reason.
BENEDICK Why then, your uncle and the Prince and Claudio have been deceived; they swore you did.
BEATRICE Do not you love me?
BENEDICK Troth no, no more than reason.
BEATRICE Why then my cousin, Margaret, and Ursula are much deceived, for they did swear you did.

(Claudio and Hero produce love letters from Benedick and Beatrice to each other)

BENEDICK A miracle! here's our own hands against our hearts. Come, I will have thee; but, by this light, I take thee for pity.
BEATRICE I would not deny you, but by this good day I yield upon great persuasion, and partly to save your life, for I was told you were in a consumption.
BENEDICK Peace; I will stop your mouth.   v. 4. 72–9, 91–7

In this scene the main contrasting themes of the play are brought together, and very lightly and quickly resolved: marriage true and false, masking and unmasking, the delusion and truth of youthful love. The harmonies may all be heard in Beatrice's and Benedick's words. The exchange is in prose, but (like the prose of Leonato's masked ball) it has a rhythm and a varied symmetry suggesting the formality of a dance figure. The key words – love, reason, day, light, pity, peace – make music both for the ear and for the understanding as they echo back and forth, deepening in meaning with each new context. The effect of the scene as a whole is epitomized in Beatrice's and Benedick's heavenly double-take: their foolish idiosyncrasy is clear, but some joyful flood of acceptance and understanding frees them, for the moment, and lifts them beyond it. Is this effect 'comic'? I do not know; I think it is intended to bring a smile, not for the wind-up of this little plot, but for the precarious human condition.

When one reads *Much Ado* in the security of one's own room, indulging in daydreams of an ideal performance, it is possible to forget the practical and critical problems which surround the question of the play's viability in our time. But it must be admitted that high-school productions are likely to be terribly embarrassing, and I do not even like to think of the play's pathetic vulnerability on Times Square. The play demands much from its performers, almost as much as Chekhov does. It demands a great deal from its audience: a leisurely and contemplative detachment which seems too costly in our hustled age. Perhaps Shakespeare should be blamed for all this: if *Much Ado* does not easily convince us on the contemporary stage, perhaps we should conclude, as Eliot once concluded of *Hamlet*, that it is an artistic failure. But on that principle we should have to rule out a great deal of Shakespeare. It was his habit, not only in *Hamlet* and *Much Ado*, but in many other plays, to indicate, rather than explicitly to present, his central theme; and to leave it to his performers and his audience to find it behind the varied episodes, characters, and modes of language which are literally presented. Everything which Shakespeare meant by *The Comedy of Errors* is immediately perceptible; the comic vision of *Much Ado* will only appear, like the faces which Dante saw in the milky substance of the moon, slowly, and as we learn to trust the fact that it is really there.

'Two Comedies' by Francis Fergusson, first published in the *Sewanee Review*, 1954, and reprinted in *The Human Image in Dramatic Literature*

Suggestions for Further Reading

BERTRAND EVANS: *Shakespeare's Comedies*, I. I. This book examines Shakespeare's use of dramatic awareness in constructing his comedies: his decisions on how much to let the audience know, and how much to let each character know.

DEREK TRAVERSI: *Shakespeare: The Early Comedies* (British Council pamphlet, 'Writers and Their Work'). Normally a subtle and often elusive critic, Traversi is more straightforward than usual in this pamphlet.

MARK VAN DOREN: *Shakespeare*. The play is an unfeeling farce. 'He could write it very well, and be hugely funny; but the heart of his interest was elsewhere'. Like most critics of the play, Van Doren lingers on those few (and untypical) details that 'point ahead to the time when Shakespeare will have found the kind of comedy in which his nature can repose'.

THE TWO GENTLEMEN OF VERONA

THREE

Shadows, Dreams and Plays in
The Two Gentlemen of Verona

... As might be expected, Shakespeare's early comedies explore play metaphors of a type different from those associated with *Titus Andronicus* or the histories of Henry VI. Yet there is one image common to all of these early plays. Deceit, whether comic or tragic, is a staple of drama and also a traditional meeting point of the actor and the ordinary man. In that initial soliloquy of his in *Henry VI, Part Three*, Richard spoke of Proteus as a model for dissemblers. It was a familiar name for the actor, one which the Puritans occasionally employed, and which Shakespeare himself chose for the actor-villain of *The Two Gentlemen of Verona*. Proteus is a far less interesting character than Richard; he is neither so cunning nor so obviously theatrical. Yet his villainy, like Richard's, is associated quite deliberately with the stage.

Towards the end of the comedy, Silvia describes Proteus as 'thou counterfeit to thy true friend' (*The Two Gentlemen of Verona*, v. 4. 53). This term 'counterfeit' possesses chameleon hues. It is another of those words, like 'act' or 'play', which can be understood in either a dramatic or a non-dramatic sense. Often, it signifies simple imitation, as it does in Othello's account of those engines of war which 'Th'immortal Jove's dread clamours counterfeit' (*Othello*, III. 3. 360), or old Capulet's description of his daughter:

> In one little body
> Thou counterfeit'st a bark, a sea, a wind.
> *Romeo and Juliet*, III. 5. 130–31

Counterfeit is also, however, a virtual synonym in Elizabethan English for the actor and his art. As such, it may be quite innocent. Antonio's sheepish 'To tell you true, I counterfeit him' (*Much*

Ado About Nothing, II. I. 100) implies a harmless masquerade. Falstaff providently saves himself from Ford by 'counterfeiting the action of an old woman' (*The Merry Wives of Windsor*, IV. 5. 110), and Edgar, disguised as the Bedlam beggar, says of his tears for the King, 'They mar my counterfeiting' (*King Lear*, III. 6. 60). Rosalind in *As You Like It*, recovering from her unmanly swoon, and trying to make it look like jest, centres her conversation with Oliver upon the word.

ROSALIND Counterfeit, I assure you.
OLIVER Well then, take a good heart and counterfeit to be a man.
ROSALIND So I do; but i'faith, I should have been a woman by right.
As You Like It, IV. 3. 169–73

Once involved, however, with the idea of malicious deceit, 'counterfeit' tends to darken, to acquire connotations of treachery. Of the cries in the night in *Othello*, Ludovico says prudently, ''Tis heavy night. | These may be counterfeits' (*Othello*, V. 1. 42–3), and Helena brands Hermia, whom she fancies a dissembler, as 'you counterfeit, you puppet' (*A Midsummer Night's Dream*, III. 2. 288). In *The Two Gentlemen of Verona*, Silvia applies the word to Proteus as a description of his duplicity and betrayal of his friend. Her use of 'counterfeit' echoes the mocking dialogue between Valentine and the foolish Thurio earlier in the comedy.

THURIO Seem you that you are not?
VALENTINE Haply I do.
THURIO So do counterfeits.
The Two Gentlemen of Verona, II. 4. 10–12

The faithful Julia also associates Proteus with the actor. In a comedy which sometimes seems almost maddening in its devotion to quibbles and intricate tricks with words, her exploitation of the theatrical connotations latent in the 'play the part' idiom is curiously – almost uniquely – moving in a way which the force of the play metaphor and the emotional reality of Julia herself among a cast of shadows together make possible. Disguised as a boy, she stands in the night outside the Duke's Palace and hears her lover Proteus serenading Silvia.

JULIA He plays false, father.

HOST How, out of tune on the strings?

JULIA Not so; but yet so false that he grieves my very heartstrings. . . .

HOST Hark, what fine change is in the music!

JULIA Ay, that change is the spite.

HOST You would have them always play but one thing?

JULIA I would always have one play but one thing.

IV. 2. 57–60, 66–9

A little later, in the guise of Proteus's page, Julia goes on her reluctant embassy to Silvia. She is charged with the mission of delivering to the lady her own ring, given to Proteus at his departure from Verona, and of claiming in return Silvia's portrait, the 'shadow' (*The Two Gentlemen of Verona*, IV. 2. 126; IV. 4. 116) of the reality already given to Valentine.

'Shadow' is a word associated not only with that painted token which is all of Silvia that Proteus can win, but also with Julia in her obscurity and disguise (*The Two Gentlemen of Verona*, IV. 2. 123). When Silvia asks the supposed page to satisfy her curiosity about Proteus's first love, the images of disguise and shadow which have gone before run almost automatically into the play metaphor.

> SILVIA How tall was she?
> JULIA About my stature; for at Pentecost,
>   When all our pageants of delight were play'd,
>   Our youth got me to play the woman's part,
>   And I was trimm'd in Madam Julia's gown,
>   Which served me as fit, by all men's judgments,
>   As if the garment had been made for me;
>   Therefore I know she is about my height.
>   And at that time I made her weep agood,
>   For I did play a lamentable part.
>   Madam, 'twas Ariadne passioning
>   For Theseus' perjury and unjust flight;
>   Which I so lively acted with my tears
>   That my poor mistress, moved therewithal,
>   Wept bitterly; and would I might be dead
>   If I in thought felt not her very sorrow.

IV. 4. 153–68

The speech depends upon a complicated overlapping of illusion and reality: the real Julia, playing the part of Proteus's page Sebastian, describes an imaginary theatrical performance in which that page appeared as Ariadne before Julia herself. The passage sets up a series of illusions receding into depth of which the most remote, the tears wrung from Julia by the stage presentation of a lover's perfidy, in fact represents reality.

from Chapter IV of *Shakespeare and the Idea of the Play* by Anne Righter, 1962

Suggestions for Further Reading

JOHN F. DANBY: 'Shakespeare Criticism and *Two Gentlemen of Verona*' (*Critical Quarterly*, Winter 1960). Defends the play as a serious treatment of the debate between love and friendship, and claims that our criticisms of it are largely due to our lack of sympathy with Elizabethan ideas.

BERTRAND EVANS: *Shakespeare's Comedies*, 1. 2. The dramatist's use of contrasting awarenesses (by audience and by characters) 'contains anxieties within a frame of warm reassurance'.

S. A. SMALL: 'The Ending of *Two Gentlemen of Verona*' (*Publications of the Modern Language Association*, Volume XLVIII, 1933). The ending is not an artistic success, since it requires of us 'a cold application of the doctrine of friendship'. The unscholarly are seldom satisfied with the ending of this play; the scholars are divided.

DEREK TRAVERSI: *Shakespeare: The Early Comedies* (British Council pamphlet, 'Writers and Their Work').

MARK VAN DOREN: *Shakespeare*. Though the play is not as good of its kind as *The Comedy of Errors*, it is the first to contain 'heaven-bred poesy', and to catch the tone of 'the golden world of gentlemen where Shakespeare's comedies will occur'.

THE TAMING OF THE SHREW

FOUR

Shakespeare's Imperfect Realism

... THE TAMING OF THE SHREW is a remarkable example of
Shakespear's repeated attempts to make the public accept realistic
comedy. Petruchio is worth fifty Orlandos as a human study. The
preliminary scenes in which he shews his character by pricking up
his ears at the news that there is a fortune to be got by any man who
will take an ugly and ill-tempered woman off her father's hands, and
hurrying off to strike the bargain before somebody else picks it up,
are not romantic; but they give an honest and masterly picture of a
real man, whose like we have all met. The actual taming of the
woman by the methods used in taming wild beasts belongs to his
determination to make himself rich and comfortable, and his
perfect freedom from all delicacy in using his strength and opportunities for that purpose. The process is quite bearable, because the
selfishness of the man is healthily goodhumoured and untainted by
wanton cruelty, and it is good for the shrew to encounter a force like
that and be brought to her senses. Unfortunately, Shakespear's own
immaturity, as well as the immaturity of the art he was experiment-
ing in, made it impossible for him to keep the play on the realistic
plane to the end; and the last scene is altogether disgusting to
modern sensibility. No man with any decency of feeling can sit it
out in the company of a woman without being extremely ashamed
of the lord-of-creation moral implied in the wager and the speech
put into the woman's own mouth. Therefore the play, though still
worthy of a complete and efficient representation, would need,
even at that, some apology.

by George Bernard Shaw, the *Saturday Review*, 6 Novem-
ber 1897; reprinted in *Shaw on Shakespeare*, edited by
Edwin Wilson

FIVE

The Taming of the Shrew

WHEN Petruchio the woman-hater is asked what gale blows him from Verona to Padua he answers airily, being a free and happy fellow with no other care than the need to find himself a wealthy wife:

> Such wind as scatters young men through the world
> To seek their fortunes farther than at home
> Where small experience grows.   I. 2. 50–52

The hilarious piece of which he is hero might so far, then, be such an excursion into the romantic universe of young Italian adventure as *The Two Gentlemen of Verona* is; for that experiment, of about the same age as *The Shrew*, starts also with youthful blades whetting their edges on the wheel of travel.

But Petruchio is hero of a farce, not of a romance. Comedy is made once more from situation: a shrew is to be tamed, a man is found to tame her, and he proceeds to do so by as many devices as can be developed in the time available. The interest of the audience will be in the devices, not in the persons who work them or upon whom they are worked. A certain callousness will be induced to form in the sensibilities of the beholder, so that whereas in another case he would be outraged he will now laugh freely and steadily for two hours. The practitioner in farce, no less than the practitioner in melodrama, must possess the art of insulating his audience's heart so that it cannot be shocked while the machinery hums.

The Taming of the Shrew, however, has a deep and curious interest such as *The Comedy of Errors* nowhere has. Formally it is as much a farce, and leans as frankly on a doctrine which Shakespeare must have adopted in cold blood, for on the evidence of the other plays it was not his own. This is the doctrine of male superiority, which Luciana had expressed in *The Comedy of Errors* when she reminded Adriana that men 'are masters to their females' (II. 1. 24), and which Petruchio expresses here not only when he declares of Katherine that

> She is my goods, my chattels; she is my house,
> My household stuff, my field, my barn,
> My horse, my ox, my ass, my any thing.   III. 2. 232–4

but indeed at all times and by all his actions; nor does Katherine fail at the end to agree. Yet the resulting play, as its popularity attests, is strangely and permanently interesting.

This is because it has hit the relation of the sexes at its livest point. Shakespeare hit the point again, and classically for him, in the story of Beatrice and Benedick; but even now he is master of the theme that lies in the war between love and pride, in the perhaps perversely fascinating spectacle of intellect and will being brought into line with instinct. Love stories are never so engaging as when their principals do not wish to love, and particularly when it is their power that prevents them. For one thing, we are never so sure as then that love is genuine; and for another, there is a peculiar delight in discovering that two persons have mistaken attraction for repulsion, and in listening to the reverse language of raillery which they employ in place of lisps and sighs. The best lovers are witty lovers who bury their perturbation under abuse; at least this is true for comedy, and by all means it is the case where situation is the thing.

Our secret occupation as we watch *The Taming of the Shrew* consists of noting the stages by which both Petruchio and Katherine – both of them, for in spite of everything the business is mutual – surrender to the fact of their affection. Shakespeare has done this not by violating his form, not by forgetting at any point to write farce, and least of all by characterizing his couple. He has left them man and woman, figures for whom we can substitute ourselves, and that is precisely what we do as we commence to understand why Katherine wants so badly to hear Bianca talk of her suitors, even beats her because she will not; as we read reservations into her scorn of Petruchio; as we wait to see her give Petruchio (V. 1) his first quiet kiss; and as we assume behind Petruchio's roughness a growing attachment to this woman he is so deliciously – we must confess it – torturing. Shakespeare has done what he has done somewhat as a general takes a city: by sheer strength, in utter confidence, and with the soundest knowledge of our outstanding weakness.

Both the man and the woman are brilliant of tongue. She can call him 'a mad-cap ruffian and a swearing Jack', 'a frantic fool', 'a mad-brain rudesby'. But his high spirits carry him as far as genius. His anger, real or pretended, leads him to the limits of language:

> You peasant swain! You whoreson malt-horse drudge!
>
> IV. 1. 132
>
> A whoreson beetle-headed, flap-ear'd knave!
>
> IV. 1. 160
>
> Why, this was moulded on a porringer. . . .
> Why, 'tis a cockle or a walnut-shell,
> A knack, a toy, a trick, a baby's cap.
>
> IV. 3. 64, 66–7
>
> Why, thou say'st true; it is a paltry cap,
> A custard-coffin, a bauble, a silken pie.
>
> IV. 3. 81–2
>
> What's this? A sleeve? 'T is like a demi-cannon.
> What, up and down, carv'd like an apple-tart?
> Here's snip and nip and cut and slish and slash,
> Like to a censer in a barber's shop.
>
> IV. 3. 88–91

The language of the play, or at any rate of the play as it concerns Katherine and Petruchio, is everywhere vigorous and vernacular, and healthily grown over with tough local terms. We hear of a chestnut in a farmer's fire, of hazel twigs and hazel nuts, of kersey boot-hose, of horses shoulder-shotten and begnawn with the bots, of sops thrown in the sexton's face, of apples and oysters, of a bottom of brown thread, of rush-candles, and of parsley in the garden to stuff a rabbit. Petruchio's crowning harangue against the tailor is stuck as full of such terms as a ham with cloves:

... Thou liest, thou thread, thou thimble,
Thou yard, three-quarters, half-yard, quarter, nail!
Thou flea, thou nit, thou winter-cricket thou! ...
Away, thou rag, thou quantity, thou remnant.

IV. 3. 107–9, 111

But the servants also are accomplished in the speech of their region, which it goes without saying is not Italy. And the Induction, wherein Christophero Sly awakes from his sleep to be Bottom in a lord's bedchamber, is as local as an inn-yard, a broken fence, a yawning dog, with its talk of old Sly's son of Burton Heath, Marian Hacket the fat ale-wife of Wincot, Peter Turph, and Henry Pimpernell. The Induction contains several of Shakespeare's later themes – music, the voices of hounds, dreams and delusions, and instructions to players; but significantly enough they are restrained within the bounds of farce, they are enriched with none of the later meaning. The hounds are hunting-dogs, music is a household affair, and dreams are funny.

But the comedy has never strayed from its path, unless the insipid story of Bianca and her suitors is to be considered an attempt, by Shakespeare or by someone else, to save the whole for romance. It is not saved. A play in which the heroine can be called a devil, a wench, a fiend of hell, a rotten apple, a thing to be boarded, an irksome brawling scold, a wildcat, and in which we nevertheless take the purest pleasure, has in fact been saved, but saved as farce. How otherwise could we behold so callously the wringing of ears and the knocking of heads which appear to be Petruchio's natural habits – and his servants', and Katherine's, for she ties her sister's hands and strikes at least three persons before she settles down? As for the settling down, there is that last long speech of hers in which she declares the humble duty of a wife in terms which would be painful to us were she a person as Portia and Imogen are persons. Katherine is a shrew. She has been tamed. And the logic of farce is that she should say so.

from *Shakespeare*, by Mark Van Doren, 1939

SIX

The Taming of the Shrew in the Theatre

... GEORGE DEVINE'S production of *The Taming of the Shrew* took a new way with the old farce. We were kept always informed that we were watching a play within a play, on this occasion in the handsome hall of an Elizabethan mansion, designed by Vivienne Kernot. The towers of Padua were to be glimpsed through the windows, but we were aware that the English alehouse was on the heath just around the corner. Marius Goring took a civilized way with Petruchio. Here was no heavyweight champion battling for a wench, but a fellow of some sensitiveness and perception. He had his own humorous values and his own sense of the dramatic. He gave the impression that Petruchio was watching this taming business with the anxious eye of an artist. When Katharina was unusually rampageous, he had a moment of hovering anxiety lest he should not be able to bring her to heel again. When he had so achieved, he let out his triumph on a fine flow of rolling speech. This was a whimsical trainer teaching his pupil how to behave for her own good. By the time that he and Katharina were on their way back to Padua and that perverse argument about the sun and the moon was being thrashed out, we realized that this couple had fallen deeply in love, and Petruchio's 'Kiss me, Kate!' was not so much a command as an invitation. Yvonne Mitchell's Katharina consorted consistently with this particular Petruchio. She was attracted by her would-be trainer, and watched him with sulky feminine interest. When she realized that she was beginning to fall in love with this unpredictable but masterful gallant from Verona, she gave him a smile which promised that the armistice, once signed, would be permanent. By reducing the whip-cracking to a minimum and keeping the circus tricks at a reasonable distance from the customary bear-baiting, the producer touched the training quite firmly with romance. This new feeling for the old farce was most agreeable.

from 'Acting Shakespeare: Modern Tendencies' by
T. C. Kemp, *Shakespeare Survey* 7, 1954

Suggestions for Further Reading

H. B. CHARLTON: *Shakespearian Comedy*, Chapter IV. Sets the play in the tradition of Italian Renaissance Comedy. 'Petruchio is different from the wooers of romance, because he remembers the grocer, the butcher, and the tailor'; and the whole play is anti-romantic.

G. I. DUTHIE: *Shakespeare* (Hutchinson's University Library), Chapter II. An extreme example of the use of orthodox Elizabethan ideas to interpret a comedy (and a good contrast to the Shaw piece above). Sees the play as a study in the order–disorder antithesis, and the taming of Katherine as the assertion of belief in hierarchy. The sophisticated members of Shakespeare's audience, claims Professor Duthie, would have seen 'the spectre of universal disintegration' hovering in the background.

BERTRAND EVANS: *Shakespeare's Comedies*, I. 4. There is a contrast in the dramatic management of the two plots. The sub-plot anticipates the later romantic comedies; the Shrew plot makes no use of gaps in awareness between audience and characters.

E. M. W. TILLYARD: *Shakespeare's Early Comedies*, Chapter IV. Sees the play as hovering uncertainly between farce (Petruchio as the brutal wife-tamer) and comedy (Petruchio as awakening Kate to self-knowledge).

DEREK TRAVERSI: *Shakespeare: The Early Comedies* (British Council pamphlet, 'Writers and Their Work').

LOVE'S LABOUR'S LOST

SEVEN

Producing *Love's Labour's Lost*

HERE is a fashionable play; now, by three hundred years, out of fashion. Nor did it ever, one supposes, make a very wide appeal. It abounds in jokes for the elect. Were you not numbered among them you laughed, for safety, in the likeliest places. A year or two later the elect themselves might be hard put to it to remember what the joke was.

THE PRODUCER'S PROBLEM

Were this all one could say of *Love's Labour's Lost*, the question of its staging today – with which we are first and last concerned – would be quickly answered, and Lose No Labour here be the soundest advice. For spontaneous enjoyment is the life of the theatre. If a performance must be accompanied by a lecture, if, for instance, when Holofernes is at the point of

Bone, bone for benè: Priscian a little scratched. 'Twill serve. . . .

we need his modern exemplar in cap and gown, standing on one side the proscenium, to interrupt with 'One moment, please! The allusion here, if you wish to appreciate its humour, is to . . .'; or if he must warn us, 'In the next scene, ladies and gentlemen, you will notice a reference to the charge-house on the top of the mountain. This is thought by the best authorities to denote . . .' not much fun will survive. For a glossary in the programme something might be said, even for a preliminary lecture. No; this last, one fears, would leave the actors with too hard a task turning class-room back to theatre. Half-digested information lies a little heavily on one's sense of humour.

It is true that with no play three hundred years old can we press our 'spontaneous' too hard. For the full appreciation of anything in

C

Shakespeare some knowledge is asked of its why and wherefore. Hamlet and Falstaff, however, Rosalind and Imogen, are compact of qualities which fashion cannot change; the barriers of dramatic convention, strange habits, tricks of speech are of small enough account with them. But what is back of these word-gymnastics of Rosaline and Berowne, Holofernes' jargon, Armado's antics? The play is a satire, a comedy of affectations. The gymnastics, the jargon and the antics are the fun. Yet a play hardly lives by such brilliancies alone. While the humour of them is fresh and holds our attention, actors may lend it a semblance of life; for there at least *they* are, alive in their kind! No play, certainly, can count on survival if it strikes no deeper root nor bears more perennial flowers. If its topical brilliance were all, Shakespeare's name tagged to this one would keep it a place on the scholar's dissecting table; in the theatre *Love's Labour's Lost* would be dead, past all question. But there is life in it. The satire beside, Shakespeare the poet had his fling. It abounds in beauties of fancy and phrase, as beautiful today as ever. We find in it Shakespeare the dramatist learning his art. To students the most interesting thing about the play is the evidence of this; of the trial and error, his discovery of fruitful soil and fruitless. The producer, pledged to present an audience with a complete something, cannot, of course, be content with promise and experiment. Measuring this early Shakespeare by the later, we may as well own there is not much more. But the root of the matter is already in him; he is the dramatist born, and all, or nearly all, is at least instinct with dramatic life. It is oftenest his calculations and his cleverness that betray him.

For satire and no more is too apt to prove dramatically fruitless. A play's values are human values, and a playwright's first task is to give his creatures being. Imaginative love for them may help him to; even hate may; but a mocking detachment cannot. If he is to shoot at their follies he must yet build up the target first; and if it is not a convincing one there will be little credit in the shooting. He cannot, of course, in a play, take direct aim himself, unless he use the method of the Moralities or its like. There is the less direct method of twisting a set of familiar heroic figures awry. Shakespeare made this experiment, not too successfully, in *Troilus and Cressida*. But his obvious plan will be to turn one or more of his creatures satirists themselves, and under their cover plant his own shafts. Even so, he must give the victims their chance, or the play will be lopsided and come tumbling down.

The Shakespeare who sets out to write *Love's Labour's Lost* is a very clever young man, a wit, a sonneteer. He is 'in the movement'. He flatters his admirers by excelling in the things they admire; he will flatter his rivals hardly less by this attention he means to pay them. But your clever young man is usually more than a little impressed by the things he mocks at; he mocks at them in self-defence, it may be, lest they impress him too much. Mockery is apt, indeed, to capitulate to the thing mocked, to be absorbed by it. And these academic follies of Navarre, the fantastic folly of Armado, the pedantic folly of schoolmaster and parson – sometimes the satire is so fine that the folly seems the clever young man's own. Yet this weakness of the would-be satirist is the budding dramatist's strength. Shakespeare cannot resist his creatures; he never quite learned to. He cannot make mere targets of them. He cannot resist his own genius, poetic or dramatic; all through the play we find the leaven of it working.

He has not written ten lines before the poet in him breaks bounds. Is this the voice of that frigid wiseacre Navarre; does this suggest the 'little academe'?

> Therefore, brave conquerors – for so you are,
> That war against your own affections
> And the huge army of the world's desires. . . .
>
> I. I. 8–10

But the clever young man recollects himself; and here, soon enough, is the sort of thing he has set out to write.

KING How well he's read, to reason against reading!
DUMAIN Proceeded well, to stop all good proceeding!
LONGAVILLE He weeds the corn, and still lets grow the weeding.
BEROWNE The spring is near, when green geese are a-breeding.
DUMAIN How follows that?

BEROWNE   Fit in his place and time.
DUMAIN In reason nothing.
BEROWNE   Something then in rhyme.

I. I. 94-9

Pretty tricksy stuff! Well enough done to show that he quite enjoyed doing it, but the sort of thing that almost anyone could learn to do. No sign-post on the road to *Hamlet*, certainly.

But mark the dramatist in his provision at the outset of the conflict and balance that every play needs, in the setting of Berowne against his companions, one man's common-sense against the crowding affectations (a sporting conflict), an ounce of reality for counterweight to a ton of shams (an instructive balance). Here also, for the moralist-critic, is the play's moral issue defined at the outset; but let us not suppose Shakespeare to have been oppressed by this. Despite his present-day idolaters he was probably not high-purposed from his cradle; moreover, he is likely to have gained most of his knowledge of life by writing plays about it. That is not a provocative paradox, but a key to the mind and method of the artist. Time and again Shakespeare tells us that he sees the world as a stage. He would not think that a belittling comparison; he takes his art too seriously. Not portentously, but as simply seriously as any man will take his purpose in life when he is lucky enough to be sure of it. We all need some centre of experience to argue from, if the world beyond our experience is to have any meaning for us. The artist transforms and multiplies experience by imagination, and may even come to think that what is true of his art will be true of the world it mirrors. This sounds absurd. But life does seem to be governed by surprisingly simple laws; and human beings, wherever and whatever they may be, do not greatly differ in essentials. That is the working hypothesis upon which art and religion, with imaginative genius to vitalize them, proceed. And let it be said of the theatre that a very short time in it will teach one how little fine clothes and fine manners may amount to. The theatre was for Shakespeare a laboratory where he worked—if but in a mimic sense— with human material. His method, his means to enlightenment, was to take a story and put the worth of it, its truth to nature, to the test of personal expression. The story might suffer; if it was not true to nature, it generally would. But Shakespeare was, on the whole, a most unconscientious story-teller, except when history bound him. Sometimes he would make a sacrifice to symmetry, as when, in *Measure for Measure*, he marries Isabella to the Duke; but he may have felt this to be poetic justice upon such a morally consistent lady. The story may be burked, neglected or finished off anyhow, as in *Much Ado About Nothing*, *Twelfth Night* and *As You Like It*. It may hang at the heels of the chief character, as in *Hamlet*. What men are, in fact, comes to concern him far more than what they do. Already in this pretty play of *Love's Labour's Lost* it instinctively concerns him, though not even doing but mere clever talk is his ostensible concern. And when he passes to the giant theme of *King Lear*, to the sweep of historic vision that is in *Antony and Cleopatra*, stretching his medium of expression till it seems to crack and break, he concerns himself, even then, with little which cannot be rendered into human passion, human pity – which cannot, in fact, be put to this laboratory test. He – literally – has no use for theories and abstract ideas. He is neither philosopher nor moralist, except as he must seem to be, making his creatures one or the other. He is a playwright; he projects character in action, and with the truth of the one to the other his power and responsibility end. If this is the playwright's limitation, it is also his strength; for to this test of human response – not mimic, truly, but real; yet the mimic but reflects the real – all philosophy and morality must finally be put.

In this earliest essay, then, we may divine the dramatist to be; and we find dramatist putting wit and poet to the proof. Shakespeare will have set out to do his best by his creatures one and all; but while Berowne grows under his hand into a figure, finally, of some dramatic stature, while the Princess, simple, straightforward, shrewd, is made flesh and blood, in the speaking of seven lines, Navarre, though a natural focus of attention and discussing himself unsparingly, remains a bundle of phrases, and Dumain and Longaville have about the substance of echoes. Of the humbler folk; Costard for three-quarters of the play is the stage Fool, but suddenly, when he comes to the acting of his Worthy, we have:

COSTARD I Pompey am, Pompey surnam'd the big —
DUMAIN The great.
COSTARD It is great, sir; Pompey surnam'd the great;
  That oft in field, with targe and shield, did make my foe to sweat;
  And travelling along this coast, I here am come by chance,
  And lay my arms before the legs of this sweet lass of France.
  If your ladyship would say 'Thanks, Pompey', I had done.
PRINCESS Great thanks, great Pompey.
COSTARD 'Tis not so much worth; but I hope I was perfect: I made a
  little fault in 'great'.
                                                 v. 2. 546-56

And these two last lines have, mysteriously and unexpectedly,
given us the man beneath the jester. Then, with another thirty
words or so, Costard (and Costard's creator) settles Sir Nathaniel
the Curate, till now little but a figure of fun, snugly in our affections.

There, an't shall please you; a foolish mild man; an honest man,
look you, and soon dashed! He is a marvellous good neighbour, in
sooth; and a very good bowler: but, for Alisander, alas, you see how
'tis; — a little o'erparted.
                                              v. 2. 574-8

And settles himself there yet more snugly in the doing it! Throughout the play, but especially towards the end, we find such outcrop-
pings of pure dramatic gold.

Drama, as Shakespeare will come to write it, is, first and last, the
projection of character in action; and devices for doing this, simple
and complex, must make up three-quarters of its artistry. We can
watch his early discovery that dialogue is waste matter unless it
works to this end; that wit, epigram, sentiment are like paper and
sticks in a fireplace, the flaring and crackling counting for nothing
if the fire itself won't light, if these creatures in whose mouths the
wit is sounded won't 'come alive'. To the last he kept his youthful
delight in a pun; and he would write an occasional passage of word-
music with a minimum of meaning to it (but of maximum emotional
value, it will be found, to the character that has to speak it). His
development of verse to dramatic use is a study in itself. He never
ceased to develop it, but for a while the dramatist had a hard time
with the lyric poet. The early plays abound, besides, in elaborate
embroidery of language done for its own sake. This was a fashionable literary exercise and Shakespeare was an adept at it. To many

young poets of the time their language was a new-found wonder; its very handling gave them pleasure. The amazing things it could be made to do! He had to discover that they were not much to his purpose; but it is not easy to stop doing what you do so well. Yet even in this play we may note the difference between the Berowne of

> Light seeking light doth light of light beguile;
> So ere you find where light in darkness lies
> Your light grows dark by losing of your eyes!
>
> I. I. 77-9

and of the soliloquy beginning

> And I forsooth in love ... III. I. 164

which, says Dr Dover Wilson, belongs to the play's revising. But this does not invalidate my point; rather the contrary. Turn also from one of the many sets of wit to Katharine's haunting answer when Rosaline twits her with rebellion against Cupid:

ROSALINE You'll ne'er be friends with him; he kill'd your sister.
KATHARINE He made her melancholy, sad, and heavy:
  And so she died: had she been light, like you,
  Of such a merry, nimble, stirring spirit,
  She might have been a grandam ere she died;
  And so may you, for a light heart lives long.

Compare it with the set of wit that follows.

ROSALINE What's your dark meaning, mouse, of this light word?
KATHARINE A light condition in a beauty dark.
ROSALINE We need more light to find your meaning out.
KATHARINE You'll mar the light, by taking it in snuff;
  Therefore I'll darkly end the argument. V. 2. 13-23

But Rosaline won't let her, and they manage to get five more rather spicier exchanges. It is all very charming; the mere sound is charming, and a 'set of wit' describes it well. Get a knowledge of the game and it may be as attractive to watch for a little as are a few sets of tennis. But pages on pages of such smart repartee will not tell us as much of the speakers as those few simple lines of Katharine's tell us – of herself and her love of her sister, and of Rosaline too. . . .

THE STAGING, COSTUME AND CASTING

The play will profit little by any departure from Shakespeare's own staging; nor is this, in its simplicity, hard to deduce. A designer may shift the period of costume fifty years or so back – or forward for that matter – if his taste dictate, and no great harm done. A certain grace may be added to Navarre and his friends by dressing them French fashion, or Italian. The Englishman was not famous for his taste in dress; though, if Portia may be trusted, he only made matters worse when he picked up notions abroad, his doublet in Italy, his round hose in France, his bonnet in Germany and his behaviour everywhere. But these scrupulous young men would be purists in tailoring too. And a comedy of affectations, of nice phrases, asks that its characters should be expressive to their boot-toes, significant in the very curl of a feather. None of the others are hard to picture. Shakespeare sets Armado before us clearly, the refined traveller from tawny Spain, dignified and mock melancholy, carrying his rapier as might a conqueror of kingdoms, though for 'remuneration' to his messengers he cannot exceed three farthings, and must go shirtless, woolward for penance; he is black-suited, of course. Figure of fun as he is, though, his pride is not pinchbeck, nor must he look merely ridiculous. He sponges on no one, and hides his poverty all he can. When Costard infamonizes him among potentates – and the potentates, we may be sure, die with laughing – Shakespeare gives him great dignity in humiliation. We can picture Moth, that well-educated infant. Navarre, we may suppose, has made him page to the tall angular Spaniard for the fun of the contrast in the looks of them. Moth knows this well enough, be sure; and just how to make the best of his own share in the composition. He should not dress like Armado, that would coarsen the joke. He might still be wearing the King's livery. So might Costard, who makes a third in this conjunction, and has a flavour of Sancho Panza about him, even as Armado every now and then sets one thinking of that greater Don, yet in the womb of imagination. To complete this group we have the harsh, drab aspect of Holofernes; Sir Nathaniel, sober-suited but well-liking; and Dull, who is dull of countenance and clothing too. These will stand in sombre contrast to the choice-garmented Court and the rainbow beauty of the Princess and her ladies; till, for their show of the Nine Worthies, they too burst into flower, and into most wondrous and gaudy flowering.

The pictorial values in the pageantry of this last scene have their dramatic value too. The Russian maskings have been laid aside, cumbrously fantastic things, convenient cloakings. Yesterday Navarre and his friends were recluse philosophers; splendid even so, no doubt, but with a pallid splendour. Today they are in love and glowingly apparelled, in which symbolism their ladies can match them; and against this delicately blended colouring the village pageant tells crude and loud. Into the midst there suddenly steps Marcade, in black from head to foot. He hardly needs to speak.

> The king your father –
> Dead, for my life!
> Even so, my tale is told.

Berowne takes order.

> Worthies, away! The scene begins to cloud. v. 2. 708–10

And it must seem to cloud; the gay colours fading out, the finery folding about its wearers like wings. But this is not the end, for the end must not be melancholy. The country-folk have yet to sing and dance their antic; a little crowd of them, dressed to match the

> . . . daisies pied and violets blue,
> And lady-smocks all silver white,
> And cuckoo-buds of yellow hue . . . v. 2. 881–3

The comedy of affectations comes to its full close upon notes of pastoral freshness and simplicity. . . .

from *Prefaces to Shakespeare I* by Harley Granville-Barker, 1930

EIGHT

Planes of Reality

... ELSEWHERE there are similar reminders of the play as play, without any ostensible design of rendering plausible an improbable incident. Indeed, in *Love's Labour's Lost*, the immediate intention is diametrically opposite: to excuse a naturalistic departure from the normal theatrical habit of ending a light comedy with wedding bells. *Love's Labour's Lost* is the most artificial of Shakespeare's comedies; the only note of ungarbled seriousness occurs at the end, when Biron is condemned to 'jest a twelvemonth in an hospital' as a cure for levity and a preliminary to marriage. The unusual task imposed by Rosaline upon her knight breaks incongruously into the abstract gaiety of a simplified play-world, bearing a sharp reminder of suffering and sorrow, ingredients of the real world hitherto unheeded through five acts of artificial wit-combat. This bitter reminder of the real world is underlined and at the same time distanced by the ensuing remarks of Biron and the King:

> BIRON Our wooing doth not end like an old play;
>   Jack hath not Jill: these ladies' courtesy
>   Might well have made our sport a comedy.
> KING Come, sir, it wants a twelvemonth and a day,
> And then 'twill end.
> BIRON   That's too long for a play.   v. 2. 884

The young Shakespeare, commenting in public on his technique, reinforces the dual consciousness of play-world and real world in the minds of his audience. A play so artificial may end quite appropriately with a reference from within to its own true nature. But, coming immediately after the hospital theme, this passage serves a more delicate purpose. With its reminder of reality, as distinguished from the play-world, it underlines the reference to human suffering by taking us back to the real world where it is to be encountered.

At the same time, by making explicit the nature of the play as a play, it preserves a threatened poise: we remember that it is a stage personage only who is to 'jest a twelvemonth in an hospital', and that personal sympathy would be misplaced. The intellectual position of the comedy has been strengthened, whilst its 'artificiality' has been satisfactorily restored.

from *Shakespeare and the Popular Dramatic Tradition* by S. L. Bethell, 1944

NINE

Navarre and His Bookmen

I

THE genius of comedy, says Socrates at the end of Plato's *Symposium*, is 'the same with that of tragedy', and the true artist in tragedy is an artist in comedy also. The interesting thesis is not developed. Socrates advances it just before the banquet finally breaks up, in the grey light of dawn. Aristodemus, who reports the occasion, was only half awake at the time, and did not hear the beginning of the discourse. Aristophanes and Agathon, to whom Socrates is addressing himself, merely assent to the proposition, 'being drowsy, and not quite following the argument'.

Comedy and tragedy alike are imitations of the actions of men, and the crucial fact about man is his dual nature. His duality makes him an incongruous figure, and if there were nothing incongruous in the human condition, there would be nothing to dramatize. The union of a spiritual essence and a corporal existence poses the initial incongruity, and from this all others flow. Infinite aspirations are subject to a finite capacity for achievement; immortal longings break upon the fact of mortality; the rational purpose gives way to irrational impulse. Incongruities such as these are the warp and the woof of human experience, and the fabric of human life reveals a pattern shot through with discrepancies: the discrepancy between the ideal and the reality, between the intention and the deed, to name those which subsume all others. To dramatize these is the purpose of tragedy and comedy alike, and this is the reason that the true artist in the one will be an artist in the other as well. In the process of dramatization, the discrepancies that I have named will appear terrible when the insolvable contradictions which they pose are urgently felt, as in *Oedipus* or *Lear*; humorous when they are eventually recognized as natural and accepted as such, as in Shakespearian comedies like *Love's Labour's Lost* or *Twelfth Night*; or grotesque when reality violates the ideal to the point of reducing it to virtual travesty, as in a tragedy like Shakespeare's *Timon of Athens* or a comedy like Ben Jonson's *Volpone*.

Love's Labour's Lost is particularly useful in defining the nature of comedy and its relation to tragedy, because the issues which this essentially merry comedy poses lead directly to that basic fact of human incongruity where comedy and tragedy equally inhere, and in the representation of which 'a change of lighting suffices to make one into the other'. Of this play, M. C. Bradbrook has said that it 'is as near as Shakespeare ever came to writing satire', and what, in addition to fine manners, pedantry, and the disguises of love, is being satirized in it is the infirmity of human purpose. Its fable, which turns on vows sworn and then forsworn under the pressure of circumstance and necessity, is the sufficient proof of this. The treatment of the fable is dry, elegant, and highly mannered, and this is as it should be. An artificial style is the only appropriate means of purveying – and in the same moment commenting on – an artificial view of life. The action of *Love's Labour's Lost* is directed at righting the balance of nature, which the proud in their simplicity would upset; it is concerned with undeceiving the self-deceived, thereby making clear the gulf that separates human intentions from deeds. In achieving so much – in enlightening the foolish without destroying them – it accomplishes the purpose which comic drama is uniquely capable of bringing to pass.

2

The play begins with the declaration of a purpose which takes the form, indeed, of a programme for regulating the life of man. It is deceptively simple. The King of Navarre with three of his attendant lords – Berowne, Longaville, and Dumain – subscribe to an oath whereby they will devote themselves for a period of three years to a life of study and fasting, during which term they renounce the company of women. The purpose they have declared is nothing less than an all-out war against the senses; and the King can address his more or less willing disciples as noble warriors, enrolled under the colours of the spirit in its eternal war with the flesh:

> Therefore, brave conquerors – for so you are
> That war against your own affections
> And the huge army of the world's desires –   I. i. 8

About the wisdom of this, Berowne, the fourth party to the high design, is doubtful from the beginning. They are 'barren tasks, too hard to keep' to which the others have pledged themselves; his fellows have 'sworn too hard-a-keeping oath'. The project is, in fact, doomed from the outset, as he alone has the wit to see. In the first place, the daughter of the King of France is due to arrive shortly at the court of Navarre on a diplomatic mission, and must be received, a circumstance which the King of Navarre has 'quite forgot'. The decree that no woman come within a mile of the court on pain of losing her tongue must of force be dispensed with 'on mere necessity', and in affirming as much, the King unwittingly names the power that will swamp his whole grand endeavour, as the wise Berowne quickly sees. 'Necessity will make us all for-sworn | Three thousand times within this three years' space', he says; and he proceeds to an all-important statement about the nature of the 'affections' against which his fellows have pledged themselves to wage war:

> For every man with his affects is born,
> Not by might mast'red, but by special grace.   I. i. 149

But Berowne, being an agreeable sort, subscribes his name to the oath at the others' urging, though he reserves the right to let necessity plead his case if he break faith.

That all four parties to the oath will end by breaking faith is, at this point, midway through the opening scene, in the nature of a foregone conclusion. The second half of Act I, Scene 1 presents us with direct evidence of how little binding the King's edicts are upon his subjects. Villainy is abroad in the King's own park, where nature is having its way. The constable Dull appears, with a letter from the fantastical knight, Don Adriano de Armado, and with the clownish rustic Costard in custody. Armado has come upon Costard in the company of the country wench Jaquenetta, and this in despite of the King's proclaimed edict decreeing a year's imprisonment for the man taken with a wench. Spurred on by his 'ever-esteemed duty',

Armado has remanded Costard to the custody of Dull, to be brought before the King for judgement. Costard, bumpkin though he be, knows what some of his more sophisticated superiors would, for the moment, deny. 'It is the manner of a man to speak to a woman', he says with unassailable logic, and it is his only adequate means of defence, being in truth but another way of saying what Berowne has already stated: that 'every man with his affects is born', and that these are not to be mastered 'by might'.

In the following scene we have further evidence of the ravages worked by passion, this time in the person of the 'magnificent' Armado himself. In his punctilious zeal he has seized upon the transgressing Costard in the name of the law, rather in the manner in which the unyielding Angelo arrests the erring Claudio and Juliet in *Measure for Measure*. And again like Angelo, Armado finds himself a prey to the same passion whose workings he would punish in others. He confesses to his page Moth that he is in love with the country girl he took in the park with Costard. The confession strikes the burlesque note appropriate to the extravagant figure of the fantastical Spaniard, but it achieves as well the very blend of aversion and desire to be noted wherever passion long withstood is yielded to. Love is here, as always on such occasions, a delicious torment, and Armado savours the bitter dose as he contemplates the baseness of the young woman who is the object of his passion.

I do affect the very ground, which is base, where her shoe, which is baser, guided by her foot, which is basest, doth tread.

It is the glory of love to subdue men, and Armado must fall, as has many another great one (Samson, Solomon, Hercules) in the catalogue of love's victims which he runs through. Thus subdued, there is nothing for it but to bid farewell to the life of knightly endeavour: 'Adieu, valour; rust, rapier; be still, drum; for your manager is in love; yea, he loveth'.

3

The proud, in comedy and tragedy alike, are forever being humbled, in one way or another. The King of Navarre explains to the Princess of France that he cannot receive her into his court by reason of an oath that he has sworn. To this she merely answers, 'Our Lady help my Lord! He'll be forsworn'. Whereupon the King replies with conviction, 'Not for the world, fair madam, by my will'. In saying as much, he has named the very faculty which can best be expected to overthrow his high resolve, for 'will' in Elizabethan usage means both 'inclination' and 'carnal appetite'; and nothing is better calculated to point up the basic infirmity of the King's purpose than the fact that it is dependent on something so dubious as the human will to carry it through. All of which the clever lady is quick to note. She is not impressed with the King's 'will' to keep his oath. 'Why, will shall break it; will, and nothing else', she says. He replies, rather feebly, that the Princess is ignorant of what he has sworn. This is not, in fact, true, as we already know. But she contents herself with stating merely that, 'Were my lord so, his ignorance were wise, | Where now his knowledge must prove ignorance'.

The words of the Princess suggest what has already been hinted more than once to this point in the play: namely, that knowledge, at least on the terms by which the King and his courtiers would seek it, will prove but folly in the end. The sufficient reason for this is that the object of their study (books) is mischosen. In the opening scene, Berowne has gone to some lengths to prove the vanity of poring painfully 'upon a book | To seek the light of truth'. And he has proceeded there to advise his fellows of the true object of study, wherein inheres the light of the only form of knowledge with which aspiring youth has any concern: a light which, if it begins by dazzling, ends by illuminating the senses:

> Study me how to please the eye indeed,
> By fixing it upon a fairer eye;
> Who dazzling so, that eye shall be his heed,
> And give him light that it was blinded by.   I. I. 80

The eye of the King of Navarre, in the course of his first interview with the French Princess, during which he tells her of his will to keep his oath, is dazzled by her fair form in just the manner Berowne has prescribed; and upon the King's departure, at the end of Act II, Boyet, the old love-mongering lord in attendance on the ladies of France, can report to the Princess that 'Navarre is infected', which is to say, 'affected'. And he recounts in detail how all the King's 'behaviours did make their retire | To the court of his eye, peeping thorough desire', with inevitable results:

> All senses to that sense did make their repair,
> To feel only looking on fairest of fair.   II. I. 239

The defection of 'Navarre and his bookmen' will thereafter follow a conventional course, from the study of books to the study of eyes. By the time the carefully patterned action of Act IV, Scene 3 is finished, each of the young men in his turn has declared his love for one of the French ladies, and has been detected by the others in so doing. Their transformation from scholars to lovers is complete; and the sometime warriors who have sworn themselves to do battle against their 'own affections | And the huge army of the world's desires' are now hailed by Berowne as 'affection's men-at-arms'. The vow that they have sworn has proved, as Dumain has roundly declared in his verses to Katharine, 'for youth unmeet', which is just what Berowne has said from the beginning; and not surprisingly, it is to him that the others turn for 'some salve' to mitigate the pain of perjury of which they are all guilty. The speech in which he sets about to prove their 'loving lawful' and their 'faith not torn' is a fine example of special pleading in defence of folly: folly which, in the context, is proved to be the highest wisdom. The lovers were fools to forswear woman; they will continue fools in 'keeping what is sworn'. The conclusion is inevitable:

> Let us once lose our oaths to find ourselves,
> Or else we lose ourselves to keep our oaths.   IV. 3. 357

But the matter is not quite so simple as Berowne suggests. They will not find themselves simply by losing their oaths, as the long fifth act will prove. They have played at being scholars; now, in the concluding act of the comedy, they play at being lovers, and with hardly more success. In Act V, Scene 2, the ladies of France are found comparing the favours they have received from their several suitors, and passing hard judgement on the conduct of the lovers, who have by now given over all pretence of abiding by their initial vow. If, in the opinion of the ladies, the young men were foolish to forswear love in the first place, their surrender to the passion exhibits folly at its height; and the folly of the lovers is compounded by their very cleverness. Had they not been so clever, they could not now prove so foolish. As the Princess declares:

> None are so surely caught, when they are catch'd,
> As wit turn'd fool; folly, in wisdom hatch'd,
> Hath wisdom's warrant and the help of school,
> And wit's own grace to grace a learned fool.   v. 2. 69

And Rosaline makes an even more penetrating pronouncement when she observes that

> The blood of youth burns not with such excess
> As gravity's revolt to wantonness.   v. 2. 73

4

This goes very deep. One wonders, indeed, if it does not go deeper than the occasion warrants. (So it seems to Mann's Adrian Leverkühn, one of whose first important musical compositions was an opera based on *Love's Labour's Lost.* cf. *Doctor Faustus* (p. 216 of the Alfred A. Knopf, New York, 1948 edition), where the passage quoted above from v. 2. 73-4 has been cited (Mann's Biron is Shakespeare's Berowne): 'he [Biron] is young and not at all grave, and by no means the person who could give occasion to such a comment as that it is lamentable when wise men turn fools and apply all their wit to give folly the appearance of worth. In the mouth of Rosaline and her friends Biron falls quite out of his role; he is no longer Biron, but Shakespeare in his unhappy affair with the dark lady [. . .]'. cf. also, pp. 231-2.) Neither Berowne, the merry mad-cap lord', nor any of his companions, has struck us as particularly grave, and their revolt to wantonness would seem to imply no great falling off from sobriety. Looking to the future of Shakespearian drama, Rosaline's words would seem to apply more appropriately to such a figure as Angelo in *Measure for Measure*, where gravity revolts to wantonness with a fury that bids fair for a time to be terrible in its consequences: the more terrible because Angelo's youthful instincts have been so long restrained. The moral here is not hard to find; and it provides the clue to the basic pattern of Shakespearian comedy; a pattern which consists in a movement from the artificial to the natural, always with the objective of finding oneself. The objective is typically accomplished in the context of a world governed by the seasonal laws of nature, where affectation gives way before the onslaught of the elements. The wonder thus worked is seen in its most mysterious form in *The Tempest* where, in Gonzalo's words near the end of the play, each of the principals has found himself 'When no man was his own'. To find oneself is to know oneself, and to know oneself is to recognize the truth about one's natural condition. In Shakespearian comedy, characters such as Angelo who never come to know themselves have never had occasion to take stock of themselves in the world of created nature; and it is no accident that the action of *Measure for Measure* never moves far beyond the city limits of Vienna. The process of self-discovery which experience of the natural world provides is best described by Duke Senior in *As You Like It*, when he declares his reaction to 'the icy fang | And churlish chiding of the winter's wind' in the Forest of Arden (where, in fact, 'the penalty of Adam | The season's difference', is no longer felt):

> ... when it bites and blows upon my body,
> Even till I shrink with cold, I smile and say
> 'This is no flattery; these are counsellors
> That feelingly persuade me what I am.'
>
> *As You Like It*, II. I. 8

For a man to be feelingly persuaded what he is, is the beginning of wisdom, and so can be nothing other than a salutary experience: salutary, because if a man does not know what he is — which involves, among other things, knowledge of his very human infirmities, his mortal frailties — he is likely to be made rudely, not to say tragically, aware of his natural condition. One thinks of Lear, the much-flattered King who has 'ever but slenderly known himself', as Regan remarks on one occasion, exposed to the wind and the rain on the heath, and brought thereby to a shattering knowledge of his mortal nature in its most essential aspects: 'the thing itself', 'unaccommodated man', 'a poor, bare, forked animal'. This is the tragic destiny of the man who does not know himself; and as is usual in tragedy, the fate that overtakes him is not lacking in irony, the irony here consisting in the incongruous distance that separates what man is in fact from what man, in his self-deceiving pride, thinks he is. But the destiny of the man who does not know himself may have, alternatively, a comic issue; for the lack of self-knowledge implies a failure to recognize the nature of human limitations, and this, like nearly everything else about the human condition, may occasion either tears or laughter.

In the comic vision of experience, the effort to transcend human limitations can never be regarded as other than folly or worse. 'People try to get outside of themselves, and escape from the man', says Montaigne at the end of his last book of essays. 'That is foolishness: instead of transforming themselves into angels, they transform themselves into beasts. Instead of raising they degrade themselves'. We are reminded once again of Angelo in *Measure for Measure*, a character for whom Montaigne's passage might well stand as an epitaph. For Angelo, as his name implies, seeks to be nothing less than angelic, and ends as something of a devil of the flesh when, after years of strictly enforced continence, necessity forces him to give his 'sensual race the rein'. Which reminds us in turn of *Love's Labour's Lost*, and Rosaline's statement that 'The blood of youth burns not with such excess | As gravity's revolt to wantonness', and of Berowne's 'For every man with his affects is born, | Not by might mast'red, but by special grace'. There is, of course, no question of Berowne and his elegant companions transforming themselves into either angels or beasts; their oath is never taken seriously enough for that; they are only made to look distinctly foolish in the eyes of the ladies of France. Still, the fact remains, the oath that they swear is against nature ('Flat treason 'gainst the kingly state of youth', as they later agree), and while the consequences of so swearing, and then finding themselves forsworn, may appear innocent enough in *Love's Labour's Lost*, they will not always be so. To see where this sort of thing leads, one must look to Angelo and *Measure for Measure*. Even in *Love's Labour's Lost*, Berowne recognizes that he and his friends must lose their oaths to find themselves; and if, as I have already said, they will not find themselves simply by losing their oaths, neither will they find themselves until the oaths have been renounced and that particular folly is behind them. To find oneself is to escape from artificiality into the natural, to leave off deceiving oneself by setting about to know oneself. The King of Navarre and his attendant lords are made to realize what Chaucer's Troilus under similar circumstances is forced to acknowledge, that 'no man [may] fordon the lawe of kynde'. Realization of this brings in its wake the realization of something else equally obvious, but hitherto equally ignored by the King of Navarre and his men: that the study of human perfection is ever being undermined by the infirmity of human purpose. 'O heaven, were man | But constant, he were perfect! That one error | Fills him with faults', says Proteus in *The Two Gentlemen of Verona*, and his name, to say nothing of his deeds, underscores the frailty that defeats resolution.

5

Navarre and his bookmen forswear their oath to study, thereby presenting incontrovertible proof of their inconstancy. 'Charity' alone can redeem them, for as Berowne says, 'charity itself fulfils the law, | And who can sever love from charity?' The charity of love repairs the imperfections wrought by the wayward will, and here it is at one with the 'special grace' which, as Berowne has declared earlier, must aid man in the mastery of his affections. Thus, it is unfortunate that the King of Navarre and his men, guilty of perjury on one count, promptly forswear themselves again, this time to the very ladies whose charitable dispositions they must appeal to if their original offence is to be forgiven. The courtiers come to the ladies disguised as Muscovites. The ladies, warned of their intent, and assuming that the gentlemen come 'but in mocking merriment', are prepared to give them 'mock for mock'. They mask themselves, and exchange the favours which each of the suitors has previously sent to his mistress. The gentlemen fall into the trap. Each unsuspectingly pays court to the wrong lady, and all are scoffed for their efforts. They retire in confusion, but return again shortly in their proper shapes. They are forced to confess to their previous disguises; and Berowne, for his part, renounces 'affectation' – where love-making is concerned – in all its forms; it has but blown him 'full of maggot ostentation'. But the worst is not yet behind, for the ladies reveal the deception they themselves have practised on the disguised lords, whereby each has sworn his faith to the wrong mistress. It is left to Berowne, typically, to put into words the enormity of this:

> Now, to our perjury to add more terror,
> We are again forsworn in will and error.   v. 2. 470

Happily, at this point, attention is directed from the folly of the lovers to folly in another guise. The show of the Nine Worthies is announced. The King fears lest the entertainment Armado, Holofernes, and the rest have undertaken to provide will shame them in the eyes of the ladies, but Berowne reassures him. By now they are shame-proof; and further, ''tis some policy | To have one show worse than the King's and his company'. Throughout the play, the affectation of the courtiers who turn scholars only to turn lovers has been parodied in the several affectations of the braggart Armado, the pedant Holofernes, and Sir Nathaniel the hedge-priest. Armado's surrender to the charms of Jaquenetta has anticipated the collapse of the courtiers' vow before the gaze of the ladies of France. The presenters of the show of the Nine Worthies are flouted by the lovers, even as the lovers have been flouted by the ladies; folly is mocked out of countenance, from the King to the pedant. But at the height of the merriment, word is brought of the death of the King of France, and the scene begins to cloud. As the ladies prepare to take their leave, the lovers press their suits in earnest, Berowne as ever serving as their spokesman, and putting their case in 'honest plain words'. The ladies, being gracious, do not reject their suits out of hand; but not unreasonably, they are determined to have some proof of the seriousness of their lovers' intentions before they enter upon 'a world-without-end bargain' with the gentlemen. The Princess speaks for all her train when, addressing herself to the King, she declares plainly that his Grace 'is perjur'd much, | Full of dear guiltiness'. If he will prove his love for her, he will remove himself 'with speed | To some forlorn and naked hermitage, | Remote from all the pleasures of the world', and there remain for a year while the Princess mourns the death of her father. At the end of the period, if the King remain constant, he may have his wish. The condition is echoed by each of the ladies in her turn: Katharine to Dumain, Maria to Longaville. The injunction Rosaline imposes on Berowne is even more explicit: he is to spend his twelvemonth term in visiting 'the speechless sick' and conversing 'with groaning wretches', ever seeking 'with all the fierce endeavour of [his] wit | To enforce the pained impotent to smile'. He promptly cries out upon the impossibility of this, which is precisely the point; if 'mirth cannot move a soul in agony', to be made aware of the fact is, of all ways, 'the way to choke a gibing spirit'. The ascetic life to which the courtiers have pledged themselves at the beginning of the play is going to be theirs after all.

The hope is that it will teach them something of human experience, and that in its grimmer aspects, where privation, suffering, and death round out the cycle of 'revels, dances, masks, and merry hours' with which *Love's Labour's Lost*, until its closing minutes, has been exclusively dealing. It is just possible that, if the frosts which the Princess anticipates for the King in his 'forlorn and naked hermitage' do not indeed nip the gaudy blossoms of his love, they may do for him what 'the icy fang | And churlish chiding of the winter's wind' do for Duke Senior in *As You Like It*: they may 'feelingly persuade' him what he is. Intimations of what a man is have been introduced into *Love's Labour's Lost* before it comes to its end. The foolish Armado, during the show of the Worthies, has turned upon his tormentors, who are ringing some of their wittiest changes on the name of Hector, and invoked respect for the memory of the vanished hero whom he is representing – and he has done so in words that should have silenced the scoffers:

The sweet war-man is dead and rotten; sweet chucks, beat not the bones of the buried; when he breathed, he was a man.   v. 2. 652

The show of the Worthies is itself interrupted by the fact of death; and from here to the end of the play the movement from the artificial to the natural is accelerated. The lovers are assigned to hermitage and hospital for the period of their trial. Armado appears and announces his vow to Jaquenetta 'to hold the plough for her sweet love three year', thereby functioning to the end in his role of zany to his betters. Whereupon he asks the company if they will 'hear the dialogue that the two learned men have compiled in praise of the Owl and the Cuckoo'.

6

Having already been treated to a poetical effusion by the more learned of the two learned men, Holofernes the pedant, in his 'affected' poem beginning 'The preyful Princess pierc'd and prick'd a pretty pleasing pricket', we are not prepared for the wondrous songs of spring and winter which close the play. They are essential to the design. With them the movement from the artificial to the natural is complete. Human nature, in all its moral, and mortal, infirmities, comes finally into focus against the world of created nature, here viewed in its seasonal aspects. There is a hint of death in 'Winter'; there is more than a hint of unsanctified copulation in 'Spring'. But the cry of the owl, funereal bird, sounding from out the dark and the cold, is 'a merry note' within the circle of the winter fire; and if the sound of the cuckoo, derisive emblem of broken marriage vows, strikes fear into the hearts of married men, it is nonetheless the basis of a venerable joke. There is a paradox here. The infirmities of the flesh would not be so troublesome if the vernal meadows were not so inviting; the hardships of winter would be less endurable than they are, were death felt as anything less than a real – though comfortably distant – presence.

To view the infirmities of human nature in perspective is the special province of comedy. In Shakespearian comedy, the perspective is provided by viewing man's moral and mortal frailties in the context of the seasonal variations of the natural world wherein they are adumbrated. Since 'the seasons' difference' is a principal consequence of the 'penalty of Adam', of which Duke Senior speaks, there is a virtually causal connexion between man's infirmities and a mutable world. To view in such a perspective all the natural shocks to which human flesh is heir is to transcend them; and in Shakespearian comedy the trick is typically turned by the most economical means, with a song. After Duke Senior has catalogued the uses of adversity, Amiens congratulates him on his ability to 'translate the stubbornness of fortune | Into so quiet and so sweet a style'. And later in *As You Like It*, Amiens himself accomplishes just such a wonder in his song beginning 'Blow, blow, thou winter wind' ('Thou art not so unkind | As man's ingratitude'). Folly, knavery, and worse are always with us, like the wind and the rain that accompany them in their several outcroppings from infancy to man's estate in Feste's song at the end of *Twelfth Night*; and nothing is better calculated to show just how appropriate a commentary on human experience, viewed tragically or comically, this is, than the fact that the same song – with its burden of 'hey, ho, the wind and the rain' and 'the rain it raineth every day' – is sung by the Fool at the height of the storm in *Lear*. Of the mad Ophelia and her songs, Laertes says: 'Thought and affliction, passion, hell itself, | She turns to favour and to prettiness', and this sums up the whole lyric achievement of the songs of Shakespearian tragedy and comedy. In the songs of Shakespearian comedy, the grimmest facts of human experience are transmuted by the lyric art, relegated to their proper place in the natural scheme of things, and thereupon dismissed, their sting having been drawn. The ugly fact of adultery, potent disturber of ordered society, is echoed back from the natural world only in the cry of the giddiest of birds. Human ingratitude is dispatched with a 'heigh-ho', as in the continuation of Amiens's song in *As You Like It* ('Heigh-ho! sing heigh-ho! unto the green holly. | Most friendship is feigning, most loving mere folly'). And death's harbinger sounds a reassuring – and therefore merry – note because, in the rural world where it is heard, it bears witness to the success of one more season's efforts to keep the enemy of life at bay. Even as it sounds its 'Tu-who; | Tu-whit, tu-who' greasy Joan keels the pot. Which is natural enough, for life, in despite of death, broken friendships, cuckolded husbands, and perjured lovers, goes on. The 'lawe of kynde' takes care of that.

from Part I ('The Ideal Unfulfilled') of *The Hyacinth Room: An Investigation into the Nature of Comedy, Tragedy, and Tragicomedy* by Cyrus Hoy, 1964

Suggestions for Further Reading

C. L. BARBER: 'The Folly of Wit and Masquerade in *Love's Labour's Lost*' (*Shakespeare's Festive Comedy*, Chapter V). Mr Barber's approach is by way of relating comedy to holiday. Holiday is a social custom in which normal responsibilities are replaced by misrule; comedy, in the hands of a serious dramatist, both expresses such release, and explores its relation to reality.

M. C. BRADBROOK: *Shakespeare and Elizabethan Poetry*, XII. 1. 'A play about courtship which turns out to be a play about love, and an attack on fine speech which is consistently full of fine speeches'.

ANNE RIGHTER: *Shakespeare and the Idea of the Play*, IV. 3. This stimulating book examines Shakespeare's use of the metaphor of the theatre in his plays, and shows how the question of stage illusion is raised in the minds of the audience to deepen and baffle their sense of what is real and what artificial. There is a much longer discussion of the play by the same author (under her maiden name, Bobbyann Roesen) in *Shakespeare Quarterly* for October 1953: a sensitive and graceful commentary that traces the contrast of Academe and outside world from the first scene to the final invocation of 'the reality of the greasy kitchen-maid and her pot, a reality which must sooner or later break through and destroy the charm of the artificial and the illusory'.

D. L. STEVENSON: *The Love Game Comedy*. Tries to distinguish the frankly romantic (even escapist) comedies – *The Merchant of Venice, Twelfth Night* – from the love-game comedies that play antagonistic attitudes to love against each other. Chapter XI discusses *Love's Labour's Lost, As You Like It* and *Much Ado*.

MARK VAN DOREN: *Shakespeare*. Suggests that the delight and excellences of the play (style, wit, topicality, 'love of language for its own intoxicating sake') are also its limitations. We demand of poetry 'that it be other than satin; even the best satin'.

G. D. WILLCOCK: *Shakespeare as a Critic of Language* (Shakespeare Association Lecture, 1935). Mostly about *Love's Labour's Lost*.

F. A. YATES: *A Study of Love's Labour's Lost*. Deals with the topical element, and attempts to identify real movements and individuals behind the play.

A MIDSUMMER NIGHT'S DREAM

TEN

The Making of *A Midsummer Night's Dream*

... HERE, then, we have a young playwright commissioned to write a wedding play – a play to be presented at court. He is naturally anxious to shine; and, moreover, though his fellow-playwrights already pay him the compliment of being a little jealous, he still has his spurs to win.

As I read the play and seek to divine its process of construction, I seem – and the reader must take this for what it is worth – to see Shakespeare's mind working somewhat as follows:

He turns over his repertory of notions, and takes stock.

'Lyly's model has had its day, and the bloom is off it; I must not repeat the experiment of *Love's Labour's Lost*. . . . I have shown that I can do great things with mistaken identity, but I cannot possibly express the fun of that further than I did in *The Comedy of Errors*; and the fun there was clever, but a trifle hard, if not in-human. . . . But here is a wedding; a wedding should be human; a wedding calls for poetry – and I long to fill a play with poetry. (For I *can* write poetry – look at *Venus and Adonis*!) . . . Still, mistaken identity is a trick I know, a trick in which I am known to shine. . . . If I could only make it poetical! . . . A pair of lovers? For mistaken identity that means two pairs of lovers. . . . Yet, steady! We must not make it farcical. It was all very well to make wives mistake their husbands. That has been funny ever since the world began; that is as ancient as cuckoldry, or almost. But this is a wedding play, and the sentiment must be fresh. Lovers are not so easily mistaken as wives and husbands – or ought not to be – in poetry.

'I like, too' – we fancy the young dramatist continuing – 'that situation of the scorned lady following her sweetheart. . . . I did not quite bring it off in *The Two Gentlemen of Verona*; but it is none the less a good situation, and I must use it again. (And he did: not only here, but in *All's Well That Ends Well*, for instance.) . . . Lovers

mistaking one another . . . scorned lady following the scorner . . .
wandering through a wood (that is poetical, anyhow). . . . Yes, and
by night; this play has to be written for a bridal eve. . . . A night
for lovers – a summer's night – a midsummer's night – dewy
thickets – the moon. . . . The moon? Why, of course, the moon!
Pitch-darkness is for tragedy, moonlight for softer illusion.
Lovers can be pardonably mistaken – under the moon. . . . What
besides happens on a summer's night, in a woodland, under the
moon?

'Eh? . . . Oh, by Heaven! Fairies! Real Warwickshire fairies!
Fairies full of mischief – Robin Goodfellow and the rest. Don't I
know about *them*? Fairies full of mischief – and for a wedding,
too! How does that verse of Spenser's go?

> Ne let the Pouke –

'Fairies, artificers and ministers of all illusion . . . the fairy ointment,
philters, pranks, "the little western flower" –

> Before milk-white, now purple with Love's wounds,
> And maidens call it Love-in-Idleness.

'These and wandering lovers, a mistress scorned – why, we scarcely
need the moon, after all!'

Then – for the man's fancy never started to work but it straight-
way teemed – we can watch it opening out new alleys of fun,
weaving fresh delicacies upon this central invention. 'How, for a
tangle, to get one of the fairies caught in the web they spin? Why
not even the Fairy Queen herself? . . . Yes; but the mortal she falls
in with? Shall he be one of the lovers? . . . Well, to say the truth, I
haven't given any particular character to these lovers. The absolute
jest would be to bring opposite extremes into the illusion, to make
Queen Mab dote on a gross clown. . . . All very well, but I *haven't
any clowns*. . . . The answer to that seems simple: if I haven't, I
ought to have. . . . Stay! I have been forgetting the Interlude all
this while. We must have an Interlude; our Interlude in *Love's
Labour's Lost* proved the making of the play. . . . Now suppose we
make a set of clowns perform the Interlude, as in *Love's Labour's
Lost*, and get them chased by the fairies while they are rehearsing?

Gross flesh and gossamer – that's an idea! If I cannot use it now, I certainly will some day. . . . But I *can* use it now! What is that story in Ovid, about Midas and the ass's ears? Or am I confusing it with another story – which I read the other day, in that book about witches – of a man transformed into an ass?'

Enough! I am not, of course, suggesting that Shakespeare constructed *A Midsummer Night's Dream* just in this way. (As the provincial mayor said to the eminent statesman, 'Aha, sir! that's more than you or me knows. That's *Latin*!') But I do suggest that we can immensely increase our delight in Shakespeare and strengthen our understanding of him if, as we read him again and again, we keep asking ourselves *how the thing was done.* . . .

. . . I once discussed with a friend how, if given our will, we would have *A Midsummer Night's Dream* presented. We agreed at length on this:

The set scene should represent a large Elizabethan hall, panelled, having a lofty oak-timbered roof and an enormous staircase. The cavity under the staircase, occupying in breadth two-thirds of the stage, should be fronted with folding or sliding doors, which, being opened, should reveal the wood, recessed, moonlit, with its trees upon a flat arras or tapestry. On this secondary remoter stage the lovers should wander through their adventures, the fairies now conspiring in the quiet hall under the lantern, anon withdrawing into the woodland to befool the mortals straying there. Then, for the last scene and the interlude of *Pyramus and Thisbe*, the hall should be filled with lights and company. That over, the bridal couples go up the great staircase. Last of all – and after a long pause, when the house is quiet, the lantern all but extinguished, the hall looking vast and eerie, lit only by a last flicker from the hearth – the fairies, announced by Puck, should come tripping back, swarming forth from cupboards and down curtains, somersaulting downstairs, sliding down the baluster rails; all hushed as they fall to work with their brooms – hushed, save for one little voice and a thin, small chorus scarcely more audible than the last dropping embers:

Through this house give glimmering light,
  By the dead and drowsy fire;
Every elf and fairy sprite
  Hop as light as bird from brier. . . .
Hand in hand, with fairy grace,
Will we sing and bless this place.

          Trip away,
          Make no stay,
    Meet me all by break of day.

from *Shakespeare's Workmanship* by Sir Arthur Quiller-
Couch, 1918

ELEVEN

The Masque Transmuted

From their gross matter she abstracts their forms,
    And draws a kind of quintessence from things;
Which to her proper nature she transforms
    To bear them, light, on her celestial wings.
                                SIR JOHN DAVIES

IN the last chapter I suggested that certain qualities in the poetry of
Spenser and Milton were the result of the close relationship between
masquing and poetry. In this chapter I shall make a special study of
A Midsummer Night's Dream and *The Tempest*, two masque-like
plays which are particularly happy examples of the transformation
of the masque by the creative imagination of the poet. For the
question as to the relation between *A Midsummer Night's Dream*,
The Tempest, and the Court masque, is not merely a matter of
classification: behind it lies the vital question as to how far the art of
a nation is dependent on the quantity and quality of its recreation,
and how far the individual genius is dependent upon the artistic
talent diffused throughout society.

The suggestion that *A Midsummer Night's Dream* and *The
Tempest* should be regarded as masques has little to recommend it.
In all probability both plays were written for the celebration of
Court weddings, but they are not masques, because there are no
masquers, because they are independent of their occasion, because
their plots are not mere inductions leading up to masque dances,
because there is nothing in them corresponding to the sudden
failure of detachment which occurs at the end of Peele's *Arraign-
ment of Paris*, and even to a lesser extent in the final scene of Milton's
Comus. On the other hand, if they are further removed from the
masque form, they are much closer to its spirit than is *Comus*. For
Shakespeare perceived, or at any rate acted upon, the principle that
the masque must die to live. Ben Jonson failed nobly in his effort to

99

exalt the soul of the masque, because he was for ever hampered by its body, but Shakespeare, being a playwright, not a masque poet, was able to disregard the masque body altogether, and instead of having to supply the place of music, carpentry, and dancing by inadequate prose description, he transmuted all these things into poetry, and wove them into the very texture of his plays.

The scenic element is almost as important in *A Midsummer Night's Dream* as in the masque, but it is treated in a very different way. The wood near Athens is not dependent upon, rather it is antagonistic to, the art of the scene painter. Even if *A Midsummer Night's Dream* was well-staged at Court, still Oberon's description of his surroundings could hardly be translated into terms of paint and canvas, for what scene painter would be quite equal to the 'bank where the wild thyme blows', or, indeed, what human actor could obey Titania's stage direction:

> Come, now a roundel and a fairy song;
> Then, for the third part of a minute, hence...?   II. 2. 1–2

The feeling of the countryside, the romantic fairy-haunted earth, has affected the very details of language.

> Your eyes are lode-stars; and your tongue's sweet air
> More tuneable than lark to shepherd's ear,
> When wheat is green, when hawthorn buds appear.
>
> I. 1. 183–5

When Bottom appears with his ass's head:

> As wild geese that the creeping fowler eye,
> Or russet-pated choughs, many in sort,
> Rising and cawing at the gun's report,
> Sever themselves and madly sweep the sky;
> So, at his sight, away his fellows fly.   III. 2. 20–24

Titania winds Bottom in her arms:

> So doth the woodbine the sweet honeysuckle
> Gently entwist; the female ivy so
> Enrings the barky fingers of the elm.   IV. 1. 39–41

'Acorn', 'canker-blossom', 'hindering knot grass', are epithets flung at each other by the quarrelsome lovers.

When Duke Theseus has left the lovers to themselves, Demetrius, still dazed and only half awake, murmurs:

> These things seem small and undistinguishable,
> Like far off mountains turned into clouds.   IV. I. 184–5

It is a fine image, giving just that suggestion of awe and uncertainty which was needed to soften the transition from dream. But the women are suffering even more than the men from that exhaustion and bedraggledness, which is so oppressive in the small hours after a sleepless night:

> *Re-enter Helena*
> HELENA O weary night! O long and tedious night,
>   Abate thy hours! Shine, comforts, from the east!
>   That I may back to Athens by daylight. . . .
>   *Re-enter Hermia*
> HERMIA Never so weary, never so in woe,
>   Bedabbled with the dew and torn with briers,
>   I can no further crawl, no further go;
>   My legs can keep no pace with my desires.
>   Here will I rest me till the break of day.
>   Heavens shield Lysander, if they mean a fray!
>   III. 2. 431–3, 442–7

The lovers are all asleep on the flowery bank, when they are joined by Titania, Bottom and the fairies. Bottom has 'an exposition of sleep' come upon him and, as he and the Fairy Queen rest together, Oberon and Puck arrive and conquer Cupid's flower by Dian's bud. Titania wakes, freed from the spell, takes hands with Oberon, and the day dawns.

> PUCK Fairy king, attend, and mark:
>   I do hear the morning lark.
> OBERON Then, my queen, in silence sad,
>   Trip we after the night's shade;
>   We the globe can compass soon,
>   Swifter than the wandering moon.   IV. I. 90–95

The fairies vanish, a horn winds, Theseus, Hippolyta, and the rest break in with a clatter of horses and hounds, the day breaks and the shadows flee away. But the broad sunlight is not suited to the Midsummer Night's Dream, the day soon passes and gives place to torchlight. It would have been a simple plan to leave the fairy part in the centre of the play as a dream interval in the waking workaday world, but Shakespeare knew better than that. There is nothing more disappointing to a child than to find that the fairy tale was only a dream after all, and children know best how a fairy tale should be conducted.

> The iron tongue of midnight hath tolled twelve;
> Lovers, to bed; 'tis almost fairy time.   v. i. 352–3

Once more the colouring changes. The mortals are gone, the bright festal lights are dimmed, 'now the wasted brands do glow', now the fire is dead and drowsy, and very quietly, very lightly, the fairies come in; dreamland has invaded reality, and who shall say which is which, for Puck left behind with his broom and his parting word sweeps the whole thing away, like the leaves of yesteryear.

To compare a very great with a very small thing, the imaginative effect of this kind of plot-weaving is like that of the transformation scenes in ballet or pantomime, where groups of dancers come in like waves of colour, melting one into another. The effect is attractive even when crudely and unbeautifully designed. Transmuted into poetry it is of surpassing charm. It could only have been so transmuted at a time when pageantry was part of the people's life, when beauty was an element in all their recreations and 'they drew it in as simply as their breath'.

Music in the Court masque was even more important than scenery. Again and again, in the accounts of Elizabethan and Jacobean revels, we are told of the entrancing quality of the music. Robert Laneham told his merchant friend how Elizabeth stood by night on the bridge at Kenilworth and listened to the music sounding from barges on the quiet water. The music which accompanied the show of the *Lady of the Lake* moved him to ecstasy:

Noow, Syr, the ditty in mitter so aptly endighted to the matter, and after by voys so deliciously deliver'd ... every instrument agayn in hiz kind so excellently tunabl; and this in the eeving of the day, resoounding from the calm waters, whear prezens of her Majesty, and longing to listen, had utterly damped all noyz and dyn; the hole armony conveyd in tyme, tune, and temper thus incomparably melodious; with what pleazure, Master Martyn, with what sharpnes of conceyt, with what lyvely delighte, this moought pears [pierce] into the heerers harts; I pray ye imagin yoorself az ye may; for, so God judge me, by all the wit and cunning I have, I cannot express, I promis yoo.... Muzik iz a nobl art!*

This music Shakespeare has transmuted into his poetry, as he has transmuted the spectacular element of Pageantry. Laneham's emotion still vibrates in the words of Oberon:

> My gentle Puck, come hither. Thou remember'st
> Since once I sat upon a promontory,
> And heard a mermaid on a dolphin's back
> Uttering such dulcet and harmonious breath,
> That the rude sea grew civil at her song,
> And certain stars shot madly from their spheres,
> To hear the sea-maid's music.   II. I. 148-54

The whole play is musically written. It is interesting to compare Milton's famous 'Sabrina' lyric with any of the fairy songs in *A Midsummer Night's Dream* and *The Tempest*. In 'Sabrina' each word is exquisitely right, each word is an entity with its own peculiar value. In Shakespeare's songs the words melt into one another, and sometimes meaning is almost lost in melody and emotion. There is the same musical quality in the flowing blank verse of *A Midsummer Night's Dream*, verse which is lyrical rather than dramatic; liquid clear, never checked in its course by some sudden, sharp, projecting thought. Milton's dialogue has the terse, stichomythic quality of Greek or Senecan drama, Shakespeare's is a part-song (cf. *A Midsummer Night's Dream*, I. I. 132 ff., with *Comus*, lines 271 ff.).

* Laneham's *Account of the Queen's Entertainment at Killingworth Castle*, 1575, reprinted in John Nichols's *Progress and Public Processions of Queen Elizabeth*, Vol. I, pp. 458, 459.

The real soul of the masque, however, was the rhythmic movement of living bodies. It is owing to this fact that *A Midsummer Night's Dream* is more nearly related to the genuine masque than is *Comus*. In *Comus*, as we have seen, though dances occur, they are merely incidental, and the play would be scarcely altered by their omission. In *A Midsummer Night's Dream* most – not all – of the dances are vitally connected with the plot. For instance, Titania's awakening in Act IV, Scene 1 is an important point in the play, for it is the point where the ravel begins to be untangled, and the occasion is celebrated by a dance of reunion between Fairy King and Fairy Queen:

> OBERON Sound, music! Come, my queen, take hands with me,
> And rock the ground whereon these sleepers be.
> Now thou and I are new in amity,
> And will tomorrow midnight solemnly
> Dance in Duke Theseus' house triumphantly,
> And bless it to all fair prosperity.
> There shall the pairs of faithful lovers be
> Wedded, with Theseus, all in jollity.
>
> IV. 1. 82–9

The rhythm of the poetry is a dance rhythm, the lines rock and sway with the movement of the fairies. Even more closely in the last scene does the verse echo the light pattering steps of the elves. There is nothing like this in *Comus*. The lyrics there are exquisite, melodious, but they are not dance-songs. Even the entry of Comus is poetry of the *Il Penseroso* order, imaginative, intellectual, reminiscent, while Shakespeare's lines are alive with movement, and suggest the repeat and turn and rhythmic beat of dancing. In a word, in *Comus* we have thought turned to poetry, while in *A Midsummer Night's Dream* we have sound and movement turned to poetry.

The influence of the dance has affected not merely isolated songs and speeches, but the whole structure of *A Midsummer Night's Dream*. Again a comparison with *Comus* is helpful. The difference in style between *Comus* and *A Midsummer Night's Dream* depends upon a difference of spirit. *Comus* is a criticism of life, it springs from an abstract idea: *A Midsummer Night's Dream* is a dance, a movement of bodies. The plot is a pattern, a figure, rather than a series of events occasioned by human character and passion, and this pattern, especially in the moonlight parts of the play, is the pattern of a dance.

> Enter a Fairie at one doore, and Robin Goodfellow at another. . . .
> Enter the King of Fairies, at one doore, with his traine; and the Queene, at another with hers.
>
> II. I. 0, 59

The appearance and disappearance and reappearance of the various lovers, the will-o'-the-wisp movement of the elusive Puck, form a kind of figured ballet. The lovers quarrel in a dance pattern: first, there are two men to one woman and the other woman alone, then for a brief space a circular movement, each one pursuing and pursued, then a return to the first figure with the position of the women reversed, then a cross-movement, man quarrelling with man and woman with woman, and then, as finale, a general setting to partners, including not only lovers but fairies and royal personages as well.

This dance-like structure makes it inevitable that the lovers should be almost as devoid of character as masquers or masque-presenters. The harmony and grace of the action would have been spoilt by convincing passion.

The only character study in *A Midsummer Night's Dream* is to be found in the portrayal of Bottom, Theseus, and perhaps Hippolyta. Even in drawing these characters Shakespeare was evidently influenced by the memory of pageants, complimentary speeches and entertainments addressed by townspeople and humble folk to the Queen or to the nobility. A glance through Nichols's *Public Progresses* shows what innumerable lengthy speeches, what innumerable disguisings and shows, Elizabeth was obliged to bear with gracious demeanour. Her experiences were similar to those of Theseus:

> Where I have come, great clerks have purposed
> To greet me with premeditated welcomes;
> Where I have seen them shiver and look pale,
> Make periods in the midst of sentences,
> Throttle their practis'd accent in their fears,
> And, in conclusion, dumbly have broke off,
> Not paying me a welcome.
>
> V. I. 93-9

One Sunday afternoon, at Kenilworth Castle, Elizabeth and her Court whiled away the time by watching the country-people at a Brideale and Morris Dance. Their amused kindly tolerance is just that of Theseus and the lovers towards the Athenian workmen. So that even in the most solid and dramatic parts of his play Shakespeare is only giving an idealized version of courtly and country revels and of the people that played a part in them.

In *A Midsummer Night's Dream* Bottom and his companions serve the same purpose as the antimasque in the courtly revels. It is true that Shakespeare's play was written before Ben Jonson had elaborated and defined the antimasque, but from the first grotesque dances were popular, and the principle of contrast was always latent in the masque. There is, however, a great difference between Jonson's and Shakespeare's management of foil and relief. In the antimasque (e.g. in *The Masque of Queens*) the transition is sudden and the contrast complete, a method of composition effective enough in spectacle and ballet. But in a play, as Shakespeare well knew, the greatest beauty is gained through contrast when the difference is obvious and striking, but rises out of a deep though unobtrusive resemblance. This could not be better illustrated than by the picture of Titania winding the assheaded Bottom in her arms. Why is it that this is a pleasing picture, why is it that the rude mechanicals do not, as a matter of fact, disturb or sully Titania's 'close and consecrated bower'? Malvolio in Bottom's place would be repellent, yet Malvolio, regarded superficially, is less violently contrasted to the Fairy Queen than is Nick Bottom. Bottom with his ass's head is grotesquely hideous, and in ordinary life he is crude, raw, and very stupid. We have no reason to suppose that Malvolio was anything but a well set-up, proper-looking man, spruce, well-dressed, the perfect family butler. His mentality too is of a distinctly higher order than Bottom's. He fills a responsible position with credit, he follows a reasoned line of conduct, he thinks nobly of the soul. Two things alone he lacks (and that is why no self-respecting fay could ever kiss him) – humour and imagination. Malvolio is, therefore, the only character who cannot be included in the final harmony of *Twelfth Night*. Bottom and his fellows did perhaps lack humour (though the interview with the fairies suggests that Bottom had a smack of it), but in its place they possessed unreason. Imagination they did have, of the most simple, primal, childlike kind. It is their artistic ambition that lifts them out of the humdrum world and turns them into Midsummer Dreamers, and we have seen how cunningly Shakespeare extracts from their very stupidity romance and moonshine. But, indeed, grotesqueness and stupidity (of a certain kind) have a kinship with beauty. For these qualities usually imply a measure of spiritual freedom, they lead to at least a temporary relief from the tyranny of reason and from the pressure of the external world. In *A Midsummer Night's Dream* the dominance of the Lord of Misrule is not marked by coarse parody, but by the partial repeal of the laws of cause and effect. By delicate beauty, gentle mockery, and simply romantic foolishness our freedom is gained.

If Shakespeare's play had, like *Comus*, been based upon an abstract idea, he might have found in Malvolio, not in Bottom, the most effective contrast to the Fairy Queen. The contrast between the prosaic man of business and the pierrot or elfin type of creature is a recurrent theme in literature. The amusement lies in putting the prosy people in charming or unconventional surroundings and laughing at their inadequacy and confusion –

> Big fat woman whom nobody loves,
> Why do you walk through the field with gloves,
> Missing so much and so much?

But either gloves or yellow stockings and cross garters would shatter Shakespeare's dream. For his play is not a criticism of life but a dance, and a dance of which the underlying motif is harmony. The contrast may be sharp as you please, but the unity must be deeper than the divergence. For, after all, the presiding deity is Hymen. His functions are performed by the fairies who are, indeed, emanations from him. Deeply rooted in folk-lore is the connexion between the fairies and fertility, and Shakespeare had a happy inspiration when he substituted them for the Ceres, Dianas, and Junos of pageantry, and also turned them into an expression of the harmony and concord which was the keynote of most Elizabethan revels.

If the descriptions do not mislead us, civic and courtly entertainments must always have been tantalizing those who witnessed them with suggestions of loveliness that were never quite realized. Just when the great gardens were about to turn into Fairyland, the poet would spoil everything with some clumsy allegory or compliment. These suggestions seem to have sunk down into Shakespeare's mind, and thence to have emerged transformed and perfected, moulded into final and satisfactory shape, a revelation of that world 'where music and moonlight and feeling are one'. . . .

. . . Through *A Midsummer Night's Dream* and *The Tempest* the loveliness of the masque is still accessible to us. How did Shakespeare bring this about? Not by imitating any one masque, not by indulging in vague rhapsodies on the beauties of the revels, but by taking his floating recollections of Court festivities and moulding them into a new, definite, concrete form. We have already seen this shaping process at work in the case of Oberon's vision, and it is particularly obvious also in the case of the fairies of *A Midsummer Night's Dream*. There they stand, clearly outlined in the moonlight, shapely, attractive, positive little creatures, but behind them, stretching back and back into the darkness, are innumerable forms, ill-defined, shifting, transitory, northern elves, haunters of burial mounds, Greek nymphs of standing lakes and groves, witches, fates, norns, gnomes, and hobgoblins of the folk, medieval fairy kings and queens, all the thoughts and fancies of the generations, crossing and re-crossing, branching off, combining, coalescing – no wonder that in this play Shakespeare cannot refrain from speaking of the arduous process of creation:

> The poet's eye, in a fine frenzy rolling,
> Doth glance from heaven to earth, from earth to heaven;
> And, as imagination bodies forth
> The forms of things unknown, the poet's pen
> Turns them to shapes, and gives to airy nothing
> A local habitation and a name.
>
> V. I. 12–17

This shaping process is most obviously at work in poetry written in the classical spirit, but it is part of all poetic creation. In poems which are pervaded by the sense of mystery, this sense of mystery is still expressed by the definite story or image or rhythm. In *The Tempest*, for instance, free play is given to all those mystical feelings which were so often evoked by the masque, but these feelings are expressed by means of one particular story, one particular background. Many travellers' tales, and many scenic splendours, have gone to the making of the Fairy Isle, vague medieval theories as to elemental spirits, half-memories of disguised musicians, seated in stage clouds, have taken individual shape in Ariel, many rumours and inaccurate yarns of Elizabethan sailors have become concrete in Caliban with his ancient and fish-like smell. The poet's pen turns them to shape.

Creation, then, is a higher kind of definition. The poet, like the theologian, is a dogmatist, for he puts into words, and so limits and preserves, the thoughts of himself and his generation and of all those whose minds are akin to his own. And by so doing he not only immortalizes the life of his time, he makes it dynamic. It is not unusual to draw a contrast between the living spirit and the dead form. But in art certainly the dynamic quality of a masterpiece is usually in direct proportion to its concreteness and comely outline. Shakespeare, by making his fairies definite, also made them fruitful, and ever since he created them, they have never ceased to influence literature and the nursery. As soon as the vague idea, or fluid revel, has been moulded into definite form, it is re-absorbed into the general consciousness, which is raised to a higher level. *A Midsummer Night's Dream* was the product of many earlier masques and entertainments, it was afterwards used to enrich the libretti of Ben Jonson. Spenser embodied a whole era of social life in his poem; his poem then proceeded to colour, not only the social life of his time, but a very great deal of the literature of his own and subsequent ages, and if his *Faerie Queene* does not quite rank with the greatest poems of the world, it is chiefly because it is too fluid. For the poet's definition is not merely conservative, it is also creative. Through *A Midsummer Night's Dream* and *The Tempest* we experience not only what the masque was, but what it might have been.

from *The Court Masque* by Enid Welsford, 1927

TWELVE

A Midsummer Night's Dream and the
Meaning of Court Marriage

THE opinion that *A Midsummer Night's Dream* is largely a shimmering fabric of 'moonlight, with a touch of moonshine' has become stock among students of Shakespeare. One rephrases habitual insights concerning gossamer and magic whenever one treats of the work. But there is more to the play than a dream. The efforts of historical scholars to place this comedy in the setting of its dramatic tradition, to see it as '*sui generis*, a "symbolical" or masque-like play' suggest that we ought to revise our romantic preconceptions of its structure and theme. Elizabethan masques usually afforded pleasures more serious than those of moonshine, and *A Midsummer Night's Dream* is not unlike them in this respect. It was created for the solemn nuptials of a noble house, perhaps for those of the Earl of Derby or the Earl of Essex. For our purposes, the specific families involved matter little. Rather it is important that the significance of the play's symbolism and the *raison d'être* of its pageantry can come clear through an examination of the occasion of its presentation.

Commensurate with its origins in a court marriage, this drama speaks throughout for a sophisticated Renaissance philosophy of the nature of love in both its rational and irrational forms. Even Bottom the fool observes that 'reason and loue keepe little company together, now a daies' (III. 1. 147–8). His sententious surmise – and it has been taken as the drama's theme – is best understood in terms of sixteenth-century marriage doctrines. When these and the symbols used to convey them are properly understood, the disparity between Reason and Love will appear figured in the distance from Athens to the woods; it is emblemized in the play's shift from light to darkness. The formal contrasts and similarities between the

Duke and Queen of Athens and their fairy counterparts depict like distinctions. However, since such structural effects are organically linked to the philosophy which informs them, the purpose of this essay must be twofold. It must first make a cursory survey of Renaissance thought concerning the function of festival drama and the significance of wedlock. Then it must indicate the methods by which symbol and masque pattern, structure and theme, work together to make luminous a traditional understanding of marriage. . . .

*

Mr Olson then links the play to Renaissance neo-Platonism through the speech of Theseus: the poet 'bodies forth airy nothings' as the Renaissance artist was thought to make available to the senses those invisible and abstract entities that were his subject: in this case, ideas of love and marriage as part of the great chain of being, perceived by reason. He analyses the first act in great detail, with an abundance of sixteenth-century parallels: Theseus is the model ruler and wise man, Lysander and Hermia – and Helena even more – are bound for confusion (symbolized by the wood) because they seek a temporal and unreasonable, not a higher, love.

In the wood, we find things topsy-turvy: Oberon ('a delicate figure for grace') has lost his sovereignty over Titania, who symbolizes the opposite, earthly love, and derives from the complex figure of Diana Proserpine, a kind of sensuous goddess of chastity. To punish her, Oberon causes her to dote on the bestial.

*

What then are the invisible and abstract entities which may be seen in the comic fairy plot? Paraphrase is always bad for a stage piece; it tends to impoverish and rationalize the richness of a dramatic symbol. Yet, if one were to apply this malpractice to the Oberon–Titania–Bottom triangle, one might say that celestial love in the form of Oberon attempts to capture the young man (the 'sprete' or the changeling) into his train and bring earthly love under his control in order that the rational and animal in man may form a proper marriage. To accomplish this, Divine Love 'providentially works through imperfect human love' as in the *Knight's*

Tale. That is, Oberon uses love-in-idleness to force Titania to release her hold upon the changeling and to seek only the carnal or physical man, Bottom. Bottom recognizes the earthy character of Titania's love when he speaks of her having little reason for loving him, and then tosses off the jest which sets the theme of the play (III. I. 145–50). The service which Titania's coterie, especially Peaseblossom, Mustardseed, and Cobweb, pay to Bottom is obviously a miniature picture of the satisfaction which the products of the earth can give to the grosser senses. There is a plot analogous to this one in Lyly's *Endimion*; there Cynthia, the higher love, forces Tellus or earthly passion to release her hold upon Endimion (the rational soul) but allows her to retain her love for Corsites (the body). Shakespeare was possibly as aware as Lyly that the body quite naturally will have its sexual appetites. He may also have recognized, as more recent dramatists sometimes do not, that these appetites need not undermine man's reason, his social responsibility, or his spiritual seeking.

Thus, having reduced physical love to her proper sphere, Oberon can use 'Dians budde' to release her from the unchaste power of 'Cupids flower'. At that point the third movement of the play begins in the fairy plot. Oberon regains his sovereignty over the fairy queen; the two loves are matched as they should be in any true marriage. The pair beats the ground in a circular dance, and Oberon calls for music which strikes 'more dead | Then common sleepe: of all these, fi[v]e the sense' (IV. I. 84–5). This harmony may be the *mundana musica* which preserves chaste loves and keeps the stars from wrong. The dance was given the same universal significance as a symbol for the concord of divine love in Sir John Davies's *Orchestra* (1595). Finally, all this is knit together when the fairies hear the song of the lark, a bird which sings at heaven's gate and which well into the seventeenth century was a symbol for the ascent of the reasonable soul toward God. Thus the king and queen of the other world arrive at the ordered condition which Theseus and Hippolita had reached at the play's beginning. Such an interpretation of the fairy plot may be incomplete, but it seems to me somewhat more consonant with what we know of the literary use of fairies in the 1590s from the *Faerie Queene* than the view we sometimes get that Shakespeare was here a slightly amateurish Warwickshire folk-lorist.

To see the mythical plot in this way is to see it as an integral part of the total dramatic meaning of the play. It amounts to a stage projection of the inner condition of the lovers, of the pattern of fall and redemption which they experience. Shakespeare is craftsman enough to establish carefully stage links between the two plots. Thus, when Demetrius and Helena first appear in the woods, Helena comes running after Demetrius (II. 1. 188); ten lines earlier Oberon has predicted that Titania will pursue the first beast she sees with the soul of love. Later Titania sleeps and receives the juice of love-in-idleness upon her eyelids; then Lysander and Hermia sleep, and Lysander is treated with the same philtre. Under its influence, Lysander worships Helena (II. 2. 83–156); the next scene gives us a Titania enamoured of Bottom's shape. Throughout, Shakespeare uses formal parallelism between scenes from the two plots to stress their inner relationship and to heighten the humour of both.

Though the flight to the woods is obviously the beginning of the lovers' fall, their subjection is not such a serious one. Shakespeare is not writing a serious play in that sense. Hermia preserves her humane modesty though Helena is less worried about the worth of her virginity. In any case, Oberon again providentially works through imperfect human love, using the philtre to transform the initial foolishness into behaviour which is more obviously irrational. The ridicule which is the most potent enemy of the wrong kind of love is intended to act both upon the lovers and, it is hoped, upon their audience. Puck makes a mistake with Lysander, but this only serves to heighten the comedy. The boy sinks to sleep protesting everlasting love for Hermia; he awakens from the herb eager to run through fire for Helena. He has arrived at that unsound condition where he can adduce scholastic arguments for his sanity, and so give the theme of the play another ironic twist:

> The will of man is by his reason swai'd:
> And reason saies you are the worthier maide.
> Things growing are not ripe, vntill their season:

> So I, being young, till now ripe not to reason.
> And touching now, the [point] of humaine skill,
> Reason becomes the Marshall to my will,
> And leads mee to your eyes. . . .   II. 2. 115–21

Incidentally, Reason in *Le Roman de la Rose* does not attempt to marshal the will to the eyes of a beautiful woman, but to a different kind of jewel.

However, the climax of the dramatization of the troubles of irrational love is reached in Act III, Scene 2. The exaggerated praise and worship of the mistress common in Ovidian satiric love poetry, the suspicions of friends are all there. Hermia even endeavours to tear out Helena's eyes (III. 2. 298). A moralist might say that the concupiscible passions have led on to the irascible. This is also what happens to Palamon and Arcite in the *Knight's Tale*. Yet, the troubles of heroic love do not lead the lovers in Shakespeare's work to the same violent end which Chaucer's Arcite suffers. It is part of Shakespeare's art that while the plight of the lovers seems more and more desperate to them, it appears increasingly comic to their audience, possibly because in this play the benevolent Oberon can send in his Robin to rescue the squabbling pairs and apply the *Remedia Amoris*:

> On the ground, sleepe sound:
> Ile aply your eye, gentle louer, remedy. . . .
> *Iacke* shall haue *Iill*: nought shall goe ill:
> The man shall haue his mare again, & all shall be well.
>
>   III. 2. 448-9, 462-3

Thus Oberon, with his servants, returns the lovers to reason; by allowing them to see for themselves the humour of their situation, he makes it possible for them to extricate themselves permanently from the fond fancy which misdirects the will and leaves one enamoured of an ass.

The lovers are ready for the type of 'bond of love' speech which Theseus gives in the third section of the *Knight's Tale*. Here again Shakespeare chooses the appropriate dramatic symbols. The song of the lark, the music, and dance symbolize the 'faire cheyne' in the fairy plot; in the other plot Theseus appears at dawn to remark the same effects:

> How comes this gentle concord in the worlde,
> That hatred is so farre from iealousie,
> To sleepe by hate, and feare no enmitie. . . .
>
> IV. I. 146–8

This concord is a reflection of the concord between Oberon and Titania, between their loves. It suggests a return of the world of nature from seasonal disorder to a similar harmony. And the state comes to its own order; Theseus now preserves hierarchy by over-ruling Egeus. His success results from a more profound under-standing of the principle of consent as the basis of marriage than he exhibited in the first scene. Finally, he proposes the ritual which will confirm a union not 'Briefe, as the lightning in the collied night . . .' (I. I. 145) but rather more lasting:

> . . . in the Temple, by and by, with vs,
> These couples shall eternally be knit.　　IV. I. 183–4

The last act is lighter in tone. The contract complete, the lovers see enacted the tragedy of Pyramus and Thisbe. But even this fits into the total pattern. For this story is, as Arthur Golding knew, a tragedy of the 'headie force of frentick love'. At one level, it is the potential tragedy of the lovers in the woods. It becomes, of course, a comedy because of the crudity in its poetry and in the stagecraft of the mechanicals; even this crudity gives Shakespeare an opportunity to show Theseus manifesting that kind of charity toward his subjects which holds societies together. It is also a comedy because the Renaissance view of marriage did not hold that fallen man must always be torn by the briars of the wild woods. Oberon's final benediction upon the wedded couples is not so specifically con-cerned with Christian theological redemption as that which the Knight gives to Palamon and Emelye:

> And God, that al this wyde world hath wroght,
> Sende hym his love that hath it deere aboght. . . .
>
> *Knight's Tale*, 3099–100

Yet the 'true loue' which Oberon promises to the newly married ones may be related to Divine Love, and the blots which are not to appear in their offspring were blots first made when Nature's hand was scarred in the fall.

Since the play operates according to no normal Aristotelian laws of psychological causality, critics have expected to find in it arcane fertility myth and ritual. But the ritual with which the work is concerned is after all the marriage rite. And the symbols come not from the Celtic twilight but from more conscious and intellectual literary traditions. Shakespeare was able to celebrate the marriage occasion at the noble mansion with archetypes more alive to the noblemen of his time than the superstitions of their Druidic ancestors. The major symbols used in *A Midsummer Night's Dream* had been made the property of the court by the works of Lyly and Spenser, authors who also exercised an influence on Shakespeare at the time he wrote the play. Shakespeare's purpose is to bring to life certain truths about wedlock which may have seemed at best abstractions, at worst clichés, to his audience. He widens their significance by mirroring them in an elaborate series of parallelisms between Athens and the woods, between the world of the fairies and the world of the lovers, between the orders of the individual family, of society, and of nature in general. The values which the drama supports are not trivial. That society in which sexual mores are governed well, in which marriage is relatively unselfish, may exhibit a deeper unity in other matters. It is in terms of such values that the dream becomes more than fanciful illusion and grows, in Hippolita's phrase, 'to something of great constancy' (v. 1. 26).

'*A Midsummer Night's Dream* and The Meaning of Court Marriage' (abridged), by Paul A. Olson, *ELH*, A Journal of English Literary History, Volume XXIV, 1957

Suggestions for Further Reading

C. L. BARBER: 'May Games and Metamorphoses on a Midsummer Night' (*Shakespeare's Festive Comedy*, Chapter VI). Barber at his best: and especially interesting on the fairies, pointing out the sceptical strain that allows us almost to disbelieve in them.

J. R. BROWN: *Shakespeare and his Comedies*. 'Our wavering acceptance of the illusion of drama' is an image of accepting the truth of love, which – like the mechanicals' play – seems the 'silliest stuff' to an outsider, but reasonable to the lover.

H. B. CHARLTON: *Shakespearian Comedy*, Chapter V. On the blending of romance and realism.

FRANK KERMODE: 'The Mature Comedies' (*Stratford on Avon Studies III: Early Shakespeare*, edited by Brown and Harris). Especially interesting on *A Midsummer Night's Dream*. Like Olson, Kermode treats the play's ideas seriously, relating them to some of the more uplifting strains of Renaissance thought.

H. A. MYERS: *Tragedy: A View of Life*. This book contains an interesting comparison between *Romeo and Juliet* and the *Dream*, reprinted in the Signet edition of the play. Tragedy discovers order and justice in the moral sphere; comedy sees disorder and reconciles us to it by laughter. So Myers is largely concerned with the Pyramus and Thisbe episode which (as others too have remarked) tells a similar story to *Romeo and Juliet*.

HOWARD NEMEROV: 'The Marriage of Theseus and Hippolyta' (*Kenyon Review*, Autumn 1956). Suggests that the view of poetry advanced in Theseus's famous speech is rather philistine, and that Hippolyta's reply may be nearer Shakespeare's own view – or that he may be uniting them in the marriage of the two characters. 'The poetry of Theseus is rational, civic-minded, discursive and tends constantly to approach prose. The poetry of Hippolyta is magical, fabulous, dramatic, and constantly approaches music. . . . Their wedded life . . . is the history of poetry in the English language'.

ANNE RIGHTER: *Shakespeare and the Idea of the Play*, IV. 3. This play offers ample scope to an approach which stresses theatre metaphors and the use of a play within a play.

MARK VAN DOREN: *Shakespeare*. Sees the *Dream* as Shakespeare's first fully mature play: it contains his best poetry yet, and also his shrewdest anti-poetic elements. 'The end of poetry is self-parody, and its wisdom is self-understanding. Never again will he work without a full comprehension of the thing he is working at'.

THE MERCHANT OF VENICE

Note

A COLLECTION like this would be lopsided if it did not admit that some plays have drawn more good criticism than others, and allot space accordingly. Partly this is a question of the plays' merits: *The Merry Wives* is a dull play, and it has not tempted many good critics. Partly, but not wholly; for it may be the very unevenness of a flawed masterpiece that has fascinated the interpreters, and led them to their most brilliant speculations. If *The Merchant of Venice* were not alive — poetically and theatrically — from start to finish, it could not have inspired the insights it has; but if it were not so controversial — if we could all agree what Shakespeare thought of Shylock — the argument could not have gone on so long and so excitingly. Whether or not this is the true cause, I have no doubt about the fact: that this play has produced more first-rate criticism than any of the other comedies. So I make no apology for giving it the most space.

Every opinion on Shylock has been canvassed. Some believe he is a simple villain, and the play anti-Semitic: this is often the view of the historically-minded, and for rather different reasons it was the view of the Nazis — Rosenberg is said to have written a preface to a school edition of the play, which I have not, unfortunately, been able to get hold of. Others believe he is a tragic hero: this, we are told, is how Henry Irving played the part. And many believe that Shakespeare could not make up his mind — that he was swept into a sympathy that threatened to destroy the play. When one looks coolly at Shylock's lines, it is hard to deny that the anti-Shylock critics have a strong case: Shylock says hardly anything of which the surface meaning is attractive. But the sympathy which actors, audience and readers persist in feeling must come from somewhere. Can it be solely the result of our humanitarianism, our modern prejudices (i.e. our lack of prejudice), our dislike of anti-Semitism? Perhaps to look coolly at his surface meaning is not the best way to respond to Shylock. And bound up with the question of what we think of Shylock, is what we think of the Christians: is Bassanio a fortune-hunter? is Gratiano vindictive? How does one answer such questions — by reconstructing Elizabethan conventions, or by using one's ears and one's knowledge of people?

It would have been easy to set a pro-Shylock essay against an anti-Shylock one, and let the extremes contend while the reader adjudicated; but it would not have been fair to the critics, and so, ultimately, not fair to the play. For the best critics have not found Shylock simple, and I have therefore preferred to include three extended discussions that are all torn both ways: all feel with Shylock that a Jew hath eyes, yet all keep a steady eye on the total effect. John Palmer is fair to the point of being judicial; Auden finds in the play's apparent contradictoriness something of the paradox of the human condition; and Mr Burckhardt (whose essay I have had to abridge shamefully) listens with a fine ear to the quality of Shylock's language, and its disturbing effect on the rest of the play. Max Plowman's little piece (also abridged) does not keep in such close touch with the play itself as the other essays in this book, but its shrewdness and subtlety make it worth including.

Shylock is not the whole of *The Merchant of Venice*, and though he has dominated criticism he has not monopolized it. Freud's brilliant passing uses of literary material can be seen at their best in the short passage about Portia, which illustrates his own modest insistence that he had not discovered the unconscious – the great poets and philosophers did that long before – but merely the method of studying it scientifically. And the apparently simple texture of the play's one song has teased from Mr Empson one of his most delicate analyses.

And finally, the play is superb theatre – none better. I have therefore allowed it two production-notices: one from a theatre-minded scholar, the other from a leading actor and producer.

THIRTEEN

Portia's Verbal Slip

ANOTHER example in which a dramatist makes use of a slip of the tongue has been discovered by Otto Rank (1910) in Shakespeare. I quote Rank's account:

A slip of the tongue occurs in Shakespeare's *Merchant of Venice* (III. 2), which is from the dramatic point of view extremely subtly motivated and which is put to brilliant technical use. Like the slip in *Wallenstein* to which Freud has drawn attention, it shows that dramatists have a clear understanding of the mechanism and meaning of this kind of parapraxis and assume that the same is true of their audience. Portia, who by her father's will has been bound to the choice of husband by lot, has so far escaped all her unwelcome suitors by a fortunate chance. Having at last found in Bassanio the suitor who is to her liking, she has cause to fear that he too will choose the wrong casket. She would very much like to tell him that even so he could rest assured of her love; but she is prevented by her vow. In this internal conflict the poet makes her say to the suitor she favours:

> 'I pray you tarry; pause a day or two,
> Before you hazard: for, in choosing wrong,
> I lose your company; therefore, forbear awhile:
> There's something tells me (*but it is not love*)
> I would not lose you . . .
>
> . . . I could teach you
> How to choose right, but then I am forsworn;
> So will I never be; so may you miss me;
> But if you do you'll make me wish a sin,
> That I had been forsworn. Beshrew your eyes,
> They have o'erlooked me, and divided me;
> *One half of me is yours, the other half yours –*
> *Mine own, I would say*; but if mine, then yours,
> And so all yours.'

The thing of which she wanted to give him only a subtle hint, because she should really have concealed it from him altogether, namely, that even before he made his choice she was wholly his and loved him – it is precisely this that the poet, with a wonderful psychological sensitivity, causes to break through openly in her slip of the tongue; and by this artistic device he succeeds in relieving both the lover's unbearable uncertainty and the suspense of the sympathetic audience over the outcome of his choice.

Observe, too, how skilfully Portia in the end reconciles the two statements contained in her slip of the tongue, how she solves the contradiction between them and yet finally shows that it was the slip that was in the right:

> But if mine, then yours,
> And so all yours.

by Sigmund Freud, first published in *Psychopathology of Everyday Life*, 1914; text from *Introductory Lectures on Psycho-Analysis* (Standard Edition Volume XV), 1915

FOURTEEN

Money and *The Merchant*

MONEY is a dangerous subject. Polite conversation avoids it. You may talk about economics, but not raw money. . . .

Money is so commonly the measure we usually apply to men that he who speaks of it critically will be quickly 'sized up'. The shrewd never tell of their own. 'Put money in thy purse', says Iago; and we take his advice, as secretly as possible. Income-tax communications are strictly private, and what a man is 'worth' is divulged only at his death. Rate money higher than wisdom, and in the world of men you will pass unreproved, for money is the token of civilized self-preservation, and fear insists upon the first law of nature. So money has a permanent place in all our thoughts. Our social roots are in money; no one can be allowed to live without it. We are tied to money. It is the shore to which every human craft is anchored, and will remain anchored until mankind has learnt the greatest lesson history can teach it – how to live by a more spiritual means of exhange. . . .

Of course the idea of living by a more spiritual means of exchange than money is highly romantic: it has never been done – at least, not successfully for any length of time. But the idea persists in spite of experience, and its persistence is prophetic. Sooner or later we shall have to translate it from the reign of romance to the world of fact, or the idea will poison us. The perpetual rule of life by money will not endure.

That is really what Shakespeare was saying in *The Merchant of Venice* – his most often misinterpreted play. . . . It is . . . a romantic comedy of heart's desire, designed to throw the life-value and the money-value into the strongest possible contrast.

A play that ends where it begins, in a world in which good-fellowship is the ruling principle. The only currency these Venetians understand is the currency of fellowship, where he who has is debtor to him who has not, where the only enemy is the man who will not accept such currency, but exalts a lower meed of worth and sanctifies it in the name of justice. He is the enemy because the gratification of his desire would drag life back from a civilized to a comparatively barbaric state. He is the enemy because he would check the free flow of money, which should move as healthfully as blood in the human body, and by the incision of usury play the vampire. Shylock is a symbol of the Mammon that can only be served by the negation of God; to sentimentalize him, after the modern fashion, is not merely to damage but to destroy the action of the play. Shakespeare made him human and so pointed the way to his redemption; but he left him inhuman as well, and thereby showed a subtlety and a truth to life which he emphasized again in the character of Iago.

Money is today what Shylock was to the world of Venice – the forbidding aspect, the dark principle, the shadow in the sun, the grim necessity. Its logic is inhuman. It has principle, but its principle is insufficient for the flexibility of human life. The problem is how to circumvent it without destroying the foundations of justice. And the answer is, by compelling it to the strictest interpretation of its own logic.

That was how Portia solved the problem. She took the Jew at his word and kept him to it. 'A verbal quibble?' Not at all; on the contrary, the turning upon itself of the weapon of logic basely misused in its attack upon life. And Shylock was convinced by the only means that would carry conviction.

By such a piece of strict rationalism would money be convinced today. 'Realize your wealth', said Portia. 'Liquidate it in the open court. If you cannot do this, your inability disproves your claim. There is no entity in money. Even as flesh is mingled with blood, so inseparably and inextricably is this, for which you claim a sovran right, woven in the fibres of life.' Compel money to be strictly honest, and it will lose its power to terrorize. Confine it to the work of exchange, and it will lose its power to beget. For money that breeds is the anomaly: in the act it has assumed an attribute of the creature, and when its life is threatened what can it do but seek compensation in flesh?

The theme of *The Merchant* is the interdependence of human beings in civilized society – an inviolable interdependence. This is the idea that Shakespeare outrages. It appears most obvious in the Trial Scene where a man stands wholly dependent upon a woman. It is shown in Portia's dependence upon her father's will, her maid's cheerfulness, and Bassanio's love. It runs like a thread through the play showing itself in the dependence of Bassanio upon Antonio, of Gratiano upon his friends, of Old Gobbo upon Launcelot, of Lorenzo upon Jessica, even of Shylock upon his daughter and his friend, and in the dependence of all of them upon favour and circumstance. All the sympathetic characters are shown as living in happy human interdependence. On them the sun of fortune shines in the end: they come to weal. All who arrogate to themselves wealth or merit (not only Shylock, but the braggart Princes of Morocco and Arragon) come to woe. . . .

from 'Money and *The Merchant*' by Max Plowman, *The Adelphi*, September 1931

FIFTEEN

'Tell me where is Fancy bred'

... WE are concerned here with a sort of dramatic ambiguity of judgement which does not consider the character so much as the audience. There is a simple example in the casket scene of *The Merchant of Venice*. Portia is far too virtuous to attempt to evade her father's devastating scheme; she fully approves of it ('If you do love me, you will find me out'); and yet, while Bassanio is choosing, she arranges that there should be a song continually rhyming with 'lead', and ending in a conceit about coffins. The audience is not really meant to think she is telling him the answer, but it is not posed as a moral problem, and seems a natural enough thing to do; she might quite well do it in the belief that he would not hear; the song is explaining to *them* the point about the lead casket, may be taken to represent the fact that Bassanio understands it, heightens the tension by repeating the problem in another form, and adds to their sense of fitness in the third man being the lucky one.

Corresponding to this doubt as to Portia's honesty is a stronger one as to Bassanio's affection; he seems superior to the other suitors only in the most incidental qualities, and is more frankly marrying for money than any of them. But Shakespeare loved his arrivistes for their success, their shamelessness and their self-deception, and Bassanio is justified by the song which leads him to choose rightly. Fancy is nothing, fancy is fleeting, and yet it is all that the dignity of poetry is based upon, and we must ring its knell as for the life of man. Lead, a fundamental mere humanity, eventual death, must be accepted, must be chosen, before one can get what one wants, and can go on with the poetry of the play; fancy can only hide lead, and lead must be enough for the maintenance of fancy.

from *Seven Types of Ambiguity* by William Empson, 1930

SIXTEEN

Shylock

SHAKESPEARE in presenting Shylock has so artfully combined the necessities of his plot with the revelation of a character that it is difficult, almost impossible, to say of any single incident or speech which of the two purposes is better served. The man lives in every word that he utters. He has a distinct language of his own and every syllable denotes his quality. His first words are of ducats; his introductory conversation with Bassanio might be cross-headed: Any usurer to any client: *Three thousand . . . ducats . . . For three months . . . Antonio shall become bound . . . Antonio is a good man . . . Yet his means are in supposition . . . The man is notwithstanding sufficient . . . Three thousand ducats – I think I may take his bond.* There is nothing here that seems to serve any other purpose than to present the comic Jew and to get the story under way. But the man is already alive. We shall know him again as soon as he opens his lips – a man whose words are stubborn in his mouth, in whose speech there is no ease or warmth or levity, who hammers out his phrases and can find no way of varying them once they are uttered. *Three thousand ducats . . . Antonio bound.* It is the utterance of a man whose mind is concentrated, obsessed, focused upon a narrow range of fixed ideas. Shylock had the trick of compulsive repetition characteristic of the man in whom imagination, such as it is, forever sits on brood. It is the speech of one who is incapable of humour, whose words will always precisely fit his meaning, in whom no play or flight of fancy is possible:

Ships are but boards, sailors but men. There be land-rats and water-rats, land-thieves and water-thieves – I mean pirates. And then there is the peril of waters, winds and rocks.

Such is the eloquence of Shylock. So literal is his habit of mind that he must interrupt his recitation of the bleak hazards of trade to explain that by water-thieves, a phrase which strikes him as possibly too picturesque to be exactly understood, he means pirates.

Meanwhile Shakespeare must come immediately to grips with his story of the comic Jew and the pound of flesh. He grasps the nettle firmly in an aside wherein Shylock discloses his intention and the motives behind it:

> How like a fawning publican he looks!
> I hate him for he is a Christian:
> But more for that in low simplicity
> He lends out money gratis, and brings down
> The rate of usance here with us in Venice. . . .
> If I can catch him once upon the hip,
> I will feed fat the ancient grudge I bear him. . . .
> He hates our sacred nation, and he rails,
> Even there where merchants most do congregate,
> On me, my bargains, and my well-won thrift,
> Which he calls interest. . . . Cursèd be my tribe,
> If I forgive him!   I. 3. 36–47

There is no hint in this speech, and there has been as yet no suggestion in the play, that Shylock has any human justification for his monstrous project. For the moment Shakespeare is satisfied with presenting his comic Jew in all the stark, ugly simplicity of the legend with which his audience was familiar. Shylock detests Antonio because he is a Christian; because he lends out money gratis and brings down the rate of usance; because he hates the Jews and dislikes their way of doing business. Shylock, in this first exhibition of his malice, is a comic figure and so he remains in the passages that follow: debating of his present store; delivering the traditional patter of the money-lender about the difficulty of making up the sum required; justifying his practice of usury by citing the trick played by Jacob on Laban over the parti-coloured lambs.

Then comes the first intimation that Shakespeare, having undertaken to supply his audience with a comic Jew committed to a barbarous enterprise, not only intends to make his conduct psychologically credible but has already realized in imagination what it means to wear the star of David:

SHYLOCK Signior Antonio, many a time and oft
In the Rialto you have rated me
About my moneys and my usances:
Still have I borne it with a patient shrug,
For suff'rance is the badge of all our tribe.
You call me misbeliever, cut-throat dog,
And spet upon my Jewish gaberdine,
And all for use of that which is mine own.
Well then, it now appears you need my help:
Go to then, you come to me, and you say,
'Shylock, we would have moneys' – you say so!
You that did void your rheum upon my beard,
And foot me as you spurn a stranger cur
Over your threshold – moneys is your suit.
What should I say to you? Should I not say
'Hath a dog money? is it possible
A cur can lend three thousand ducats?' or
Shall I bend low, and in a bondman's key,
With bated breath, and whisp'ring humbleness,
Say this:
'Fair sir, you spet on me on Wednesday last –
You spurned me such a day – another time
You called me dog: and for these courtesies
I'll lend you thus much moneys'?   I. 3. 101-24

That is perhaps the most remarkable speech in the play. It
suggests for the first time on any stage that the Jew has a case. The
Jew, moreover, puts that case with a deadly logic, sharpened by
persecution to the finest edge, and with a passion which no amount
of suff'rance can conceal. It reveals a mind so intensely concentrated
upon itself, so constricted in its operation, that it can only express
itself in repetitions of a rhythmic, almost hypnotic, quality. *You
have rated me about my moneys . . . Shylock, we would have moneys . . .
moneys is your suit. . . . You call me misbeliever, cut-throat dog. . . .
Hath a dog money? . . . You called me dog and, for these courtesies, I'll
lend you thus much moneys. And spet upon my Jewish gaberdine. . . .
You that did void your rheum upon my beard. . . . Fair sir, you spet on
me on Wednesday last.*

The ease with which Antonio is trapped into the bond with
Shylock is a good example of the way in which Shakespeare turns to

advantage the limitations imposed upon him by his material. Antonio is predestined to sign a contract which will put his life at the mercy of a mortal enemy whom he has every reason to distrust. That is a tall order. Shakespeare does not evade the difficulty, but uses it to serve perhaps the most striking purpose of his play, which is to contrast the narrow, alert and suspicious character of the Jew, member of a persecuted race, with the free, careless and confident disposition of the Christian sure of his place in the sun. It is a contrast maintained in every scene of the play. Shylock in word and deed is typical, intense and precise; the Christians are impulsive, sentimental and wayward. Shylock trusts in his bond; the Christians trust to luck – whether it be Bassanio staking love and fortune on the choice of a casket or Antonio gambling on the ships which fail to come home. Shylock tells us of his 'bargains' and his 'well-won thrift', but riches fall from a window on to the head of Lorenzo. The characteristic qualities on either side are respectively those of the oppressed and the oppressor. If in Shylock we stand appalled by the warping of mind and spirit which oppression inflicts on those who suffer it, we are not less repelled by the infatuated assumption of Antonio and his friends that to them all is permitted in the best of possible worlds. The point is constantly emphasized in the minutest particulars of dialogue and incident. When Shylock, justifying his bargains, cites the case of Jacob and the parti-coloured lambs:

> This was a way to thrive, and he was blest:
> And *thrift* is blessing if men steal it not

Antonio rejoins:

> This was a venture, sir, that Jacob served for –
> A thing not in his power to bring to pass,
> But swayed and fashioned by the hand of heaven.

I. 3. 84-8

Here, incidentally but in a nutshell, the careful husbandry of the Jew is contrasted with the careless genial improvidence of the Christian. Such touches of character, constantly repeated, not only prepare us for Antonio's easy acceptance of the bond but dispose us to swallow the whole preposterous story as entirely natural to the persons conceived.

From the sealing of the merry bond we pass to the story of Jessica. No incident in the play has so richly contributed to the transformation of Shylock, the comic Jew, into a lamentable victim of Christian bigotry and licence. This metamorphosis reached its literary climax in Heine:

I heard a voice with a ripple of tears that were never wept by eyes. It was a sob that could come only from a breast that held in it all the martyrdom which, for eighteen centuries, had been born by a whole tortured people. It was the death-rattle of a soul, sinking down dead tired at heaven's gates. And I seemed to know the voice, and I felt I had heard it long ago when in utter despair it moaned out, then as now, 'Jessica, my girl'.

On the stage it attained its theatrical climax, for those who re-member it, when Henry Irving returning by the light of a lantern knocked on the door of an empty house. Where, now, is your monster with a large painted nose? This is a patriarch of Israel, wronged in his most sacred affections. Small wonder if, after this, the afflicted Jew grows blind to the quality of Christian mercy.

Alas for those who, seeking to find Shakespeare in one part only of his design, lose or pervert the whole! There is as little warrant for the voice that moaned in Heine's ear as for the Irving interpolation which made of that tragic figure beating on the door a sublime and pathetic incident to wring your hearts.

What are the facts?

Shylock bidding farewell to his daughter, is more truly comic than at any point of the story so far reached. . . .

Shylock's farewell to Jessica, which established him for Heine as a tragic figure, leaves him still comic in the play that Shakespeare wrote. Shakespeare has done no more in this scene – but how much it is – than humanize the stage qualities of the comic Jew. Every stroke aims at our sense of comedy. 'Thou shalt not gormandize, as thou hast done with me', he tells Launcelot who is quitting him to serve Bassanio, and, in bidding farewell to this 'huge feeder', he exhibits a malevolence which, like all fixed ideas in a living creature, is at the same time ludicrous and terrible:

> ... Drones hive not with me.
> Therefore I part with him, and part with him
> To one that I would have him help to waste
> His borrowed purse.
>
> II. 5. 47–50

Is Shylock, mourning his daughter's flight, any less comic than Shylock bidding his daughter to shut his doors and windows? A careful study of the scene with Salerio and Tubal provokes conclusions profoundly disconcerting to the heirs of the romantic tradition. It is supremely comic in itself and Shakespeare deliberately contrived in advance that the comic element should prevail over its emotional implications. Far from intending us to sympathize with an afflicted father, he has emphasized before the event that Shylock's affection is abnormally possessive and, in depicting the Jew's reaction to her flight, he subordinates even this self-centred affection to the fury of a man of property upon whose well-won thrift an unspeakable outrage has been committed. *My own flesh and blood to rebel. . . . I say, my daughter is my flesh and blood.* This chimes perfectly with 'Jessica, my girl, look to my house'. . . .

There is one other point to be noted in Shakespeare's handling of Jessica. It is often insinuated, by commentators who are determined to elevate the issue between Shylock and Antonio, that the Jew was goaded into claiming his pound of flesh by the abduction of his daughter. Here, again, Shakespeare has, in the biblical sense, prevented them. Shakespeare uses the Jessica incident to make Shylock's behaviour in court more acceptable to the audience. We must have seen for ourselves some reason for the Jew's hatred of Antonio made real and visible in dramatic form. Having witnessed the flight of Jessica and Shylock's reaction to it, we shall be more likely to believe in the inexorable dog who sharpens the knife on his sole. But Shakespeare having used the incident to make the Jew's conduct in court seem less improbable suddenly realizes that, in so doing, he may have left us with an impression that Shylock was moved to extremity by paternal anguish, and, as though he foresaw the use to be made of this episode by a romantic posterity, he slips in an explicit repudiation of any such interpretation. When the news of Antonio's arrest reaches Belmont and is discussed with Portia, Jessica assures Bassanio:

When I was with him, I have heard him swear
To Tubal and to Chus, his countrymen,
That he would rather have Antonio's flesh
Than twenty times the value of the sum
That he did owe him.   III. 2. 286–90

Shakespeare here goes out of his way to inform us expressly that
Shylock had made up his mind to kill Antonio long before Jessica's
flight with Lorenzo – that he had, in fact, been in the habit of delivering at home speeches of the kind which he was shortly to
repeat in the court-house:

If every ducat in six thousand ducats
Were in six parts and every part a ducat,
I would not draw them, I would have my bond!
                                    IV. I. 85–7

Shylock, carrying his hatred to extremes, exposes the injustice and
ferocity of the social institutions from which it springs. He appeals
to the twin laws of retribution and property on which the society
in which he lives is based. Nothing is further from Shakespeare's
mind than to convey a lesson. But the lesson is there, product of a
perfectly balanced and sensitive mind intent upon the dramatic
presentation of human realities. The debated question whether
Shakespeare writing certain passages of *The Merchant of Venice* was
pleading for toleration or indicting Christian hypocrisy, exalting
equity above the law or divine mercy above human justice, does not
arise. He presents a situation in which all these issues are involved,
characters in which their effects are displayed, arguments appropriate to the necessary incidents and persons of the comedy; and
leaves it to his critics to draw the indictment or convey the apology.
His purpose was to write a comedy and he is never more intent on
this purpose than in the scene whose moral implications have
excited so much interest among those who study the play in the
light of their own ethical and social standards. Shylock eagerly
producing the bond for Portia's inspection – the bond which is to
prove his own undoing – is undeniably comic. So is Shylock
examining the bond to verify that the flesh must be cut from
Antonio nearest his heart. So is Shylock looking in vain for any

mention of a surgeon. So is Shylock applauding the wisdom of the judge who is about to ruin him. So, above all, is Shylock promptly asking for the return of his money when he realizes that his claim to Antonio's flesh will not be allowed.

And behind all this obvious comedy is the indifferent irony of the comic spirit which, in presenting the human realities of a situation, necessarily exposes the blindness of human beings to their own inconsistencies: Portia, singing the praises of mercy when she is about to insist that the Jew shall have the full rigours of justice according to the strict letter of the law; Antonio, congratulating himself on his magnanimity in the very act of imposing on his enemy a sentence which deprives him of everything he values; Christian and Jew mutually charging one another with an inhumanity which is common to both parties.

How Shylock, imagined by Shakespeare as a comic figure and sustaining his comic character to the last, was yet able to become a depositary of the vengeance of his race (Hazlitt), the ruins of a great and noble nature (Hudson) and the most respectable person in the play (Heine) is now perhaps sufficiently evident. The question when and how, if ever, Shylock ceases to be comic answers itself as we read the play. To the question when? the answer, if we bear in mind that Shakespeare's comedy springs from imaginative sympathy and not from intellectual detachment, is: never for an instant. The question how? should not therefore arise. But alas for logic and the categories! No one can remain wholly insensible to the emotional impact of the play. The imaginative effort expended by Shakespeare in making his Jew a comprehensibly human figure has imparted to him a vitality that every now and then stifles laughter and freezes the smile on our lips. If these passages are rightly handled by the actor or accorded their just place and value by the reader, the comedy remains intact. If, on the contrary, these passages are thrown into high relief and made to stand out of their context, the comedy is destroyed. Heine maintained that Shakespeare *intended* to write a comedy but was too great a man to succeed. This comes very near the truth, but what really happened was something rather more subtle and difficult to describe. Shakespeare took the comic Jew for a theme, and wrote a true comedy. But it was a comedy after his own pattern and desire – a comedy in which ridicule does not exclude compassion, in which sympathy and detachment are reconciled in the irony which is necessarily achieved by the comic spirit in a serene presentation of things as they are. . . .

from *Comic Characters of Shakespeare* by John Palmer, 1946

SEVENTEEN

Brothers and Others

The possible redemption from the predicament of irreversibility – of being unable to undo what one has done – is the faculty of forgiving. The remedy for unpredictability, for the chaotic uncertainty of the future, is contained in the faculty to make and keep promises. Both faculties depend upon plurality, on the presence and acting of others, for no man can forgive himself and no one can be bound by a promise made only to himself.

HANNAH ARENDT

THE England which Shakespeare presents in *Richard II* and *Henry IV* is a society in which wealth, that is to say, social power, is derived from ownership of land, not from accumulated capital. The only person who is in need of money is the King who must equip troops to defend the country against foreign foes. If, like Richard II, he is an unjust king, he spends the money which should have been spent on defence in maintaining a luxurious and superfluous court. Economically, the country is self-sufficient, and production is for use, not profit. The community-forming bond in this England is either the family tie of common blood which is given by nature or the feudal tie of lord and vassal created by personal oath. Both are commitments to individuals and both are lifelong commitments. But this type of community tie is presented as being ill suited to the needs of England as a functioning society. If England is to function properly as a society, the community based on personal loyalty must be converted into a community united by a common love of impersonal justice, that is to say, of the King's Law which is no respecter of persons. We are given to understand that in Edward III's day, this kind of community already existed, so that the family type of community is seen as a regression. Centuries earlier, a war between Wessex and Mercia, for example, would have been regarded as legitimate as a war between England

and France, but now a conflict between a Percy and a Bolingbroke is regarded as a civil war, illegitimate because between brothers. It is possible, therefore, to apply a medical analogy to England and speak of a sick body politic, because it is as obvious who are aliens and who ought to be brothers as it is obvious which cells belong to my body and which to the body of another. War, as such, is not condemned but is still considered, at least for the gentry, a normal and enjoyable occupation like farming. Indeed peace, as such, carries with it the pejorative associations of idleness and vice.

> Now all the youth of England are on fire
> And silken dalliance in the wardrobe lies.
> Now thrive the Armourers and Honour's thought
> Reigns solely in the breast of every man.
> They sell the pasture now to buy the horse.
> *Henry V*, II. 1. 1–5

The only merchants who appear in *Henry IV* are the 'Bacon-fed Knaves and Fat Chuffs' whom Falstaff robs, and they are presented as contemptible physical cowards.

In *The Merchant of Venice* and *Othello* Shakespeare depicts a very different kind of society. Venice does not produce anything itself, either raw materials or manufactured goods. Its existence depends upon the financial profits which can be made by international trade,

> . . . the trade and profit of the city
> Consisteth of all nations . . .
> *The Merchant of Venice*, III. 3. 30–31

that is to say, on buying cheaply here and selling dearly there, and its wealth lies in its accumulated money capital. Money has ceased to be simply a convenient medium of exchange and has become a form of social power which can be gained or lost. Such a mercantile society is international and cosmopolitan; it does not distinguish between the brother and the alien other than on a basis of blood or religion – from the point of view of society, customers are brothers, trade rivals others. But Venice is not simply a mercantile society; it is also a city inhabited by various communities with different loves

– Gentiles and Jews, for example – who do not regard each other personally as brothers, but must tolerate each other's existence because both are indispensable to the proper functioning of their society, and this toleration is enforced by the laws of the Venetian state.

A change in the nature of wealth from landownership to money capital radically alters the social conception of time. The wealth produced by land may vary from year to year – there are good harvests and bad – but, in the long run its average yield may be counted upon. Land, barring dispossession by an invader or confiscation by the State, is held by a family in perpetuity. In consequence, the social conception of time in a landowning society is cyclical – the future is expected to be a repetition of the past. But in a mercantile society time is conceived of as unilinear forward movement in which the future is always novel and unpredictable. (The unpredictable event in a landowning society is an Act of God, that is to say, it is not 'natural' for an event to be unpredictable.) The merchant is constantly taking risks – if he is lucky, he may make a fortune, if he is unlucky he may lose everything. Since, in a mercantile society, social power is derived from money, the distribution of power within it is constantly changing, which has the effect of weakening reverence for the past; who one's distant ancestors were soon ceases to be of much social importance. The oath of lifelong loyalty is replaced by the contract which binds its signatories to fulfil certain specific promises by a certain specific future date, after which their commitment to each other is over.

The action of *The Merchant of Venice* takes place in two locations, Venice and Belmont, which are so different in character that to produce the play in a manner which will not blur this contrast and yet preserve a unity is very difficult. If the spirit of Belmont is made too predominant, then Antonio and Shylock will seem irrelevant, and vice versa. In *Henry IV*, Shakespeare intrudes Falstaff, who by nature belongs to the world of *opera buffa*, into the historical world of political chronicle with which his existence is incompatible, and thereby, consciously or unconsciously, achieves the effect of calling in question the values of military glory and temporal justice as embodied in Henry of Monmouth. In *The Merchant of Venice* he gives us a similar contrast – the romantic fairy-story world of Belmont is incompatible with the historical reality of money-making Venice – but this time what is called in question is the claim of Belmont to be the Great Good Place, the Earthly Paradise. Watching *Henry IV*, we become convinced that our aesthetic sympathy with Falstaff is a profounder vision than our ethical judgement which must side with Hal. Watching *The Merchant of Venice*, on the other hand, we are compelled to acknowledge that the attraction which we naturally feel towards Belmont is highly questionable. On that account, I think *The Merchant of Venice* must be classed among Shakespeare's 'Unpleasant Plays'.

Omit Antonio and Shylock, and the play becomes a romantic fairy tale like *A Midsummer Night's Dream*. The world of the fairy tale is an unambiguous, unproblematic world in which there is no contradiction between outward appearance and inner reality, a world of being, not becoming. A character may be temporarily disguised – the unlovely animal is really the Prince Charming under a spell, the hideous old witch transforms herself into a lovely young girl to tempt the hero – but this is a mask, not a contradiction: the Prince is *really* handsome, the witch *really* hideous. A fairy-story character may sometimes change, but, if so, the change is like a mutation; at one moment he or she is this kind of person, at the next he is transformed into that kind. It is a world in which people are either good or bad by nature; occasionally a bad character repents, but a good character never becomes bad. It is meaningless therefore to ask why a character in a fairy tale acts as he does, because his nature will only allow him to act in one way. It is a world in which, ultimately, good fortune is the sign of moral goodness, ill fortune of moral badness. The good are beautiful, rich and speak with felicity, the bad are ugly, poor and speak crudely.

In real life we can distinguish between two kinds of choice, the strategic and the personal. A strategic choice is conditioned by a future goal which is already known to the chooser. I wish to catch a certain train which will be leaving in ten minutes. I can either go by subway or take a taxi. It is the rush hour, so I have to decide which I believe will get me sooner to the station. My choice may turn out to be mistaken, but neither I nor an observer will have any difficulty in understanding the choice I make. But now and again, I take a decision which is based, not on any calculation of its future consequences, for I cannot tell what they will be, but upon my immediate conviction that, whatever the consequences, I must do this now. However well I know myself, I can never understand completely why I take such a decision, and to others it will always seem mysterious. The traditional symbol in Western Literature for this kind of personal choice is the phenomenon of falling-in-love. But in the fairy-tale world, what appear to be the personal choices of the characters are really the strategic choices of the storyteller, for within the tale the future is predestined. We watch Portia's suitors choosing their casket, but we know in advance that Morocco and Arragon cannot choose the right one and that Bassanio cannot choose the wrong one, and we know this, not only from what we know of their characters, but also from their ordinal position in a series, for the fairy-tale world is ruled by magical numbers. Lovers are common enough in fairy tales, but love appears as a pattern-forming principle rather than sexual passion as we experience it in the historical world. The fairy tale cannot tolerate intense emotions of any kind, because any intense emotion has tragic possibilities, and even the possibility of tragedy is excluded from the fairy tale. It is possible to imagine the serious passion of Romeo and Juliet having a happy ending instead of a tragic one, but it is impossible to imagine either of them in Oberon's Wood or the Forest of Arden.

The fairy tale is hospitable to black magicians as well as to white; ogres, witches, bogeys are constantly encountered who have their temporary victories but in the end are always vanquished by the good and banished, leaving Arcadia to its unsullied innocent joy where the good live happily ever after. But the malevolence of a wicked character in a fairy tale is a given premiss; their victims, that is to say, never bear any responsibility for the malice, have never done the malevolent one an injury. The Devil, by definition malevolent without a cause, is presented in the medieval miracle plays as a fairy-story bogey, never victorious but predestined to be cheated of his prey.

Recent history has made it utterly impossible for the most unsophisticated and ignorant audience to ignore the historical reality of the Jews and think of them as fairy-story bogeys with huge noses and red wigs. An Elizabethan audience undoubtedly still could – very few of them had seen a Jew – and, if Shakespeare had so wished, he could have made Shylock grotesquely wicked like the Jew of Malta. The star actors who, from the eighteenth century onwards, have chosen to play the role, have not done so out of a sense of moral duty in order to combat anti-Semitism, but because their theatrical instinct told them that the part, played seriously, not comically, offered them great possibilities.

The Merchant of Venice is, among other things, as much a 'problem' play as one by Ibsen or Shaw. The question of the immorality or morality of usury was a sixteenth-century issue on which both the theologians and the secular authorities were divided. Though the majority of medieval theologians had condemned usury, there had been, from the beginning, divergence of opinion as to the correct interpretation of Deuteronomy 23. 19–20:

Thou shalt not lend upon usury to thy brother; usury of money, usury of victuals, usury of any thing that is lent upon usury: Unto a stranger thou mayest lend upon usury . . .

and Leviticus 25. 35–7, which proscribe the taking of usury, not only from a fellow Jew, but also from the stranger living in their midst and under their protection.

Some Christian theologians had interpreted this to mean that, since the Christians had replaced the Jews as God's Chosen, they were entitled to exact usury from non-Christians.*

Who is your brother? He is your sharer in nature, co-heir in grace, every people, which, first, is in the faith, then under the Roman Law. Who, then, is the stranger? the foes of God's people. From him

* *N.B.* For the quotations which follow, I am indebted to Benjamin Nelson's fascinating book *The Idea of Usury* (Princeton University Press).

demand usury whom you rightly desire to harm, against whom weapons are lawfully carried. Upon him usury is legally imposed. Where there is the right of war, there also is the right of usury. (St Ambrose)

Several centuries later, St Bernard of Siena, in a statement of which the sanctity seems as doubtful as the logic, takes St Ambrose's argument even further.

Temporal goods are given to men for the worship of the true God and the Lord of the Universe. When, therefore, the worship of God does not exist, as in the case of God's enemies, usury is lawfully exacted, because this is not done for the sake of gain, but for the sake of the Faith; and the motive is brotherly love, namely, that God's enemies may be weakened and so return to Him; and further because the goods they have do not belong to them, since they are rebels against the true faith; they shall therefore devolve upon the Christians.

The majority, however, starting from the Gospel command that we are to treat all men, even our enemies, as brothers, held that the Deuteronomic permission was no longer valid, so that under no circumstances was usury permissible. Thus, St Thomas Aquinas, who was also, no doubt, influenced by Aristotle's condemnation of usury, says:

The Jews were forbidden to take usury from their brethren, i.e., from other Jews. By this we are given to understand that to take usury from any man is simply evil, because we ought to treat every man as our neighbour and brother, especially in the state of the Gospel whereto we are called. They were permitted, however, to take usury from foreigners, not as though it were lawful, but in order to avoid a greater evil, lest to wit, through avarice to which they were prone, according to Isaiah 56. 7, they should take usury from Jews, who were worshippers of God.

On the Jewish side, talmudic scholars had some interesting interpretations. Rashi held that the Jewish debtor is forbidden to pay interest to a fellow Jew, but he may pay interest to a Gentile. Maimonides, who was anxious to prevent Jews from being tempted into idolatry by associating with Gentiles, held that a Jew might borrow at usury from a Gentile, but should not make loans to one, on the ground that debtors are generally anxious to avoid their creditors, but creditors are obliged to seek the company of debtors.

Had Shakespeare wished to show Shylock the usurer in the most unfavourable light possible, he could have placed him in a medieval agricultural society, where men become debtors through misfortunes, like a bad harvest or sickness for which they are not responsible, but he places him in a mercantile society, where the role played by money is a very different one.

When Antonio says:

> I neither lend nor borrow
> By taking or by giving of excess ... I. 3. 56–7

he does not mean that, if he goes into partnership with another merchant contributing, say, a thousand ducats to their venture, and their venture makes a profit, he only asks for a thousand ducats back. He is a merchant and the Aristotelian argument that money is barren and cannot breed money, which he advances to Shylock, is invalid in his own case.

This change in the role of money had already been recognized by both Catholic and Protestant theologians. Calvin, for example, had come to the conclusion that the Deuteronomic injunction had been designed to meet a particular political situation which no longer existed.

> The law of Moses is political and does not obligate us beyond what equity and the reason of humanity suggest. There is a difference in the political union, for the situation in which God placed the Jews and many circumstances permitted them to trade conveniently among themselves without usuries. Our union is entirely different. Therefore I do not feel that usuries are forbidden to us simply, except in so far as they are opposed to equity and charity.

The condemnation of usury by Western Christendom cannot be understood except in relation to the severity of its legal attitude, inherited from Roman Law, towards the defaulting debtor. The pound-of-flesh story has a basis in historical fact for, according to the Law of the Twelve Tables, a defaulting debtor could be torn to pieces alive. In many medieval contracts the borrower agreed, in the case of default, to pay double the amount of the loan as a forfeit, and imprisonment for debt continued into the nineteenth century. It was possible to consider interest on a loan immoral because the defaulting debtor was regarded as a criminal, that is to say, an exception to the human norm, so that lending was thought of as normally entailing no risk. One motive which led the theologians of the sixteenth century to modify the traditional theories about usury and to regard it as a necessary social evil rather than as a mortal sin was their fear of social revolution and the teachings of the Anabaptists and other radical utopians. These, starting from the same premiss of Universal Brotherhood which had been the traditional ground for condemning usury, drew the conclusion that private property was unchristian, that Christians should share all their goods in common, so that the relation of creditor to debtor would be abolished. Thus, Luther, who at first had accused Catholic theologians of being lax towards the sin of usury, by 1524 was giving this advice to Prince Frederick of Saxony:

It is highly necessary that the taking of interest should be regulated everywhere, but to abolish it entirely would not be right either, for it can be made just. I do not advise your Grace, however, to support people in their refusal to pay interest or to prevent them from paying it, for it is not a burden laid upon people by a Prince in his law, but it is a common plague that all have taken upon themselves. We must put up with it, therefore, and hold debtors to it and not let them spare themselves and seek a remedy of their own, but put them on a level with everybody else, as love requires.

Shylock is a Jew living in a predominantly Christian society, just as Othello is a Negro living in a predominantly white society. But, unlike Othello, Shylock rejects the Christian community as firmly as it rejects him. Shylock and Antonio are at one in refusing to acknowledge a common brotherhood.

I will buy with you, sell with you, talk with you, walk with you, and so following, but I will not eat with you, drink with you, nor pray with you.   (Shylock: I. 3. 30–32)

146

> I am as like . . .
> To spit on thee again, to spurn thee, too.
> If thou wilt lend this money, lend it not
> As to thy friends . . .
> But lend it rather to thine enemy,
> Who if he break, thou mayst with better face
> Exact the penalty.   (Antonio: I. 3. 125–8, 130–32)

In addition, unlike Othello, whose profession of arms is socially honourable, Shylock is a professional usurer who, like a prostitute, has a social function but is an outcast from the community. But, in the play, he acts unprofessionally; he refuses to charge Antonio interest and insists upon making their legal relation that of debtor and creditor, a relation acknowledged as legal by all societies. Several critics have pointed to analogies between the trial scene and the medieval *Processus Belial* in which Our Lady defends man against the prosecuting Devil who claims the legal right to man's soul. The Roman doctrine of the Atonement presupposes that the debtor deserves no mercy – Christ may substitute Himself for man, but the debt has to be paid by death on the cross. The Devil is defeated, not because he has no right to demand a penalty, but because he does not know that the penalty has been already suffered. But the differences between Shylock and Belial are as important as their similarities. The comic Devil of the Mystery play can appeal to logic, to the letter of the law, but he cannot appeal to the heart or to the imagination, and Shakespeare allows Shylock to do both. In his 'Hath not a Jew eyes . . .' speech in Act III, Scene 1, he is permitted to appeal to the sense of human brotherhood, and in the trial scene, he is allowed to argue, with a sly appeal to the fear a merchant class has of radical social revolution:

> You have among you many a purchased slave
> Which, like your asses and your dogs and mules,
> You use in abject and in slavish parts . . .   IV. I. 90–92

which points out that those who preach mercy and brotherhood as universal obligations limit them in practice and are prepared to treat certain classes of human beings as things.

Furthermore, while Belial is malevolent without any cause except love of malevolence for its own sake, Shylock is presented as a particular individual living in a particular kind of society at a particular time in history. Usury, like prostitution, may corrupt the character, but those who borrow upon usury, like those who visit brothels, have their share of responsibility for this corruption and aggravate their guilt by showing contempt for those whose services they make use of.

It is, surely, in order to emphasize this point that, in the trial scene, Shakespeare introduces an element which is not found in *Pecorone* or other versions of the pound-of-flesh story. After Portia has trapped Shylock through his own insistence upon the letter of the law of Contract, she produces another law by which any alien who conspires against the life of a Venetian citizen forfeits his goods and places his life at the Doge's mercy. Even in the rush of a stage performance, the audience cannot help reflecting that a man as interested in legal subtleties as Shylock would, surely, have been aware of the existence of this law and that, if by any chance he had overlooked it, the Doge surely would very soon have drawn his attention to it. Shakespeare, it seems to me, was willing to introduce what is an absurd implausibility for the sake of an effect which he could not secure without it: at the last moment when, through his conduct, Shylock has destroyed any sympathy we may have felt for him earlier, we are reminded that, irrespective of his personal character, his status is one of inferiority. A Jew is not regarded, even in law, as a brother.

If the wicked Shylock cannot enter the fairy-story world of Belmont, neither can the noble Antonio, though his friend, Bassanio, can. In the fairy-story world, the symbol of final peace and concord is marriage, so that, if the story is concerned with the adventures of two friends of the same sex, male or female, it must end with a double wedding. Had he wished, Shakespeare could have followed the *Pecorone* story in which it is Ansaldo, not Gratiano, who marries the equivalent of Nerissa. Instead, he portrays Antonio as a melancholic who is incapable of loving a woman. He deliberately avoids the classical formula of the Perfect Friends by making the relationship unequal. When Salanio says of Antonio's feelings for Bassanio

> I think he only loves the world for him . . .   II. 8. 50

we believe it, but no one would say that Bassanio's affections are equally exclusive. Bassanio, high-spirited, elegant, pleasure-loving, belongs to the same world as Gratiano and Lorenzo; Antonio does not. When he says:

> I hold the world but as the world, Gratiano,
> A stage, where every man must play a part,
> And mine a sad one . . .   I. I. 77–9

Gratiano may accuse him of putting on an act, but we believe him, just as it does not seem merely the expression of a noble spirit of self-sacrifice when he tells Bassanio:

> I am a tainted wether of the flock,
> Meetest for death; the weakest kind of fruit
> Drops earliest to the ground, and so let me.
>
> IV. I. 114–16

It is well known that love and understanding breed love and understanding.

> The more people on high who comprehend each other,
> the more there are to love well, and the more
> love is there, and like a mirror, one giveth
> back to the other.   *Purgatorio*, XV

So, with the rise of a mercantile economy in which money breeds money, it became an amusing paradox for poets to use the ignoble activity of usury as a metaphor for love, the most noble of human activities. Thus, in his Sonnets, Shakespeare uses usury as an image for the married love which begets children.

> Profitless usurer, why does thou use
> So great a sum of sums, yet canst not live?
> For having traffic with thyself alone
> Thou of thyself thy sweet self dost deceive.   Sonnet 4

> That use is not forbidden usury
> Which happies those that pay the willing loan,
> That's for thyself, to breed another thee,
> Or ten times happier, be it ten for one.   Sonnet 6

And, even more relevant, perhaps, to Antonio are the lines

> But since she pricked thee out for women's pleasure
> Mine be thy love, and thy love's use their treasure.
>
> Sonnet 33

There is no reason to suppose that Shakespeare had read Dante, but he must have been familiar with the association of usury with sodomy of which Dante speaks in the Ninth Canto of the Inferno.

> It behoves man to gain his bread and to prosper. And because the usurer takes another way, he contemns Nature in herself and her followers, placing elsewhere his hope. . . . And hence the smallest round seals with its mark Sodom and the Cahors. . . .

It can, therefore, hardly be an accident that Shylock the usurer has as his antagonist a man whose emotional life, though his conduct may be chaste, is concentrated upon a member of his own sex.

In any case, the fact that Bassanio's feelings are so much less intense makes Antonio's seem an example of that inordinate affection which theologians have always condemned as a form of idolatry, a putting of the creature before the creator. In the sixteenth century, suretyship, like usury, was a controversial issue. The worldly-wise condemned the standing surety for another on worldly grounds.

> Beware of standing suretyship for thy best friends; he that payeth another man's debts seeketh his own decay: neither borrow money of a neighbour or a friend, but of a stranger.
>
> (Lord Burghley)

> Suffer not thyself to be wounded for other men's faults, or scourged for other men's offences, which is the surety for another: for thereby, millions of men have been beggared and destroyed. . . . from suretyship as from a manslayer or enchanter, bless thyself.
>
> (Sir Walter Raleigh)

And clerics like Luther condemned it on theological grounds.

> Of his life and property a man is not certain for a single moment, any more than he is certain of the man for whom he becomes surety. Therefore the man who becomes surety acts unchristian-like and deserves what he gets, because he pledges and promises what is not his

and not in his power, but in the hands of God alone. . . . These sureties act as though their life and property were their own and were in their power as long as they wished to have it; and this is nothing but the fruit of unbelief. . . . If there were no more of this becoming surety, many a man would have to keep down and be satisfied with a moderate living, who now aspires night and day after high places, relying on borrowing and standing surety.

The last sentence of this passage applies very well to Bassanio. In *Pecorone*, the Lady of Belmonte is a kind of witch and Gianetto gets into financial difficulties because he is the victim of magic, a fate which is never regarded as the victim's fault. But Bassanio has often borrowed money from Antonio before he ever considered wooing Portia and was in debt, not through magic or unforeseeable misfortune, but through his own extravagances,

> . . . 'Tis not unknown to you, Antonio,
> How much I have disabled my estate
> By something showing a more swelling port
> Than my faint means would grant continuance . . .

I. I. 122–5

and we feel that Antonio's continual generosity has encouraged Bassanio in his spendthrift habits. Bassanio seems to be one of those people whose attitude towards money is that of a child; it will somehow always appear by magic when really needed. Though Bassanio is aware of Shylock's malevolence, he makes no serious effort to dissuade Antonio from signing the bond because, thanks to the ever-open purse of his friend, he cannot believe that bankruptcy is a real possibility in life.

Shylock is a miser and Antonio is openhanded with his money; nevertheless, as a merchant, Antonio is equally a member of an acquisitive society. He is trading with Tripoli, the Indies, Mexico, England, and when Salario imagines himself in Antonio's place, he describes a possible shipwreck thus:

> . . . rocks . . .
> Would scatter all her spices on the stream,
> Enrobe the roaring waters with my silks.

I. I. 31, 133–4

The commodities, that is to say, in which the Venetian merchant deals are not necessities but luxury goods, the consumption of which is governed not by physical need but by psychological values like social prestige, so that there can be no question of a Just Price. Then, as regards his own expenditure, Antonio is, like Shylock, a sober merchant who practises economic abstinence. Both of them avoid the carnal music of this world. Shylock's attitude towards the Masquers:

> Lock up my doors and when you hear the drum
> And the vile squeaking of the wry-necked fife
> Clamber not you up the casement then . . .
> Let not the sound of shallow foppery enter
> My sober house . . .   II. 5. 28–30, 34–5

finds an echo in Antonio's words a scene later:

> Fie, fie, Gratiano. Where are all the rest?
> 'Tis nine o'clock: our friends all stay for you.
> No masque tonight – the wind is come about.
>
>   II. 6. 62–4

Neither of them is capable of enjoying the carefree happiness for which Belmont stands. In a production of the play, a stage director is faced with the awkward problem of what to do with Antonio in the last act. Shylock, the villain, has been vanquished and will trouble Arcadia no more, but, now that Bassanio is getting married, Antonio, the real hero of the play, has no further dramatic function. According to the Arden edition, when Alan McKinnon produced the play at the Garrick theatre in 1905, he had Antonio and Bassanio hold the stage at the final curtain, but I cannot picture Portia, who is certainly no Victorian doormat of a wife, allowing her bridegroom to let her enter the house by herself. If Antonio is not to fade away into a nonentity, then the married couples must enter the lighted house and leave Antonio standing alone on the darkened stage, outside the Eden from which, not by the choice of others, but by his own nature, he is excluded.

Without the Venice scenes, Belmont would be an Arcadia without any relation to actual times and places, and where, therefore, money and sexual love have no reality of their own, but are symbolic signs for a community in a state of grace. But Belmont is related to Venice though their existences are not really compatible with each other. This incompatibility is brought out in a fascinating way by the difference between Belmont time and Venice time. Though we are not told exactly how long the period is before Shylock's loan must be repaid, we know that it is more than a month. Yet Bassanio goes off to Belmont immediately, submits immediately on arrival to the test of the caskets, and has just triumphantly passed it when Antonio's letter arrives to inform him that Shylock is about to take him to court and claim his pound of flesh. Belmont, in fact, is like one of those enchanted palaces where time stands still. But because we are made aware of Venice, the real city, where time is real, Belmont becomes a real society to be judged by the same standards we apply to any other kind of society. Because of Shylock and Antonio, Portia's inherited fortune becomes real money which must have been made in this world, as all fortunes are made, by toil, anxiety, the enduring and inflicting of suffering. Portia we can admire because, having seen her leave her Earthly Paradise to do a good deed in this world (one notices, incidentally, that in this world she appears in disguise), we know that she is aware of her wealth as a moral responsibility, but the other inhabitants of Belmont, Bassanio, Gratiano, Lorenzo and Jessica, for all their beauty and charm, appear as frivolous members of a leisure class, whose carefree life is parasitic upon the labours of others, including usurers. When we learn that Jessica has spent fourscore ducats of her father's money in an evening and bought a monkey with her mother's ring, we cannot take this as a comic punishment for Shylock's sin of avarice; her behaviour seems rather an example of the opposite sin of conspicuous waste. Then, with the example in our minds of self-sacrificing love as displayed by Antonio, while we can enjoy the verbal felicity of the love duet between Lorenzo and Jessica, we cannot help noticing that the pairs of lovers they recall, Troilus and Cressida, Aeneas and Dido, Jason and Medea, are none of them examples of self-sacrifice or fidelity. Recalling that the inscription on the leaden casket ran, 'Who chooseth me must give and hazard all he hath', it occurs to us that we have seen two characters do this. Shylock, however unintentionally, did, in fact, hazard all for the sake of destroying the enemy he hated, and Antonio, however unthinkingly he signed the bond, hazarded all to secure the happiness of the friend he loved. Yet it is precisely these two who cannot enter Belmont. Belmont would like to believe that men and women are either good or bad by nature, but Shylock and Antonio remind us that this is an illusion: in the real world, no hatred is totally without justification, no love totally innocent. . . .

'Brothers and Others' (slightly abridged) from *The Dyer's Hand* by W. H. Auden, 1963

EIGHTEEN

The Gentle Bond

I

THE danger of literary source-hunting is that it abets our natural tendency to discount things we believe we have accounted for. The source, once found, relieves us of the effort to see what a thing *is*; we are satisfied with having discovered how it got there. Shakespeare's plots – especially his comedy plots – have generally been at a discount; we have been content to say that the poet took his stories pretty much as he found them and then, as the phrase goes, 'breathed life' into them, enriched them with his subtle characterizations and splendid poetry. That the dramatist must make his plot into the prime metaphor of his meaning – this classical demand Shakespeare was magnanimously excused from, the more readily because by the same token we were excused from the labour of discovering the meaning of complex and 'improbable' plots.

But with the plot thus out of the way, other problems often arose. *The Merchant of Venice* is a case in point. Audiences persist in feeling distressed by Shylock's final treatment, and no amount of historical explanation helps them over their unease. It is little use telling them that their attitude towards the Jew is anachronistic, distorted by modern, un-Elizabethan opinions about racial equality and religious tolerance. They know better; they know that, in the play itself, they have been made to take Shylock's part so strongly that his end seems cruel. Nor does it do them much good to be told that Shakespeare, being Shakespeare, 'could not help' humanizing the stereotype villain he found in his sources; Richard III and Iago are also given depth and stature, but we don't feel sorry for them. If we regard *The Merchant* as a play of character rather haphazardly flung over a prefabricated plot, we cannot join, as unreservedly as we are meant to, in the joyful harmonies of the last act; Shylock spooks in the background, an unappeased ghost.

The source of our unease is simple enough: Shylock gets more than his share of good lines. This is nowhere more evident than in the court-room scene, where he and Antonio, villain and hero, are pitted against each other in a rhetorical climax. Shylock is powerful in his vindictiveness:

> You'll ask me why I rather choose to have
> A weight of carrion flesh than to receive
> Three thousand ducats. I'll not answer that;
> But say it is my humour. Is it answer'd?
> What if my house be troubled with a rat
> And I be pleas'd to give ten thousand ducats
> To have it ban'd? What, are you answer'd yet?
> Some men there are love not a gaping pig;
> Some, that are mad if they behold a cat;
> And others, when the bagpipe sings i'th'nose,
> Cannot contain their urine: for affection,
> Master of passion, sways it to the mood
> Of what it likes or loathes. Now, for your answer:
> As there is no firm reason to be render'd
> Why he cannot abide a gaping pig;
> Why he, a harmless necessary cat;
> Why he, a swollen bagpipe; but of force
> Must yield to such inevitable shame
> As to offend, himself being offended;
> So can I give no reason, nor I will not,
> More than a lodg'd hate and a certain loathing
> I bear Antonio, that I follow thus
> A losing suit against him. Are you answer'd?   IV. 1. 40–62

Antonio is grandiloquent:

> I pray you, think, you question with the Jew.
> You may as well go stand upon the beach
> And bid the main flood bate his usual height;
> You may as well use question with the wolf
> Why he hath made the ewe bleat for the lamb;
> You may as well forbid the mountain pines

To wag their high tops and to make no noise
When they are fretten with the gusts of heaven;
You may as well do anything most hard,
As seek to soften that – than which what's harder? –
His Jewish heart.   IV. 1. 70–80

Both men use the triple simile in parallel structure, but the similarity
serves only to bring out the difference. The toughness of Shylock's
argument is embodied in the toughness of his lines, his passion in
their speed and directness; this is a man who *speaks*. We might
simply say that Shakespeare here is writing close to his dramatic
best; but if by this time he was able to give his devils their due, why
does he leave his hero shamed? Antonio's lines are flaccidly ora-
torical; his similes move with a symmetry so slow and pedantic that
our expectations continually outrun them. He strains so hard for
the grand that when he has to bring his mountainous tropes around
to the point of bearing, they bring forth only a pathetic anti-climax:
'You may as well do anything most hard'. True, the burden of his
speech is resignation; but it is feeble rather than noble, a collapse
from overstatement into helplessness.

The historical critic may protest at this point that such a judgement reflects a modern bias against rhetoric, a twentieth-century
preference for the understated and purely dramatic. But the qualities
which make us rank Shylock's lines over Antonio's have long been
accepted among the criteria by which we seek to establish the
sequence of Shakespeare's plays, on the assumption that where we
find them we have evidence of greater maturity and mastery. Nor is
this only an assumption. In *The Merchant* itself there is a crucial
occasion where these qualities are preferred and where, had the
choice been different, the consequence would have been disaster for
Antonio. The occasion is Bassanio's choice of the right casket; he
rejects the golden one, because it is 'mere ornament', and prefers
lead:

          thou meagre lead,
     Which rather threat'nest than dost promise aught,
     Thy plainness moves me more than eloquence.
                                            III. 2. 104–6

(My interpretation here rests on an emendation; the Folio and the Quartos read 'paleness', not 'plainness'. But the emendation has the support of most editors since Warburton – and of sound sense. Bassanio means to contrast the three metals; and though both silver – 'thou pale and common drudge' – and lead are pale, it is contrary to his purpose, and to the logical structure of his speech, to fix on the one quality in which lead is *like* silver. The line as the Folio has it would have to be read with a strong emphasis on 'Thy'; but even then there is no reason why the paleness of lead should move Bassanio, when that of silver left him unmoved. Moreover, and most decisively, the word is clearly antithetical to 'eloquence'; and while 'plainness' yields a natural antithesis, 'paleness' does not.) At a decisive moment, Bassanio's critical judgement is the same as ours; so that, when we find ourselves more moved by Shylock's plainness than by Antonio's eloquence, we have the best possible reason for feeling sure that Shakespeare intended us to be.

For Bassanio's judgement is 'critical' in more senses than one: the play's happy outcome hangs on his taste. Had he judged wrongly, Portia could not have appeared in court to render her second and saving judgement. In the casket scene, the action turns on the *styles* of metals, conceived as modes of speech; the causalities of the play assume a significance which is, initially at least, only obscured by our being told that Shakespeare's plot is to be found in *Il Pecorone* and the *Gesta Romanorum*. Why does Portia come to Venice? Because Bassanio chooses plainness over eloquence. And how is Bassanio put into the position to make that choice? By Antonio's having bound himself to Shylock. That is how the causal chain of the story runs; it does not run from Fiorentino to Shakespeare.

And, as in any good play, so here the causality reveals the meaning of the whole. It shows that the plot is *circular*: bound in such a way that the instrument of destruction, the bond, turns out to be the source of deliverance. Portia, won through the bond, wins Antonio's release from it; what is more, she wins it, not by breaking the bond, but by submitting to its rigour more rigorously than even the Jew had thought to do. So seen, one of Shakespeare's apparently most fanciful plots proved to be one of the most exactingly structured; it is what it should be: the play's controlling metaphor. As the subsidiary metaphors of the bond and the ring indicate, *The Merchant* is a play about circularity and circulation; it asks how the vicious circle of the bond's law can be transformed into the ring of love. And it answers: through a literal and unreserved submission to the bond as absolutely binding. It is as though Shakespeare, finding himself bound to a story already drawn up for him in his source, had taken it as the test of his creative freedom and had discovered that this freedom lay, not in a feeble, Antonio-like resignation, which consoles itself with the consciousness of its inner superiority to the vulgar exigencies of reality, but in a Portia-like acceptance and penetration of these exigencies to the point where they must yield their liberating truth. The play's ultimate circularity may well be that it tells the story of its own composition, of its being created, wholly given and intractably positive though it seems, by the poet's discovery of what it is.

2

The world of *The Merchant* consists of two separate and mostly discontiguous realms: Venice and Belmont, the realm of law and the realm of love, the public sphere and the private. Venice is a community firmly established and concerned above all else with preserving its stability; it is a closed world, inherently conservative, because it knows that it stands and falls with the sacredness of contracts. Belmont, on the other hand, is open and potential; in it a union – that of lovers – is to be founded rather than defended. The happy ending arises from the interaction of the two realms: the bond makes possible the transfer of the action to Belmont, which then *re*-acts upon Venice. The public order is saved from the deadly logic of its own constitution by having been transposed, temporarily, to the private sphere.

But it is not a matter merely of transposition. Each realm has, as it were, its own language, so that the process is better described as a re-translation. Antonio's bonding is a necessary condition for Bassanio's winning Portia, but it is not a sufficient cause; the riddle of the caskets must be correctly *interpreted*. And in exactly the same way the winning of Portia is a necessary condition but not a sufficient cause for the redemption of the bond; it likewise cannot be bought but must be correctly interpreted. The language of love and liberality does not simply supersede that of 'use' (=usury) and law; it must first be translated from it and then back into it. Love must learn to speak the public language, grasp its peculiar grammar; Shylock, to be defeated, must be spoken to in his own terms. That he compels this retranslation is his triumph, Pyrrhic though it turns out to be.

The Jew draws his eloquence and dignity from raising to the level of principle something which by its very nature seems to deny principle: *use*. Antonio's most serious mistake – or rather failure of imagination – is that he cannot conceive of this possibility. He takes a fearful risk for Bassanio, but he cannot claim full credit for it, because he does not know what he is risking. Not only is he confident that his ships will come home a month before the day; he is taken in by Shylock's harmless interpretation of the 'merry jest', the pound-of-flesh clause:

> To buy his favour, I extend this friendship.   I. 3. 163

He is sure that the Jew wants to *buy* something, to make some kind of profit, and pleasantly surprised that the profit is to be of so 'gentle' (=gentile) a kind; he cannot conceive that a greedy usurer would risk three thousand ducats for a profitless piece of carrion flesh. His too fastidious generosity prevents him from reckoning with the generosity of hatred:

> . . . his flesh – what's that good for?
> To bait fish withal!   III. 1. 44–5

So he blindly challenges the usurer – the very man he is about to use – to do his worst:

> I am as like to call thee so again,
> To spit on thee again, to spurn thee too.
> If thou wilt lend this money, lend it not
> As to thy friends; for when did friendship take
> A breed of barren metal of his friend?

But lend it rather to thine enemy,
Who, if he break, thou mayest with better face
Exact the penalty.   1. 3. 125–32

(Little wonder that his later words about Shylock's hardness come off so feebly.) The worst he expects is the exacting of 'barren metal'; that it will turn out to be a pound of his own flesh does not enter his haughtily gentle mind.

But the play, thanks largely to Shylock's imagination, insistently makes the point that metal is not barren; it does breed, is pregnant with consequences and capable of transformation into life and even love. Metal it is which brings Bassanio as a suitor to Belmont, metal which holds Portia's picture and with it herself. When Shylock runs through Venice crying, 'My ducats and my daughter', we are as shallow as Venetian dandies and street urchins if we simply echo him with ridicule. Jessica and Lorenzo turn fugitive thieves for the sake of these ducats; it is only at the very end, and by the grace of Portia, that they are given an honest competence:

> Fair ladies, you drop manna in the way
> Of starved people.   v. 1. 294–5

In this merchant's world money is a great good, is life itself. When Antonio, again through Portia, learns that three of his argosies are 'richly' come to harbour, he is not scornful of mere pelf but says:

> Sweet lady, you have given me life and living.   v. 1. 286

(Which makes him Shylock's faithful echo; 'You take my life, | If you do take the means whereby I live'.) Bassanio, with Shylock's ducats, ventures to Belmont to win 'a lady richly left' and so to rid himself of his debts; it is a good deal worse than irrelevant to blame him (as some gentlemen critics, of independent income no doubt, have done) for being a fortune hunter. One, perhaps *the* lesson Antonio is made to learn is a lesson in metal-breeding.

Shylock is imaginative not only about money and flesh but about speech. We are, I am convinced, meant to understand that he draws his bloody inspiration directly from Antonio. In the lines just before the stating of the clause, we are shown how intimately and subtly the Jew responds to words, how they trigger his imagination, which

THE MERCHANT OF VENICE

thus proves more charged and sure than Antonio's. (That is why he has the better lines.) When Antonio proudly says: 'I do never *use* it', Shylock begins his story of Jacob's *ewes*; shortly thereafter, when his calculations – 'Let me see, the *rate* . . .' – are brusquely interrupted by Antonio's impatient: 'Well, Shylock, shall we be beholding to you?', he picks up the thread again but with a new twist:

> Signior Antonio, many a time and oft
> In the Rialto you have *rated* me. I. 3. 101–2

This is how he is brought to the idea of making his metal breed flesh. Unlike Antonio, he does not speak in set pieces leading to sententious commonplaces, 'as who should say: "I am Sir Oracle, | And when I ope my lips, let no dog bark."' *His* speech is for *use*, as it is of ewes; that is the secret of its effectiveness. Out of context his lines are not as quotable as many of Antonio's; but then we have reason to be suspicious of Shakespeare's quotable lines; Polonius is probably the most quoted of his characters. Shylock and Antonio provide the first major instance of Shakespeare's exploration of the conflict between noble-minded orators and less scrupulous but more effective speakers: between Brutus and Antony, Othello and Iago. The words of genuine speakers are so fully part of the dramatic situation, so organically flesh of the play's verbal body, that they resist excision. They grow, as truly dramatic speech must, from their circumstances and in turn change them; since the literal meaning of 'drama' is 'action', they are what they ought to be: language in action. It is because Shylock speaks this language that he is able to transform barren metal into living substance; the very mode of his speaking here becomes the mode of his doing. . . .

3–4

After this discussion of Shylock's language, Mr Burckhardt deals with the two most important changes made by Shakespeare in his sources. Since the main source (a play called *The Jew*) is now lost, these changes are only speculative, but there is some evidence that Shakespeare made them. Why did he add the story of Lorenzo and Jessica? As a foil to the love of the principals, suggests Mr Burckhardt – a love that undergoes no test, an inversion of true, bonded love. And why did he change the inscription on the leaden casket from a religious to a secular one? To answer this, he returns to Shylock's language. I give the whole of Section 5 of his article, and most of Section 6 (omitting his concluding discussion of the ring episode).

5

If the Jessica story is thus a kind of inverse demonstration of the play's point, the changed inscription goes directly to the core of Shakespeare's meaning.

In writing *The Merchant* Shakespeare learned, by my interpretation, that his work as a commissioned playwright need not be servile, money-grubbing prostitution of his talent, that he need not make himself a motley to the view, gore his own thoughts and sell cheap what was most dear. There was dignity in his trade, truth and worth in the two hours' traffic of the stage. Antonio's sadness at the outset is, by his own description, that of a man who has to play a 'part' arbitrarily assigned him; his restitution to happiness begins when he – though not fully aware of what he is doing – pledges his life to a binding contract and a literal 'deadline'. With this pledge things start to happen; 'circulation' sets in. Trading with his talent is not in itself contemptible, an exploitation of something that should be employed only freely, for 'gentle', liberal ends. It is, or can be, the beginning of action.

But this discovery entailed another – and a formidable risk. It meant that Shylock, the prophet of use and the bond, had to be built up – that his language had to be given the force and dignity which would sustain the claim Shakespeare was entering for profit-poetry. (Marlowe's Barabas was of no help to him; Barabas was a merchant-prince, with a language much more like Antonio's than like the lowly usurer's:

> What more may Heaven do for earthly men
> Than thus to pour out plenty in their laps,
> Ripping the bowels of the Earth for them,
> Making the Sea their servant, and the winds
> To drive their substance with successful blasts?
>
> *The Jew of Malta*, I. I. 108–12

That is Antonio's grandiloquence, as Antonio's humbling is the humbling of Marlowe's 'mighty line'.) Characters who spoke in Shylock's idiom and cadence had been comic figures, meant to earn good-natured smiles if they were good and to be despised if they were malicious. For the language they spoke was that in 'common use', employed by common men for the mean and illiberal ends they are compelled to pursue. It was not gentle, noble – the idiom designed to give the poet's patrons and protectors a properly idealized image of themselves. The language of the stage – at least of characters deserving serious regard – was one of representation rather than action, or if action, then of 'actions of state'. Or it was a language of feelings – the 'gentle' feelings allowed for within the conventions of courtly love. It moved in set pieces – lofty commentaries on an action that moved independently. If the action ended tragically, it was because the protagonists were star-crossed, or because the wheel of Fortune turned, or because they were guilty of *superbia* or some similar grand and splendid sins and crimes. If it ended happily, it did so because the proper feelings, dressed in the properly gentle language, had won out over loud-mouthed braggarts, mealy-mouthed parasites, foul-mouthed usurers and other ill-spoken folk. In either case the dramatic question was begged; the convention predetermined the issue and the judgement of the audience. Gentle was as gentle did; gentle talked as gentle did; ergo: gentle was as gentle talked – the syllogism of aristocratic sentimentality.

Had Shakespeare written three hundred years later, he might have had to fight free of a different kind of sentimentality – that of the naturalists. As it was – and because he was Shakespeare – he confronted the word 'gentle' in all its tricky ambiguity: as meaning something purely external (well-born; Christian) as well as kind, generous, loving. He did not think that churlishness proved a man honest and uncorrupted; nor was he satisfied with making the tritely pious point that, alas! not every gentleman is a gentle man. His problem was a different one: to vindicate gentleness under conditions – social and (it is the same thing) linguistic conditions – which did not beg the question but put it.

Shylock puts the question. In his mouth the common language

assumes a force which puts all genteel speech to shame and reduces gentle speech to impotence. It mocks, and makes a mockery of, all sentimental claims to a 'higher truth', clothed in elevated and elevating rhetoric, which cannot produce its credentials in the only court there is: the state's. Shylock's language is positivism triumphant, scornful of gentle pretensions, forcing the gentles to confess that, when all the ornament is stripped away, they too have been relying on the positive laws of the social order. If Shylock were silenced by force or fiat – even by divine intervention – his triumph would only be more complete; for he would then have compelled the gentiles, or their god, openly to profess his own faith: positivism. An overruled Shylock would be what (I think it safe to guess) his predecessor of *The Jew* could never have been: a tragic hero.

The question the Jew puts is not confined to the class meaning of 'gentle'; it probes with equal rigour the religious meaning. We have good reason to suppose that the language of Shakespeare's source begged the question of gentility: we *know* that it begged the question of Christianity. That is the point of the changed inscription. Simply by making the clearly labelled Christian choice, by proving himself a devout rather than a worldly chooser, the gentile of the earlier play gained the truth by which the Jew was vanquished. The test did not involve a risk but asked for a correct response; so that *The Jew* as a whole was not a drama, an action (with the absolute risk all true action involves), but a teaching machine, which in the end rewarded and reinforced the right answer with redemption, bliss and victory over the evil one. The Christian proved his superiority over the Jew merely by showing that he *was* a Christian and had learned his catechism – a religious tautology exactly analogous to the social one. To sum up: Shakespeare sees that the word 'gentle' evades the social and religious issue by institutionalizing it. Through the power he gives to Shylock's dramatically ungentle speech and through the elimination of the religious solution, he submits to the hazard of a genuine test – not a schoolmaster's but a chemist's. His play is, so to speak, the *aqua regia* into which the word 'gentle' is dropped to see if it is more than fool's gold.

To return to the plot. Belmont, left to itself, would end in sterile

self-absorption; Venice, left to itself, would end in silence. There is
an odd logic working in Shylock's bond: with its seal and letter it
gradually deadens even the Jew's powerful speech. Increasingly his
lines become monotonous and monomaniacal; where we heard him,
earlier, responding acutely and flexibly to Antonio's hard scantness,
he now grows deaf:

> ANTONIO I pray thee, hear me speak.
> SHYLOCK I'll have my bond; I will not hear thee speak.
> I'll have my bond; and therefore speak no more . . .
> I'll have no speaking; I will have my bond.
>
> III. 3. 11–13, 17

The theme is continued in the trial scene:

> I'll not answer that . . .
> I am not bound to please thee with my answers . . .
> Till thou canst rail the seal from off my bond,
> Thou but offend'st thy lungs to speak so loud.
>
> IV. I. 42, 65, 139–40

And finally:

> There is no power in the tongue of man
> To alter me. I stay here on my bond. IV. I. 236–7

Thus 'bond', in Shylock's mouth, comes to mean the opposite of
speech and hearing; and since the state must sustain him, we come
to the point where the community, to preserve itself, must prohibit
communion. He who stands on the bond is no longer answerable
and need no longer listen; the instrument of exchange threatens to
render the body politic tongue-tied. A gap opens between the
private and utterly ineffectual speech of men as men and the
deadening, unalterable letter of the law. Portia's oft-quoted lines
about the quality of mercy are remarkable not so much for their
eloquence as for their impotence; they are of no use, fall on deaf
ears, *do* nothing and so remain, in the literal sense, un-dramatic.

It may be objected here that changing the inscription was, after
all, no real risk. The plot was laid out for the poet and was sure to
lead to a happy ending; not even the device by which that ending
was achieved – Portia's judgement – had to be invented. But beyond

the risk involved in changing the moral and dramatic balance between the usurious Jew and the noble Christian, Shakespeare had to confront, in simple fidelity to his source, the hazard that was its very meaning. He did not alter the story but restored it to itself by freeing it from a pious falsification. For its meaning was that it sprang from a series of ventures, of hazards; it was propelled by the risks Antonio, Bassanio, Portia and, up to a point, Shylock were willing to take. Its ethic was that of venture capitalism raised to the moral level; so that to make it pivot, at the decisive juncture, on an option to invest in God's own, gilt-edged securities was to deprive it of its truth. Shakespeare's change here, though of a kind opposite to that of the Jessica plot, is directed towards the same end: while through the 'free lovers' he accented the outlines of the composition by adding shadows, in the test scene he removed a layer of pious overpainting. The picture as he leaves it is not changed but more itself than when he took it in hand; he is a restorer, not an adapter.

But at this point there is a reversal. Very much as Shylock learned, from Antonio's hardness, how to transform metal into flesh, so Portia now learns from Shylock himself the art of winning life from the deadly letter. So far she has given no hint that she has come with the solution ready; her last plea, interrupting as it does her already begun judgement, has the desperate urgency of a final, hopeless effort. When she asks Shylock to provide a surgeon to staunch the blood, does she know yet that it is on this point she will presently hang him? Or is it not rather Shylock himself who leads her to the saving inspiration?

> SHYLOCK Is it so nominated in the bond?
> PORTIA It is not so express'd; but what of that?
> 'Twere good you do so much for charity.
> SHYLOCK I cannot find it; 'tis not in the bond.   IV. I. 254–7

We cannot read Portia's mind and purposes, but this much is clear: here the crucial word is forced from her which then recurs in:

> This bond doth give thee here no jot of blood;
> The words *expressly* are 'a pound of flesh'.
>
> IV. I. 301–2

The same process is at work as that which led to the framing of the bond; language, and with it Antonio and the state, have been revived and freed to act.

If we read Portia's judgement as a legal trick and Shylock's defeat as a foregone conclusion, the Jew's final humiliation must appear distressingly cruel. But there is good reason for reading the scene differently. Portia's ruling is one more hazard, and Shylock's moral collapse does not demolish the bond and all it stands for, but rather proves him unequal to the faith he has professed. Even after the judgement the issue is in doubt; it is still in Shylock's power to turn the play into a tragedy, to enforce the letter of the bond and to take the consequences. But at this point and before this choice he breaks, turns apostate to the faith he has so triumphantly forced upon his enemies. Having made the gentles bow before the letter of the law, he is now asked to become, literally, a blood witness. But he reneges and surrenders the bond's power, and like a renegade he is flogged into gentleness.

from 'The Merchant of Venice: The Gentle Bond' by Sigurd Burckhardt, E L H, A Journal of English Literary History, Volume XXIX, 1962

NINETEEN

The Merchant of Venice in the Theatre, I

EDWARDS ... Do you remember the eight pierrots in our *Merchant of Venice*?

MACLIAMMÓIR I was about to remind you of them. The *Merchant of Venice*, although we used no apron-stage, seems to me by far the nearest approach to what we are both seeking than anything else that we have done.

EDWARDS I always felt you resented the eighteenth-century innovation.

MACLIAMMÓIR Only at first. The idea on paper or in words smacks of pointlessness and affectation, and there is still to my ears something a little odd about handing over Shakespeare's characters to Goldoni, especially in settings that were like a series of Veronese pictures; yet how well it all worked out. And what a reality the snuff-boxes and the three-cornered hats lent to those awful Salarios and Salanios and Salerinos; what conviction there was in the scene where Shylock returns to find an empty house, fighting his way through the crowds of masked and garlanded revellers under showers of streamers and petals; what solidity the more precise and easily understood period lent to the relations of Bassanio and Antonio, and to the Charles Perrault fairy-tale atmosphere of the casket scenes. When the first curtain rose on Molly MacEwen's setting of Renaissance arches with their looped and festooned curtains and wreaths and gilded cupids, and one saw the figures of the *Commedia dell' Arte* dance forward with the great banner bearing the words 'The Tragical-Comical History of the Merchant of Venice by William Shakespeare', and all to the accompaniment of Frescobaldi's languorous gaiety so divertingly pointed to by the background of masked and lace-shrouded dancers, one felt the authentic Venetian thrill and knew that one was in for something that, however incongruous, was going to be good. Then the pierrots pulled a little café with chairs and tables on to the pavement, and one of them, throwing a napkin over his arm, became a waiter; Harlequin beat with his wand upon an enormous *portière* swung between the marble pillars and lo! we were in a public place in Venice, and the dandies and idlers came sauntering over a ridiculous little bridge (also set by the pierrots to one of Scarlatti's brisker moods), tapping with their canes upon the table, ordering their wine, and discussing the anatomy of melancholy. Yes, I was easily won over to the swinging forward of the story to the grand century: it gave at the same time lightness and brilliance and conviction to a play of which we are all secretly a little tired, and did not obscure the action or the characterization as a still more beautiful and far more mechanically elaborate production at Stratford some years ago tended to do; and the Dublin audience, as weary as any in the world of the pseudo-Renaissance literal treatment of Shakespeare and of this play in particular, rewarded us by thronging to the doors. Of course this was mainly to see your Shylock and Ginette Waddell's Portia; but the gaiety and the freedom of the handling, the Scaramouche-like Gobbo, the pierrots who turned into Spanish courtiers or Moorish guards, the Harlequinesque changes of scene, had something to do with it too. It was completely your production, more even than most, and the settings were Molly MacEwen at her very best, so I can praise for once with no fear of the clutching hand of modesty or self-mistrust at my heart.

EDWARDS The critics didn't agree with you. At least not all of them. Wait though; the daily papers as far as I remember approved, but some of the monthly magazines ignored it altogether and at least one weekly objected to the idea of dressing up the Bard in order to intrigue the public, the writer adding bluntly that he preferred his Shakespeare straight. What, I should like to know, is straight Shakespeare? Only one: the Elizabethan, open-air stage and all; and it is unlikely that this was what any Dublin weekly would have in view. Possibly what was meant was a rehash of the Benson school with new curtains if essential. But the Benson school was in itself an innovation, and was no straighter than any other innovation thought out by generations of distracted producers since the day when the wooden O, the three doorways, and the central balcony were deserted. We cannot wholeheartedly return to this austerity, partly because the weather in our islands must have changed or the public hardiness deteriorated since Elizabeth's day, and partly because we have nowadays, among other less excellent things, certain mechanical advantages of the stage that it would seem foolish to resist using; and also because the plays are not in their essence confined to their period, and there seems no good reason beyond those of scholarship on the one hand or on the other of mere artiness to present them simply as museum-pieces. Their endless complications, however, once the producer leaves their original form of presentation behind him, have become not only a delight, but a torment to him, and though I share with you a small satisfaction in remembering our *Merchant*, especially the idea of having a band of actors who are in and yet not of the play to do the work usually allotted, in a childish hide-behind-the-curtain secrecy that deceives nobody, to the scene-shifter, I do not believe for a second that this is a final answer to the question of how to do the plays. At present there is a perpetual quarrel between representational scenery and the demand for continuity, between the theatre of the spoken word, which is slowly but surely finding its expression in the radio, and that of visual appeal which has already given satisfaction in the cinema. In fact the theatre, that should give voice to what is happening now, as opposed to the art of the screen, which is, as you yourself have often complained, a mere record of what has already happened in the past, the modern theatre is faced with how to discover continuity, beauty, and consistency when dealing with the works of Shakespeare; and this problem we have so far not solved ourselves, nor indeed have we seen it solved by others. A revolving stage occurs to one's mind, but I have an instinctive mistrust of a question that is fundamentally artistic being handed over lock, stock and barrel to the inventiveness of the engineer. This is what has happened in the world of the cinema, with the result that the film is becoming more and more the product of the laboratory and less and less the medium for the art of acting. No, we must rediscover the secret of Shakespeare for ourselves; and though I know you do not altogether agree with me in this, I still believe that somewhere lies the formula, close to the one for which Shakespeare wrote, yet more beautiful, more evocative, and more varying, that would be a key to them all. It would be a manner further removed from that of the cinema than any used by the stage since the end of the seventeenth century, for its first principle would be that contact of the player with his audience that is the most precious quality of the living theatre, and that survives today, ironically enough, only in the music-hall; and whenever an actor has objected to the direct address, the direct appeal, the calling of the public into his confidence and the sharing with them of his secret, which is a vital part of the soliloquy, I feel it in my bones that what prompts his objection is the framed-in isolation of the proscenium and footlighted stage that sets a barrier between itself and the auditorium, and that renders any attempt on the actor's part to break that barrier down a self-conscious and artificial process. Therefore the big oval-shaped apron would be one of the first things which in the theatre I really want I would insist upon; and I am not at all certain that Shakespeare and the other Elizabethans are the only authors for whom it could be used.

from 'Three Shakespearean Productions: A Conversation (with Hilton Edwards)' by Michael MacLiammóir, *Shakespeare Survey* 1, 1948

TWENTY

The Merchant of Venice in the Theatre, II

BY one stroke Michael Langham in directing *The Merchant of Venice* at Stratford-upon-Avon showed that he was concerned to give meaning and form to the production: in the trial scene, after Shylock has said that he is 'content' and Gratiano that he would have had him hanged, a crowd circles round the Jew jeering at him, and he stumbles to the ground; Portia moves across, the crowd falls back silent, and Shylock rises face to face with the boy-like lawyer who has spoken of mercy and of fines. There were no words for them to speak, but the point of the moment was to show that all had been done, that the two were irreconcilable. Possibly such an emphasis would have been better made earlier, where Shakespeare directed the two to confront each other, but, together with other details, it ensured that the trial was as exciting as it usually is and more clearly the necessary centre of both the Venetian and Belmont strands of the plot.

The merriment of the fifth act at Belmont often seems detached and irrelevant after the drama of the fourth, and here again Langham's resource was to emphasize a theme, that of friendship. This was long prepared for: for example, Antonio's 'Fie, fie' in the first scene, when Salerio accuses him of being in love, was forcefully spoken and followed by an emphasizing moment of embarrassed silence, and the description of the parting of Antonio and Bassanio was listened to in such a way that the answering 'I think he only loves the world for him' sounded no less than a measured truth. By such means Langham was able to present Antonio's silent figure in Act V as the merchant of Venice who had just given all his wealth in love to Portia; at the end he was left alone on the stage, seated and idly playing with the piece of paper which had given him the irrelevant news that all his argosies were 'richly come to harbour'. This silent, isolated drama had something of the force of the silent, isolated drama as the other merchant of Venice departed from the court of law without the 'means of which *he* lived'. While the confrontation of Shylock and Portia gave meaning to a moment, the treatment of Antonio throughout the play allowed the end to draw strength from the whole.

Nevertheless, the outstanding aspect of the production was Peter O'Toole's Shylock. The reprieve from a persistent quest of vitality, which enabled individual points to be emphasized, also allowed one performance to tower above the others. This was less through the longer speeches than in short phrases, snatches or bites at single words: 'I *hate* him . . . If I can *catch* him . . . Even on *me* . . . I have an oath in *heaven* . . . Is *that* the law?' Sometimes this effect was delayed or reversed, as when he waited for the third 'let him *look* to his *bond*' before fully realizing and uttering his hatred, slowly and quietly. Occasionally the sudden snarl seemed irrational or perverse, as in '. . . who *then* conceiving'. His was not a pathetic Jew: 'no tears but of my shedding' was not said for sympathy, but with ritualistic beating on his breast. He expressed pain here and at the memory of Leah by showing his effort to bear it himself, with clenched control. After this the trial disappointed at first, for Shylock had not the intellectuality to carry off the long, quietly taunting speeches; these were broken with movement and self-regarding feeling, as when 'If every ducat . . .' was said with quiet voice and almost closed eyes. But as Portia drew the trial towards an issue, the shorter phrases – a shouted 'I stand for judgement . . .' stilled an angry court – and the intense sharpening of the knife had full power. After the collapse of his 'rights' Shylock regained some of his strength with his dignity; he laughed at the sparing of his life and prided himself still on his sense of right – 'send the deed after me, | And I *will* sign it'.

All along O'Toole was aided by his director. The tripping music of a masque off stage gave strength by contrast to his farewell to Jessica. His costume was more dignified than usual, so that when he returned after his daughter's flight with his gown torn and muddied the audience was at once aware of a great reversal. Neither director nor actor stressed the 'inhumanity' of Shylock: his rapaciousness was not evident, for he was dressed too well for a miser; he walked too upright to suggest cunning or unbridled hatred; in the savagery of the court scene he was controlled. Moreover, this 'magnificent Shylock', as one review called him, was opposed by a gushing, nervous, trivial band of Christians.

Presumably this was another of the director's ideas for the play, for it was consistently maintained. Antonio, who was given considerable prominence, was a sombre figure, with little joy in his generosity. The others were light. Lorenzo was brisk and Jessica unaccommodating. The crowd in the trial scene was callow, mechanical in its reactions, and cheaply exultant. The first two casket scenes were played for the comedy that could be extracted from, or given to, the wooers, while Portia's predicament and desires were almost lost to sight. The caskets did not stand still and mysterious, but were carried around by three pretty girls. Lest the audience took the Bassanio casket scene too intently, Portia was dressed in swirling pink, moved about and often spoke loudly across the stage to Bassanio. While Bassanio was 'commenting on the caskets' and the song was sung, a collapsible arbour was carried across the stage to encircle Portia. During the soliloquy, 'How all the other passions fleet to air', attention was drawn away from the speaker to a crowd of servants moving around stage to encircle Bassanio. There was little opportunity for warm intimacy, modesty, deep intelligence. In Act V there was such emphasis on gaiety, with chasing round in circles and patronizing Antonio, that Portia's underlying confidence and pleasure in Bassanio, and her good sense, could scarcely show through. Fortunately Miss Tutin played the role, and through the ebullience managed to suggest a star-eyed eagerness, and in the trial scene, without the dignity of the usual robes, spoke the mercy speech with clarity and a solemnity that seemed to come from beyond Portia's own powers or consciousness.

In all this Langham directed consistently and with an intellectual grasp of the basic conflicts of the play. While the Shylock was not cunning, rapacious or inhuman in pursuit of revenge and the Portia did not appear wise in love, by pointing the form of the play, its crises, contrasts, repetitions, developments, the director ensured that the audience was involved in the play as a whole; under this condition, false emphasis and wayward characterization cannot destroy its holding power.

For the last five years Michael Langham has directed plays at Stratford, Ontario, and this has probably influenced some details of his work. His choice of a low, dark setting, changing little except in lighting and furniture as the action moves from Venice to Belmont, might be explained by his familiarity with Ontario's open, basically unchanging stage. At the Memorial Theatre, the single set gave fluency, as did Hall's for *Troilus*, but lacked emotive, visual appropriateness – a considerable loss on a picture-frame stage. The eighteenth-century costumes are more difficult to explain; they may have been chosen to give elegance to the gaiety of this Belmont, or possibly the example of Tyrone Guthrie, his predecessor as Director of the Canadian Festival, encouraged Langham to experiment in this way. Indeed Guthrie, who directed *The Merchant of Venice* in Ontario's Stratford in 1955, often seemed to be behind this production: he had directed the caskets to be carried by three maids who moved about 'freely'; his Arragon was accompanied by 'three black-clad tutors' (Langham's had one and a mother); for cutting the pound of flesh, his Antonio was tied to a 'sort of frame' which seemed 'symbolical of crucifixion' (Langham used a simpler pillory); his crowd indulged itself in 'jeering and jostling and even spitting' at the trial; his Antonio was left 'lonely and dispirited' at the close of the play. In both productions a 'choir' sang on stage for Portia's pleasure and the lovers 'wreathed' around during the ring-jests of Act V. If these details represent direct indebtedness, it is still quite clear that in total effect, especially in their Shylocks and the oppositions of the trial scene, the two productions were wholly disparate. Besides giving strong and embracing form to his production, Langham had learned and assimilated the experience of another director and of the opportunity of working on another kind of stage.

from 'Three Directors' by John Russell Brown, *Shakespeare Survey* 14, 1961

Suggestions for Further Reading

C. L. BARBER: 'Wealth's Communion and an Intruder' (*Shakespeare's Festive Comedy*, Chapter VII). 'The Jew . . . expresses just the things about money which are likely to be forgotten by those who have it, or presume they have it, as part of a social station'.

HARLEY GRANVILLE-BARKER: *Prefaces to Shakespeare I*. Very sensitive to Shylock's language; and uses this not to defend or attack his character, but to point out Shakespeare's theatrical skill.

M. C. BRADBROOK: *Shakespeare and Elizabethan Poetry*, x. 2. Firmly anti-Shylock, on historical grounds. 'The personal responsibility of Shylock for his horrible state is very small; it is the result of his wrongs, his birth, and his creed. But to remove all guilt from him on this account, and to treat him as a sympathetic criminal, would not have occurred to any Elizabethan'.

PHILIP BROCKBANK: 'Shakespeare and the Fashion of these Times' (*Shakespeare Survey* 16). A sensitive use of contemporary thought to illuminate, among other things, the trial scene of *The Merchant of Venice*. 'Shakespeare like Spenser carries on tip-toe his burden of Renaissance thought'.

J. R. BROWN: *Shakespeare and his Comedies*. Points out the use of commercial imagery in the love poetry.

H. B. CHARLTON: 'Shakespeare's Jew' (*Shakespearian Comedy*, Chapter VI). Claims that Shakespeare's intention was to exhibit Shylock as 'an inhuman scoundrel', but that in the writing this intention was overwhelmed by the sympathy that Shakespeare the artist was forced into showing. Charlton in fact has written one of the most eloquent of the pro-Shylock pieces.

NEVILL COGHILL: 'The Basis of Shakespearean Comedy' (*Essays and Studies*, 1950, reprinted in *Shakespeare Criticism 1935–1960*, World's Classics). Sees the play as a presentation of the theme of Justice and Mercy, the Old Law and the New.

WILLIAM POEL: 'Shakespeare's Jew and Marlowe's Christians' (*Westminster Review*, January 1909). An essay in literary history by the father of modern Shakespeare production. Poel suggests that the play is a reply to *The Jew of Malta*, and aimed to correct not Marlowe's attitude to the Jew, but his too harsh portrayal of the Christians.

SIR ARTHUR QUILLER-COUCH: *Shakespeare's Workmanship*, Chapter V. Not one of Quiller-Couch's favourite plays. 'Why are these Venetians so empty-hearted? I should like to believe . . . that Shakespeare was purposely making his Venice a picture of the hard, shallow side of the Renaissance'.

HERMANN SINSHEIMER: *Shylock: the History of a Character*, or *The Myth of the Jew*.

JANET SPENS: *An Essay on Shakespeare's Relation to Tradition*, pages 44–5. Antonio as the scapegoat.

MARK VAN DOREN: *Shakespeare*. Without the apparatus of scholarship used by Mr Brown, Van Doren makes the same point about the close link between love and money in the poetry of the Venetians. Points out the rasping quality of Shylock's language ('like a file') but refuses to decide where Shakespeare's sympathies lay.

MUCH ADO ABOUT NOTHING

TWENTY-ONE

Much Ado About Nothing

THE play's date (1598 seems secure: because (a) Meres would have mentioned it, had it been acted by 1597; and he does not. (b) in Q (1600) Dogberry and Verges are described in speech-headings as Kempe and Cowley; and Kempe left the Company during 1599. (c) Jonson's *Everyman in his Humour* (performed 1598) had repopularized the humour of Humours; and uses of it in *Much Ado*, though the word was not at all new, certainly sound like easy allusions to a newly fashionable interest in it) invites one of two general approaches to interpretation. *Either* this is all trivial, however clever: the author is totally disengaged throughout, and we are foolish to look for anything in any way deep, ourselves solemnly making ado about nothing: *or* it is a brilliantly superficial and deliberately *limited* 'Italian' love-fantasia on the theme of deception by appearances (all sorts of deceptions, by several sorts of appearances): and we remember that seeming and being will provide plots in very different tones from this, in the plays that Shakespeare goes on to write in 1599 and later.

In 1923 (*Much Ado: New Cambridge* edition) Dover Wilson advanced the hypothesis of an Old Play in verse, put through 'prose revision' which left loose tags and oddments that no longer had meaning, as well as 'verse fossils'. This revision made the most of the Benedick–Beatrice sub-plot; less of Hero and Claudio; and reduced the original Borachio–Margaret 'sub-sub-plot' (on the parallel loves of the serving-man and maid pattern) to next to nothing. Undeniably there are some discrepancies in the text which this hypothesis explains away nicely. But on one important point I have my objections. In Act II, Scene 2, Borachio, sketching the defamation-scheme, says that 'instances' will be offered: he is to be seen at Hero's window, and they are to 'hear me call Margaret Hero, hear Margaret term me Claudio'. On pages 105–7 of 'The Note on the Copy', Dover Wilson makes this 'slip' the one certain evidence for the existence of a Borachio–Margaret sub-plot in 'the unrevised text', which Shakespeare here repeated accidentally: aware only that in the old play 'Margaret was deceived as well as the Prince and Claudio' (as Pryene is in *The Faerie Queene*, Book II, Canto iv, the Claribell tale), when vanity would make her dress as Hero, and welcoming 'Borachio' would look like Hero's being faithless with him. Theobald substituted 'Borachio' for 'Claudio': the original Cambridge editors were not satisfied. Theobald wanted to know how it could displease Claudio to hear his mistress using *his* name tenderly; and the Cambridge editors commented that 'Hero's supposed offence would not be enhanced by calling one lover by the name of another'. With respect, I find both attitudes obtuse. It *would* offend Claudio to hear his name misused (and to a servant) and while adultery-in-advance is a severe offence to any bride-groom, it *is* made more offensive if the morrow's marriage is mocked in the meeting of the guilty lovers. The Cambridge editors went on to suggest that Shakespeare may have meant Borachio to persuade Margaret to play, 'as children say, at being Hero and Claudio'; but they did not see that this was a *sufficient* explanation, which it surely is. The use of Hero's name would have convinced the onlookers that what they saw was not just her dress; and that of Claudio's would have the most powerful effect on those who knew the real Claudio was with them. It would seem the acme of jadish-ness. Indeed, all Borachio need do is to deliver the names in a mocking tone of soupy infatuation.

If this convinces, the difficulty vanishes; and the best evidence for the Borachio–Margaret sub-plot with it. Shakespeare had a reason-ably clear idea of how he *could* present the scene (which he never did); and it is not significant enough, as Dover Wilson claims, that 'we are not informed' of the 'detail' of 'Margaret in Hero's gar-ments' till Act V, Scene 1 (line 232). It shows what was in Shake-speare's mind: if he *had* written the scene to be played out, then we do not need informing of what we *see* (for Margaret must, obviously, have appeared in whatever Hero had worn before: probably the ball-dress from Act II, Scene 1).

This weakens the Old Play hypothesis: although it remains

possible that the 1598 composition may have been from an earlier draft (perhaps a mere sketch); and true that writing of distinguishably different sorts is juxtaposed in it, together with the uncertainties and dead-ends which result from quick composition. Detective-story consistency, and the elimination of all redundancies and contradictions, are not to be expected of an Elizabethan and especially not of a dramatist. The question, for example, of how Beatrice came not to sleep with Hero on the fatal pre-marital night is simply improper in terms of stage-convention. Dramatists would emphasize seeming guilt in such ways, without realizing that another convention would want to have the answers to 'Why?', 'Where was she?', etc. In short, the slight internal contradictions seen on reading do not signify (if Shakespeare saw them); and do not matter much, if we do. The 'old' matter (if it was old) suited certain contrasts which Shakespeare wanted to draw around 1598, and gave the 'main' plot the right lack of emphasis for the task in hand. There is no reason to doubt that the emphasis on Benedick and Beatrice is deliberate, whether he worked from a draft, a sketch, or in some other way. Nor, I think, can we fail to observe that in the 'main' plot *some* passages of a tone too disturbed or disturbing for the 'Old Play', or for early work, 'arrived' in the course of writing out, because there were already in his mind feelings and reflections on, say, 'what men daily do, not knowing what they do': feelings which were, after 1598, to lead his work towards tragi-comedy (of a sort that this play is *not*).

Deception by appearances in *love* is patently what most of *Much Ado* is 'about'. As Hero puts it:

> Of this matter
> Is little Cupid's crafty arrow made,
> That only wounds by hearsay. ...   III. I. 21–3

Cupid is not responsible for calumny; but 'hearsay' is a main force in both love-plots: each is about its effects on proud, self-willed, self-centred and self-admiring creatures, whose comedy is at bottom that of imperfect self-knowledge, which leads them on to fool themselves. Is it exaggeration to bring even Dogberry into this pattern? to point to his manifest self-admiration ('a fellow that hath had losses; and one that hath two gowns, and everything handsome about him'), and to hint that the little arrow that wounds *him* 'by hearsay' is magnificent language and 'wit'? Are not words and wisdom his Cupids? No doubt that stretches 'love' too far. But self-love is a common term to all three of the splendid comedians of the piece.

The play's wit has been justly praised and is worth some examination in detail. It is of several distinguishable sorts: the simpler important only in so far as contributing to the cumulative effect, one of impetuous exuberance, a kind of competitive vitality, expressing itself in quick manipulations of language. The Messinans have dancing minds, and make words dance or caper to their unpremeditated tunes. At its simplest level, it is mere quibble: where A has used a word capable of two meanings in different contexts, and B shows his awareness of both, by displacing it. This may be no more than a conventional game, 'comic wit degenerating into clenches', and though editors explain them, 'the mind', as Johnson says, 'is refrigerated by interruption'. *Much Ado* suffers but little from this. It may, again, be an elaboration of that: when A and B are the same person, as when Beatrice 'takes herself up' on Claudio: 'The Count is neither sad, nor sick, nor merry, nor well; but civil count – civil as an orange, and something of that jealous complexion' (II. I. 262–4). That is exactly at the point where mere verbal cleverness, non-significant quibble, passes over into relevant wit: evocative here either of Beatrice's vitality (the 'character' view) or of the exuberant quality of lively minds which strike fire by scoring off each other: the quality I called *competitive* vitality, as of a 'college of wit-crackers'.

In the wit-game Benedick and Beatrice rightly regard themselves as 'seeded' players. Beatrice makes this clear in the scene in Hero's apartment before the wedding (III. 4), when Margaret scores off her for once. Shown Hero's new gloves, she is not interested (her mind is bothered with Benedick), and unguardedly pretends to have a cold:

BEATRICE I am stuff'd, cousin, I cannot smell.
MARGARET A maid and stuff'd! There's goodly catching of cold.
BEATRICE O, God help me! God help me! How long have you profess'd apprehension?

('Since when have you been a wit-cracker in this line?' – which Beatrice regards, with good reason, as her own.) Beatrice gets more of her own medicine later, over the prescription of 'Carduus Benedictus': here the wit is both verbal and something more – we might call it the wit of situation. No precise *double-entendre* is made; but Beatrice's state of mind is such that she feels (like Benedick before her) 'there's a double meaning in that'; and she lays herself open to another laugh by again using the wrong word:

BEATRICE Benedictus! why Benedictus? You have some moral in this 'Benedictus'.

MARGARET Moral? No, by my troth, I have no moral meaning.

It is a notable point in Shakespeare's contrivance that he gives both wits their off-day, as soon as love has disturbed their freedom.

As a rule, bawdy quibble outlives its contemporaries – simply because of 'human nature'; or because the fundamental situation is practically constant. In this play, jesting about sex is apposite: its subjects are sex-opposition, wooing, wedding, wiving (with due attention to the dangers of the last in making sport of a man). The audience certainly laughed at Benedick's 'Well, a horn for my money, when all's done' (II. 3. 56), the *second* time they saw the play. It becomes comic dramatic irony, if you read Elizabethanly. Yet, quite often, I see no great gain by doing so. There is something pathetic in the detailed scholarship which laboriously strives to conjure from its grave every ghost of an expired laugh. The smutty puns, for example, humourlessly expounded by Kökeritz in *Shakespeare's Pronunciation* are often so far-fetched as to be linguistically dubious and not worth the carriage. 'Lighthearted bawdry' has its point in *Much Ado* (as in Mercutio); but only the best of points can stand heavy-handed annotation. Much of it turns on obsolete phrases: the fuse of the whole firework has to be replaced with a dry note; and the verbal transaction, by losing all its speed, loses nearly all its crack. Quibble in slow-motion ceases to be witty. None the less, by noticing or examining the dexterities of verbal switch required, we are speeded up to a better awareness of the Elizabethan manipulations of language; and, at the same time, made more conscious of the vitality evoked individually by characters, and cumulatively by quibble, pun and jest together.

Shakespeare's wit in devising the linguistic mishaps and semantic excesses of Dogberry is the other side to the flat and despised 'mere quibble'. Dogberry exaggerates, by accident and in self-satisfied ignorance, the processes by which the true wits divert the meanings of words deliberately, knowingly, and with pride in their craft. But the one is the antithesis to the other; and both sides could be told, 'Thou hast frighted the word out of his right sense, so forcible is thy wit' (Benedick to Beatrice, v. 2. 48). Wit and nitwit share a common obsessive delight in the wonders of words. This is largely what makes Dogberry the apposite farce-fool for a play in which all three plots turn on understandings and misunderstandings: quite apart from his being a marvel of the official numbskull's capacity to make extreme ado about genuine nothing.

But has the 'Malaprop' had its day? It took the stage in *Woodstock* (? 1594), was cornered by Sheridan, survived to Dickens. It is perhaps funniest in hierarchical societies, where clever and witty management (or mismanagement) of language distinguishes the *élite*; and aping this makes the linguistic lower orders flatteringly absurd. My impression is that Malaprops are only comic nowadays to over-language-conscious school-masters; or, of course, when bawdily Dogburian: when the right idea comes out in very much the wrong word. But, unless I mistake, Dogberry's skids are never improper. Impropriety in this play is the privilege of the educated.

The wit that does *not* turn on word-play is best shown by examples. Essentially it is the exuberance which leaps beyond expectation in 'improving the occasion'. Not only Benedick and Beatrice have this hyperbolic comic inventiveness: the former his strokes of Falstaffian invention, the latter her alarming opportunism (she is likely to score suddenly off anyone, at any time). The qualities of swiftness and unexpectedness are just as neatly shown by old Leonato's perfectly timed shot at Benedick. Don Pedro asks if Hero is Leonato's daughter. 'Her mother hath many times told me so', is the conventional formula in reply. 'Were you in doubt, sir, that you ask'd her?' asks Benedick. 'Signior Benedick, no; for then were you a child' (a palpable hit). They appear equally in Beatrice's magnificent impertinence to Don Pedro. She must cry 'Heigh ho for a husband!' –

DON PEDRO Lady Beatrice, I will get you one.
BEATRICE I would rather have one of your father's getting . . . .

II. I. 300

And the quality of 'comic inventiveness' is shown immediately after when he teasingly offers himself, and she says she will not have him unless she can have another for working-days: he is so costly she would have to keep him for best.

Both quickness of repartee and comic inventiveness (hyperbolic feats of exaggeration and elaboration) are intrinsic to the attitudes of self-dramatization upon which the comedy of character depends. Energy is delight and accomplished dexterity a pleasure to watch. Benedick and Beatrice have both: all the more because they are playing a part before themselves, and playing it high in an infectious sort of daring: figures of pride, which is at once humanly splendid, and 'goes before a fall'. There is no need to repeat what others have said of their proud hearts as a source of misogamy, because marriage means submission and commonplaceness. Benedick shows a more delicately amusing self-conceit than this in, for example, the admirable lines (v. 2. 63 ff.), where the two mock-solemnly agree (a) that they are too wise to woo peaceably, and (b) that not one wise man among twenty will praise himself. Benedick then hits the high note impeccably with 'Therefore is it most expedient for the wise, if Don Worm, his conscience, find no impediment to the contrary, to be the trumpet of his own virtues, as I am to myself' – a pause, to let the conceit of it shock all modest minds; then he goes one better – 'So much for praising myself, who, I myself will bear witness, is praiseworthy'. Here he is playing the Falstaffian game of carrying outrageousness as far as it will go. The *other* side of this self-conceit is in Act II, Scene 3 (lines 200 ff.), his solemn resolutions to profit morally by what he has overheard on his character: 'I must not seem proud; happy are they that hear their detractions and can put them to mending'; and the heroic resolve to make the supreme sacrifice: 'No; the world must be peopled'. There, he is magnificently *absurd*, and totally unaware of himself.

I stress the point to bring out the unappreciated fact that the common distinction between persons we laugh *at* and those we laugh *with* is too naïve and crude, at any rate for Shakespeare. Benedick's subsequent efforts to extract a double meaning from two snubbing sentences of Beatrice's repeat this vista of ingenious absurdity. Besides being excellent comedy of mistaken meanings, the last speech in Act II, Scene 3 is a perfect miniature sample of the love-humour racing a man past himself: 'I will go get her picture' (*exit*).

It may seem a wantonly paradoxical view, in so verbally brilliant a piece, but I would contend that some of the wittiest work is to be found in the interrelations and inter-inanimations of the plots. Of the three, the one that takes attention foremost is technically a sub-plot. We hardly notice that it gets going before the 'main' plot, but Beatrice is 'at' Benedick before Claudio appears; and this sex-antagonism in a fencing match between experts with sharp words is musically 'the first subject'. The comedy of this Benedick and Beatrice plot is not the simple, sentimental indulgence of the 'boy meets girl' pattern, although that is included; rather it lies in the entertaining, good-natured, critically aware contemplation of the bents in human nature shown in (*a*) their antagonism (their incapacity to leave one another alone); (*b*) their deception by contrived intrigue; (*c*) the revelations which spring from this, under the pressure of circumstances (that arise from the main plot): leading to (*d*) reversal of all their first positions. The audience is always in a slightly superior position, *not* identifying itself with either of them, though sympathetic. When all the analysers have anatomized, and perhaps reconstructed Benedick and Beatrice, they remain 'just representations of general nature', and hence, as Johnson says, 'please many and please long'.

If I were to answer in a word what the Benedick and Beatrice plot turns on, I should say *misprision*. Benedick and Beatrice misapprehend both each other *and* themselves: each misprizes the other sex, and misapprehends the possibility of a complete agreement between them, as individuals, on what causes that misprision: love of freedom and a superior conceit of themselves as 'wise' where others are fools; as 'free' and untied; and as having a right to enjoy kicking over other people's traces. They fancy they are quite different *from*, and quite indifferent *to* each other. Indifferent they are not; and the audience is 'superior' in seeing their humours *as* humours; and in being aware that the opposite to love (as passionate, obsessive interest) is not hate (another passionate interest), but cool or unnoting indifference. How little Beatrice's 'disdain' for Benedick is truly disdainful is shown in her immediately thinking of him as a measure for Don John (II. I. 6 ff.).

Because the mind of each runs on the other, they can both be simply gulled by hearsay; provided that it is overheard and includes the sort of freedom of comment we all use on absent friends: mildly malicious in tone, unspiteful in intent, and near enough true on their recognizable oddities and shortcomings. The overhearers, for all their sharpness of wit, know that the *comments* have some truth, and naturally accept the rest as also true: cf. Aristotle on lying, *Poetics*, 24. 9: 'Homer more than any other has taught the rest of us the art of telling lies in the right way. I mean the use of a fallacy'. Thus the introduction of love-thoughts into both results from a species of misapprehension. They take the *sense* of the words, but totally fail to apprehend their *intention*. The two gulling scenes belong to the comedy of advertisement. Even the advertisers' nice touches of flattery are not lacking. The criticism is spiced with proper appreciation, as when Don Pedro hints – a very subtle inducement – that he would quite like to have Beatrice himself.

That the 'main' plot of Hero and Claudio turns on misapprehension leading to the misprision of violent disprizing, is too obvious to need commentary: but much of the play's total effect hangs on the structural mainness of this plot being displaced. As in Mannerist pictures sometimes, the emphasis is made to fall on what appears structurally to be a corner. This displaced emphasis helps to maintain the sense that the 'Ado' is about 'Nothing' (it is only through the distortion that reading gives that much attention is given to the 'character' of Claudio).

But though the misapprehension from judging by appearances is quite obvious, it is easy to overlook the incidental touches by which the theme of false report, misunderstanding and jumping to conclusions is strengthened. Not logically strengthened: the 'incidents' are not necessary to the *story*; but the whole sub-episode of the proxy wooing does chime in cleverly with what is to follow. Don Pedro agrees to woo Hero; *immediately* Leonato's 'good sharp fellow' overhears and misreports (I. 2. 5 ff.); the correct report gets into the wrong ears, Borachio's; he tells Don John, who straightaway uses it maliciously on Claudio (pretending to think him Benedick behind the masque-vizor). And Claudio at once anticipates his later violent and self-regarding impetuosity by assuming that Don Pedro *has* cheated him of Hero. Call this 'atmosphere', if you like; say, perhaps, that Messina is no place to trust any man's word; whatever you say, it strengthens the theme; and the ready *and perhaps drastic* misapprehensions of quick and apprehensive minds appear as of major importance in the play, as a play and not as a merely logical story.

I say 'perhaps drastic' to suggest how the matter of this part is balanced neatly on a tonal frontier: not between comedy and tragedy, but between comedy and tragi-comedy. Hence the 'limited' of my description of the play at the beginning: the drastic possibilities are so lightly touched that there is a sense of withholding – as if the author, in another mood, could give these incidents quite another tone: but not now; not yet. This feeling is most evident in the church scene, which is *not* tragic. T. W. Craik's line, in *Scrutiny*, xix, 1953, here is mainly sound; and his interpretation that *all* the passions are presented to be viewed with comic detachment is preferable to the conventional explanation, that 'the audience is throughout in the know', etc. So is the audience in *Othello*, for what that is worth!

Without striving to make too much of it, the dance in Act II, Scene 1 is beautifully apposite. The couples walk their round: two by two, all masked; and all are using words to back the disguise of false faces with trivial deceit. The play-acted defamation of Hero, by means of a false dress on the wrong woman and names used falsely, is exactly parallel. In both, the truth is *behind* the looks and words. The *bal masqué* is only a game of seeming; yet it is a most apt symbol of the whole. The vizor is half deceit, half no deceit: you can never be sure. Believe it, and you make ado about what is nothing. And in the social order and shared delight of the dance –

all moving to the controlling rhythm, in their appointed patterns –
there is too the emblem of the harmony in which all will conclude:
as the play does, with another dance, all the vizors laid aside. The
real play is not ended with 'Strike up, pipers'. The very movement
of Act II, Scene 1, where all the main misapprehensions started, is
repeated and completed; and even the professed misogamists are
dancing to the same tune. It is as neat and pretty as 'Sigh no more,
ladies, sigh no more'.

The third plot – Dogberry, Verges, the Watch – though mainly
Dogberry, is not a mere farcical variety-turn: there *is* a thread of
connected episode. The Watch overhear Borachio's scheme and
hear it correctly enough (their invention of a thief named 'Deformed' is a nice touch: he has arrived at official constabulary
existence by the end). They only overhear because they carry out
Dogberry's ridiculous orders and make the policeman's lot a not-
unhappy one by, as far as possible, doing nothing whatever.
Despite their superb stupidity they do disentangle the plot: though
only because, Don John having fled, Borachio tells everything, and
gives them the game hands down. This is very natural and well-
managed. For had Borachio set out to bluff, the Watch would have
been utterly bamboozled in no time. *Superb* stupidity, however,
belongs more rightly to Dogberry alone. One side of him is his art
of 'comprehending vagrom' *words*: there a more 'senseless and fit
man' could not be found. But this is not the whole of him; though
a part entirely harmonious with the whole. Dogberry is a perfect
instance of the comic mirth which Plato explained in *Philebus*:
'mirth', he says, 'is generally evoked by the sight of self-ignorance
or self-conceit, as when a man fancies himself richer, more handsome, more virtuous or wiser than he really is; and this mirth must
be present in one who is powerless to inflict hurt on others, otherwise he would cease to be a source of mirth and become a source of
danger instead'. As a *real* official Dogberry would be a terror.
Conceited ignorance and vast self-importance in local government
officers is – and was, in the time of Elizabeth – as good a joke in
fiction as a very bad joke in fact.

But misprision and misapprehension are present here too, in a
different guise. The incomprehension of the stupid ass is a limiting

case of failure to apprehend; and over and above his miscomprehensions of language, Dogberry's own view of Dogberry is a vast misprision. To himself a superb creature, a wise fellow, as pretty a piece of flesh as any in Messina, he is superbly asinine in the Messina of wit and word-play. Yet, while apparently an *opposite* to the wit-crackers, he is also a parallel: in that pride of self-opinion and a nice appreciation of one's own wisdom and cleverness is as much theirs as his. There is no caustic correction of self-love in Benedick or Beatrice. But the parallel gives another common term, showing on analysis how the three plots have their implicit correspondences, how they genuinely belong together.

'Nothing can permanently please, which does not contain in itself the reason why it is so, and not otherwise'. I have been trying to probe down to the nervous system of those interrelations which *Much Ado* contains within itself, and which give it, as comedy, the poetic unity Coleridge there demands. I find a complex harmony of interdependent themes, some parallels, some direct oppositions; and it seems to me that misapprehensions, misprisions, misunderstandings, misinterpretations and misapplications are the best names for what the comedy *as a whole* is 'about'. The misapprehensions of language are one side of the play; those of human beings and states of affairs the other. At root the two are one; and both you can regard with Dogberry's formula for obdurate drunks: 'You may say they are not the men you took them for'. A step or stage beyond this, and what a different pattern of seemings might result: where neither looks nor words are to be trusted, but everything distrusted. . . . But *Much Ado* touches that for only a moment, and that unsymptomatic of the whole: for a few lines of Claudio's in the church scene. They only point to what *might* be thought and felt: in the real tragi-comedies it *will* be. Yet even in *Much Ado*, all appearances *are* equivocal.

Before leaving the plots, mark how deftly they are intertwined. Benedick and Beatrice misapprehend themselves and misprize each other. Claudio's contrived misprision of Hero, the result of intrigue, is finally dissipated by the *coup* of the Watch, which reduces all the ado to nothing. But at its zenith this same disprizing is the catalyst which liquidates the mutual misprisions of Benedick and Beatrice in the church scene. But the reactions to that scene (the confessions of love and Beatrice's implicit admission that she needs a man – to 'kill Claudio') only occur because Benedick and Beatrice have been prepared to 'apprehend': prepared by intrigue, which, like Don John's, is dependent on hearsay and overhearing, taking appearances at their face-value, and being led or misled by words: cf. the fusing of plot with plot in the *Miller's Tale*.

Words I must stress, because Dogberry is no essential part of this intertwining as I have summarized it. I suppose you could formulate it all again by saying that the controlling theme might be styled 'mistaken identities'; for, in their pride or conceit, all the principals in some degree mistake themselves: as they mistake or wrongly take situations, and mistake or wrongly take words, on purpose and wittily or accidentally and absurdly. Leonato and Antonio, the two old men lashing themselves back into a youthful fury, and threatening duels, equally mistake themselves: they are pathetic and laughable at once. And, in a way, they reflect on Benedick's sternly assuming the role of truculent executioner to Claudio – and having a comical difficulty in maintaining the part. This is a good example of Shakespeare's detachment in this play: of the amused distance at which his creations should be held, if we are to take *Much Ado* as an artistic whole.

Despite Coleridge's too often quoted comment, 'The interest in the plot is always in fact on account of the characters, not vice versa, as in almost all other writers; the plot is a mere canvas and no more', I still think that plot (in a deeper sense than 'story') is here even more important. His implied contention that the 'interest' in the main plot is 'on account of the characters' (Hero and Claudio, chiefly; and I suppose Don John) seems to me simply untrue. Against Coleridge and his echoers we might set Jonson, putting Aristotelian principle in his own words, and answering the question 'What is a Poet?': 'A poet . . . is a maker, or a feigner: his art, an art of imitation or feigning; expressing the life of man in fit measure, numbers, and harmony. . . . Hence he is called a poet, not he which writeth in measure only, but that feigneth and formeth a fable, and writes things like the truth. For the fable and fiction is, as it were, the form and soul of any poetical work or poem.' In a later note, 'the very fiction itself', he says, is 'the reason or form of the work'. 'Reason' and 'form' are abstractions from the apprehended, 'felt' interrelations between distinguishable parts of a whole. Such interrelations I have made the central matter of my examination, attempting to resolve the theme to which the three 'plots' are subservient.

Much Ado is not a 'serious' play: it is 'limited' in managing potentially serious matters with a deft nonchalance which passes by the possibility of some being sharp things that might cut. At the same time, it is a play full of themes which are to have sufficiently serious explorations and consequences in Shakespeare's later work. Othello's situation, for example, is a variant of Claudio's; just as Claudio's behaviour to Hero is a sketch of Bertram's (hurt pride turned spiteful: providing we do not see Claudio as only 'mechanical'). Deceit by words (especially words of great meaning) is a constant in the tragi-comedies; and the comedy or farce of crediting too much of what is heard, or thought to be heard, is only the other side to 'O love's best habit is in seeming trust', and the self-imposed deception by seeming and fair words which are found in the Sonnets.

Seeming and being in the later plays have a quite different seriousness. But such a theme exists here, as it does in *Henry IV, Part One*; and if we say that the one is on *love* (and sex), the other on *honour*, then, looking ahead, the change in Shakespeare's play-writing is partially represented by *Much Ado* leading to *Measure for Measure*; and *Henry IV, Part One* leading to *Troilus and Cressida*. By this I suggest that potentially serious and distressing human situations (involving love and honour) are in *Much Ado* and *Henry IV, Part One* handled 'lightly', as we say: contrived so as to keep them amusing, diverting, stimulating; but also so as to hold them more or less insulated from the deeper and more trenchant inquisitions into values of the tragi-comedies.

The place where we can hardly not notice little *points* of contact with the tragi-comedy outlook is the church scene. 'Seeming' is harshly emphasized; Claudio seems on the edge of playing a part that would make it quite another *sort* of play; and the Friar's moral lines on lost affections – sad, uncomfortable thoughts – are echoed by the King in *All's Well*. But those points mark the real insulation of *Much Ado*. The disturbed feeling of *Measure for Measure* – its troubled thinking – is not here. We can hardly speak of 'lack of feeling' in so bright, lively, glittering a piece: but is there not a certain *hard* quality, as with the bright colours of some Italian painting?

It is a *Decameron*-like story (barring the Watch), with some of the *Decameron* qualities of volatility in the persons, no wasting of sympathy on victims of jests, and the expectation of swift, unreflecting volte-faces of attitudes and emotions at the call of Fortune's pipe. That usually leaves an impression of shallowness, of a lack of *depth* of emotion, in northern European minds. The people seem rather heartless, while not in the least 'cold'; and the stories are apt to leave us thinking more about 'Now what did X really feel when . . . ?' than we know we *should*. In *Much Ado*, the brushing aside of the tone of calamity, the expectations of volatile changes of feeling in Claudio, the jocular (for so it is) 'Think not on him till tomorrow. I'll devise thee brave punishments for him. Strike up, pipers', only catch up a bright hardness (the result of a *deliberate* limitation of sympathies in the author?) which runs through the play.

Much Ado is a fantasy of equivocal appearances in a glittering world of amiable fools of all sorts. As naturally as Italians talk Italian, the Messinans talk 'equivocal'; but their 'double tongues' are as harmless as those of the 'spotted snakes' in *A Midsummer Night's Dream*. This equivocal quality, moreover, is deftly restricted to appearances: there are only the slightest touches of suggestion of any intrinsic equivocation in things themselves (in love, for example). Ambivalence is not a term to apply here.

These qualities urge me to 'place' the play in the course of Shakespeare's writing as follows. In the breaking down of sensitive endurance, and of mental resistance to the revelation of the unfairness of human nature, there is a point where a sense of humour *fails*; where to see life and the world in humorous proportions is no longer possible: it cannot be assumed by an act of will, or, if so, the assumption cannot be maintained. At this point distresses distress, and cannot be accepted tolerantly as the world's way, muffled by an easy 'they soon get over it' and by the cant of time. (I think of John Keats, of course; but without 'Keatsifying' Shakespeare. In the *later* plays the 'miseries of the world | Are misery'; but not here in *Much Ado*.) Immediately *before* that point, the besieged mind and invaded heart may defend themselves by the assumption of a certain hardness: assume the *Decameron virtu* – the trappings and the suits of *joy* – though they hath it not within. They may also find a certain high-flown gaiety – not hysterical, but making the best, and most, of the farce of human misunderstanding, deception, misprision – in the comedy of language (devised, so one may suppose, to communicate: but often used for just the reverse, either in game or in earnest). It is as if the sensitive mind and heart sought to persuade themselves by demonstration that life is a jest, and that the wider the comic net the likelier it is to resolve all the unmentioned but implied and subjective troubles in one great humorous or laughable plan, in which Fortune favours the laughers. This is the point at which great clowns who are melancholic – Chaplin, Raimu, Jouvet, Fernandel – stand and abide. One step from that strange equilibrium may turn to 'cynicism' (especially in England): the cynicism where the attitudes I called 'hardness' (self-defensive) and 'farce' (offensive, debunking) combine to 'place' love, honour, truth, only to devalue them. *Much Ado* stands in the Shakespearian canon just at that point.

from *Angel With Horns* by A. P. Rossiter, 1961

TWENTY-TWO

Awareness and Unawareness in *Much Ado About Nothing*

No comedy of Shakespeare's is more aptly named than *Much Ado About Nothing*, all the ado of which, from our vantage-point, is indeed about nothing. The Prince of Arragon and his party arrive to visit the Governor of Messina. If guests and hosts saw with our eyes, nothing memorable would occur during the visit. Claudio would marry Hero and remain at Messina. The other visitors, including Benedick, would go their way at month's end – unless monotony dispatched them earlier. Beatrice would die an old maid.

But because the inhabitants of the Messinan world do not see with our eyes, monotony finds no time to afflict them. All the action is impelled by a rapid succession of 'practices' – eight in all, the first of which is introduced at the end of the opening scene, the last exploited in the final moments. These practices are the means by which multiple discrepancies in awareness are created and sustained, some briefly, some over long periods. Sharing the practisers' confidence in each case, we hold advantage over some participants during fourteen of seventeen scenes, and at some time we hold advantage over every named person. Not only heroines and villains – the inveterate practisers in Shakespearian comedy – but very nearly all participants, including old fathers, uncles, and the Friar, take turns at deceiving others; and, conversely, each takes a turn at being deceived. No crowd of characters in a Shakespearian world exhibits more universal predilection for the game, such readiness to exchange and then exchange again the roles of deceiver and deceived. Nor does any play demonstrate more conclusively the dramatist's devotion to situations characterized by exploitable differences in awareness.

The first practice is devised by Don Pedro within minutes of the opening, after Claudio – having first ascertained that she is Leonato's only heir – has confessed that he loves Hero; says Don Pedro:

> I know we shall have revelling tonight.
> I will assume thy part in some disguise
> And tell fair Hero I am Claudio.
> And in her bosom I'll unclasp my heart
> And take her hearing prisoner with the force
> And strong encounter of my amorous tale;
> Then after to her father will I break;
> And the conclusion is, she shall be thine.   I. I. 322–9

The basis of this practice is hardly more than a pretext. Though young, Claudio is no shy Orlando, incapable of wooing for himself. He is a brash and ambitious would-be sophisticate, who might be thought more likely to ravish a heroine than be speechless. Don Pedro's gratuitous offer, then, is the first expression of that alacrity to perpetrate a practice which infects the people of this world.

The next scene presents the first example of the converse alacrity, that of seizing on and believing in what is false. Antonio reports to his brother Leonato:

> The Prince and Count Claudio, walking in a thick-pleached alley in mine orchard, were thus much overheard by a man of mine. The Prince discovered to Claudio that he loved my niece your daughter and meant to acknowledge it this night in a dance; and if he found her accordant, he meant to take the present time by the top and instantly break with you of it.   I. 2. 8–16

'Hath the fellow any wit that told you of this?' asks Leonato – but does not bother to question the servant. He hurries to tell Hero of her good fortune, and thus, abruptly, Leonato, Antonio, and Hero have dropped to a level below ours. Inevitably, they have also pushed down Don Pedro, who proceeds with his wooing, ignorant that his device has been overheard and misconstrued.

By the end of the second scene, then, from a servant's mis-overhearing and a readiness of Antonio and Leonato to mistake, a tissue of error has grown. To this point all persons involved are well intentioned, their aims honourable, and the worst result of their error should be only disappointment for Hero and Leonato when they discover that Claudio is the real suitor. But in the third scene wicked fingers insinuate themselves into the tangle. Borachio, follower of Don John, has also overheard Don Pedro and Claudio arrange their innocent deception; but, unlike Antonio's man, he has not mistaken:

... as I was smoking in a musty room, comes me the Prince and Claudio, hand in hand, in sad conference. I whipt me behind the arras, and there heard it agreed upon that the Prince should woo Hero for himself, and having obtain'd her, give her to Count Claudio.   I. 3. 60–66

'That young start-up hath all the glory of my overthrow', says Don John. 'If I can cross him any way, I bless myself every way. . . . Shall we go prove what's to be done?' At the end of Act I, then, an innocent plot set by amateurs has become snarled with a wicked one, woven by professionals.

At the opening of Act II, we share our vantage-point only with villains, other participants being ignorant both of Don John's threats and of other aspects of the suddenly complex situation. The Prince and Claudio suppose themselves sole proprietors of their innocent plot, not knowing that it has been misunderstood by Leonato and perverted by Don John; Leonato and Hero, believing a false report, are of course ignorant of the Prince's true purpose and know nothing of Don John's malicious interest. During the opening dialogue, while the gay, sharp wit of Beatrice is featured, Shakespeare repeatedly prods recollection of the secrets he has given us to hold. Thus, in the first line, Leonato inquires after Don John: 'Was not Count John here at supper?' These are the first words we have heard since Don John's threats closed the preceding act, and inevitably they remind of the immediate danger to this gay, unwitting group preparing for revels. Through remarks that twice interrupt Beatrice's flashing wit, we are reminded also of the widespread misunderstanding of the Prince's purpose; thus Leonato addresses Hero: 'Daughter, remember what I told you. If the Prince do solicit you in that kind, you know your answer'. And again, Antonio speaks to Hero: 'Well, niece, I trust you will be rul'd by your father'. Even Beatrice's sharp vision is blurred by the general error: 'If the Prince be too important, tell him there is measure in everything, and so dance out the measure'. More remarkable than that Beatrice should embrace false belief, however, is that even Don John, whose henchman had told him of the Prince's true purpose, himself slips into error: 'Sure my brother is amorous on Hero and hath withdrawn her father to break with him about it'. In a minor practice, pretending to mistake him for Benedick, he accosts Claudio:

DON JOHN Are not you Signior Benedick?

CLAUDIO You know me well; I am he.

DON JOHN Signior, you are very near my brother in his love. He is enamour'd on Hero. I pray you, dissuade him from her; she is no equal for his birth. You may do the part of an honest man in it.

CLAUDIO How know you he loves her?

DON JOHN I heard him swear his affection.   II. I. 167–75

No incident in the play better exposes the stuff of which *Much Ado About Nothing* is made, the mutually complementing alacrities in deceiving and being deceived: Don John had known the Prince's plan but permits the slightest evidence to the contrary to deceive him; Claudio, who had been the Prince's partner in the plan, falls instantly into the general error on the testimony of one he knows to be a villain: ''Tis certain so; the Prince woos for himself'. When in the next moment Benedick enters to add his misapprehension to the rest – 'the Prince hath got your Hero' – the 'proof' is superfluous. Claudio has already been convinced and slinks away 'to creep into sedges'.

At this point, midway through Act II, everything indicates that the main plot of *Much Ado About Nothing* will grow from the misunderstanding that has occurred. Act I and more than half of Act II have been used to bring about this situation. Every principal person has become involved in an error of which it appears that the inevitable consequence must be conflict between the two friends. Even the villain has made it his purpose to separate Don Pedro and Claudio – and ordinarily a villain's declaration of interest in an issue is proof enough that it will become central. It can scarcely be other than startling, therefore, that after another flurry of exploitation, Shakespeare suddenly destroys the error that he has taken nearly two acts to make general; thus Don Pedro:

Here, Claudio, I have wooed in thy name, and fair Hero is won. I have broke with her father, and his good will obtained. Name the day of marriage, and God give thee joy!   II. I. 309–12

Even so abruptly is the affair ended – and momentarily the play, two acts nearly spent, is left without the beginning of a plot. Even the villain must start anew.

The termination of what seemed the beginning of a main action suggests that Shakespeare changed his mind while writing the opening acts; for if, at the outset, he did not intend to base his plot on the misunderstanding between Claudio and the Prince, why did he give this breach such large emphasis? Elsewhere, in comedies, histories, and tragedies alike, his way is to use Act I to lay the basis for the main action; nowhere else is there occasion for such surprise as is caused by the termination of the conflict between Claudio and the Prince. It is possible, of course, that the dramatist did change his mind. The idea of making Don John's slander of Hero the heart of the plot may not yet have occurred to him. He had already told one story of division between friends, in *The Two Gentlemen of Verona*; he may have become bored with the Claudio–Don Pedro division almost at once and sealed it quickly in order to take a fresh start.

On the other hand, the best evidence that he did not change his mind, but intended from the outset to drop the Claudio–Don Pedro conflict and to make the slander of Hero his principal matter is, first, the very excessiveness of his initial emphasis on the alacrity of persons to perpetrate practices and to be deceived by others' practices; and, second, the fact that these are precisely the human conditions out of which the slander of Hero rises and is taken for truth. Though the threatened breach is healed in Act II, yielding to different matter that becomes central, yet there is continuity in the means and the environment. The major incident of Hero's slander depends as completely on the mutually complementing factors of practice and susceptibility to practice as does the Claudio–Don Pedro division. The initial, swift-moving tangle of confusions is thus illustrative of the world in which the later, greater misunderstanding is set. Its purpose is to establish the character of this world and its inhabitants, to condition our minds for the general acceptance of Hero's slander and its consequences. And it must be said that this purpose is achieved: after the initial demonstration of the Messinan predilection for deceiving and being deceived, we can believe that any falsehood will thrive in the Messinan climate. The opening incident has demonstrated that here much ado can arise from nothing. Perhaps Shakespeare allowed the initial misunderstandings to grow too great; it is certainly bad that their abrupt breaking-off causes surprise. But the gain is greater than the loss if we have been conditioned to accept a world in which Hero's slander can be perpetrated and believed. What at first seemed a fumbling start may appear in view of the total work to be a calculated introduction.

Nor is the initial tropical growth of error the only means by which Shakespeare illustrates the character of this world: Beatrice and Benedick, lights of the first magnitude in Shakespeare's universe, may attract us so strongly that we will be sorry to find them and their affair also, like the Claudio–Prince affair, primarily a means of high-lighting this character. It is true that, whereas the initial business is snuffed out and abandoned, that of Beatrice and Benedick grows to the end; even so, it is secondary: these sparkling lovers help make the environment credible in which occurs the story of the nearly speechless Hero and the insufferable Claudio. Again, it is possibly a structural fault that Beatrice and Benedick, resembling stars but serving as planets, outshine those about whom they revolve. Yet Shakespeare's subordinate devices are often memorable in their own right: besides these, witness Falstaff and Mercutio.

The illustrative initial incident is barely closed when Don Pedro – such is the way of the world – whose practice precipitated it and threatened disaster, falls to devising anew:

I will teach you how to humour your cousin, that she fall in love with Benedick; and I, with your two helps, will so practise on Benedick that, in despite of his quick wit and his queasy stomach, he shall fall in love with Beatrice.   II. I. 395–400

Immediately, residents and guests alike, all incurably addicted to practising, are plunged into another indulgence. The new practice, like the first, is innocent enough. But even as Don Pedro – who has

never even learned of the ado stirred up by his previous practice –
prepares to unite Beatrice and Benedick by deceiving them, Don
John and Borachio devise a wicked practice against Hero and
Claudio. 'How canst thou cross this marriage?' the bastard asks his
shadow; and Borachio outlines a plot 'to misuse the Prince, to vex
Claudio, to undo Hero, and kill Leonato'. Though the purposes of
Don Pedro and Don John stand in direct contrast, their means are
parallel. Says the Prince: 'If we can do this, Cupid is no longer an
archer. His glory shall be ours, for we are the only love-gods'. And
of Borachio's plot Don John speaks thus: 'Grow this to what
adverse issue it can, I will put it in practice'. The repetition of the
pattern of practices with which the play opened is striking: then Don
Pedro devised an innocent practice to win Hero for Claudio, and
Don John countered with a sinister scheme to divide and destroy
Don Pedro and Claudio; now Don Pedro devises an innocent
practice to unite Beatrice and Benedick, and Don John counters
with a sinister plot aimed to destroy all the innocents there are.

At the beginning of Act II, Scene 3, then, Shakespeare has completed preparations for claiming varied and conflicting responses of
us, who are perched high above the action. The first of these effects
is simply comic. Benedick speaks at length, to prove his immunity
to Cupid's arrow:

> I do much wonder that one man, seeing how much another man is a
> fool when he dedicates his behaviours to love, will, after he hath
> laugh'd at such shallow follies in others, become the argument of his
> own scorn by falling in love. . . .   II. 3. 6–11

This, with twenty-five lines more, is uttered directly after Don
Pedro's promise that Benedick, 'in despite of his quick wit and his
queasy stomach, he shall fall in love with Beatrice' – and our
recollection of this promise overcasts the speech. Moreover, here as
elsewhere, Shakespeare ensures against our drowsily neglecting to
use our advantage: when Benedick, hearing 'the Prince and Mon-
sieur Love' coming, retires to watch unseen – as he supposes – and
the practice designed to snare him is begun, our awareness is sharply
prodded from both sides by comments of practisers and victim.
When the Prince, Claudio, and Leonato have outdone one another

in telling the degree of Beatrice's passion, the gull who thinks himself an eagle is made to speak – shrewdly, as he supposes – from the shadows:

> I should think this a gull, but that the white-bearded fellow speaks it. Knavery cannot, sure, hide himself in such reverence.　　II. 3. 123–5

And from the other side, baldly reminding us that this is a gull indeed, Claudio's whisper encourages his fellow practisers: 'O, ay, stalk on, stalk on; the fowl sits'. The practice continues through a scene of nearly 200 lines, until Benedick 'hath ta'en th'infection'. When Beatrice comes to call him to dinner, knowing nothing of what has happened, she inevitably becomes joint victim of the gulling. He takes her sharpest lashes for expressions of love, and each remains ignorant of the other's mind.

So much for the comic, which is only part of the total effect; a shadow hangs over the action, unsuspected by either the practisers or the victims: the wicked plot hatched by Don John and Borachio. That this cloud might not escape our notice, Shakespeare has set Borachio's explanation of the plot immediately before the scene of Benedick's gulling:

> ... tell them that you know that Hero loves me; intend a kind of zeal both to the Prince and Claudio, as – in love of your brother's honour, who hath made this match, and his friend's reputation, who is thus like to be cozen'd with the semblance of a maid; – that you have discover'd thus. They will scarcely believe this without trial. Offer them instances; which shall bear no less likelihood than to see me at her chamber-window, hear me call Margaret Hero, hear Margaret term me Claudio; and bring them to see this the very night before the intended wedding. ...
> 　　II. 2. 34–46

The effect of this plot – designed to hurt the very persons who are having holiday sport with Benedick and Beatrice – is a dark over-casting of the comic effect of that scene. Shrewdly, the dramatist keeps our awareness of the menacing cloud active during the scene, not only through the presence of those who will be hurt – Claudio, most of all, and Leonato – but also by repeated naming of Hero, and, more pointedly, of Hero's chamber-window, mentioned earlier by Borachio; thus Don Pedro: 'I pray thee, get us some excellent music; for tomorrow night we would have it at the Lady Hero's chamber-window'. Our sense of the enveloping danger is further alerted by the careful paralleling of Benedick's gulling and the practice by which Don John intends to precipitate general catastrophe. It is only in their purposes that the two practices contrast.

The stair-stepped disposition of awarenesses thus makes possible here the double and conflicting effects that Shakespeare seeks in the climactic scenes of the mature comedies. The same purpose governs the opening scene of Act III, which presents the gulling of Beatrice. Unaware that Benedick has already been gulled in a way that affects herself, Beatrice is herself tricked as the scene proceeds, hence is doubly deceived at the end. Like Benedick, she thinks herself a practiser in that she hears while unseen; thus Hero: '... Look where Beatrice, like a lapwing, runs | Close by the ground, to hear our conference'. And, as in the parallel scene, through pointed comments, Shakespeare makes assurance doubly sure that we will savour the situation fully; thus Ursula:

> The pleasant'st angling is to see the fish
> Cut with her golden oars the silver stream,
> And greedily devour the treacherous bait.
> So angle we for Beatrice, who even now
> Is couched in the woodbine coverture.   III. 1. 26–30

And again, like Benedick, Beatrice swallows completely 'the false sweet bait'; thus, at the end:

> ... Benedick, love on; I will requite thee,
> Taming my wild heart to thy loving hand.
>   III. 1. 111–12

The comic effect created by exploitation of her unawareness matches that created by exploitation of Benedick's. But even darker now is the overcasting of the comic effect by our enforced recollection of Don John's wicked plot. It is darker partly because the danger is nearer, but principally because of the presence in the scene of Hero herself, who is to be most injured. Elsewhere reserved and nearly silent, in this scene Hero is active and gay, taking the lead in gulling Beatrice in that same pleached orchard where, as we know, she is herself to be undone by a practice the mechanics of which are like these. So emphatic is her participation in the present business, and so strongly does the pattern of the practice parallel that threatened by Borachio, that the glow of irony smoulders steadily; only once, when she suggests a mild slandering of Beatrice to discourage Benedick's passion, does the more typical flash of irony occur:

> ... I will go to Benedick
> And counsel him to fight against his passion;
> And, truly, I'll devise some honest slanders
> To stain my cousin with.   III. 1. 82–5

The gulling of both wits contributes the more effectively to rendering the success of Hero's defamation plausible because these two are as they are – quick, alert, sceptical by nature. The point is persuasive: if such as these can be deceived thus, then surely the world of *Much Ado About Nothing* is one in which a Don John can propose a monstrous falsehood and have it believed. The very success of the practices by which amateurs unite Benedick and Beatrice builds anxiety for Hero, against whom, as the dramatist will not let us forget, a plot has been mounted by professionals.

In *The Merchant of Venice*, anxiety for Antonio grows during the opening portion of the court scene and is most intense just before Nerissa's arrival. During this period our awareness, though superior to that of the participants, holds nothing comforting; on the contrary, Shylock's menace is drawn in such strong colours and the helplessness of the City is so emphasized that we must think Antonio's doom inescapable. So, in *Much Ado About Nothing*, anxiety is most intense during the closing portion of Act III, Scene 2, when Don John makes his first move, beginning, Iago-like, with insinuation:

DON JOHN (*to Claudio*) Means your lordship to be married tomorrow?
DON PEDRO You know he does.
DON JOHN I know not that, when he knows what I know.

III. 2. 91–5

He slanders Hero; and just as the underscoring of Shylock's vindictiveness and the helplessness of Venetian law inspired fear for Antonio's safety, so now our repeated proofs of Messina's susceptibility to gulling deepen anxiety for Hero. That defamation will be taken for truth in such a world appears certain; indeed, so apt are Claudio and Don Pedro to believe false report that we might expect them to take Don John's word even without waiting for the proof he promises. The gullible Claudio needs only to hear it breathed that Hero is false; as if exhilarated, he devises a practice as inhumane as the villain's:

> If I see anything tonight why I should not marry her tomorrow, in the congregation, where I should wed, there will I shame her.
>
> III. 2. 126–8

Don Pedro quickly agrees; their recent participation in the practice on Beatrice and Benedick has taught them nothing of wariness: their alacrity in believing still balances their alacrity in deceiving. Claudio's manner carries a hint of eagerness for the morrow; possibly he would be disappointed if, Don John's 'proof' failing, he were prevented from going on with the denunciation. In short, Hero appears as good as doomed at the first breath of calumny, even from a known villain's throat.

The ominous note on which Act III, Scene 2 closes marks an important dividing line. Up to this point our knowledge of Don John's plot against Hero and Claudio shadowed the bright scenes of the gulling of Beatrice and Benedick very much as in *The Merchant of Venice* our knowledge of Antonio's peril in Venice shadowed the casket scenes at Belmont. Now, abruptly, the dramatist reverses the use of our superior awareness: where formerly it darkened light scenes, hereafter it lightens dark ones. It was the source whence discomfort swelled; it now brings a flood of reassurance.

In *The Merchant of Venice* Nerissa's arrival, announcing Portia's, changed the use of our awareness and enabled us to watch the trial of Antonio with confidence. In *Much Ado About Nothing* it is the arrival of Dogberry and his assistants that makes the change. Says Dogberry, instructing those assigned to the Prince's watch:

> One word more, honest neighbours. I pray you, watch about Signior Leonato's door; for the wedding being there tomorrow, there is a great coil tonight. Adieu! Be vigitant, I beseech you.   III. 3. 97–100

sense of these facts darkens the gaiety of the scene, since it reminds us of the anguish that must come to this Hero who is just now so brightly unsuspecting. Yet above the shadow is another light: all will yet be well, for Don John's henchmen are in custody. We hold assurance that, however sharp the pain, Hero's injury will not be permanent. As we were assured that Portia would ultimately curb the menace of Shylock, so we have been assured that Dogberry will ultimately expose Don John's plot.

Yet Dogberry is no Portia! It is one thing to share our vantage-point with an Oberon, a Portia, a Vincentio, a Prospero – and quite another to share it with a Dogberry: the use of precisely this bumbler in a position of authority, in precisely this place, where he inspires simultaneous reassurance and exasperation, is a Shake-spearian masterstroke. Because both constable and 'compartners' are inordinately blundering, suspense is added to other effects, already multiple and conflicting, created by the scenes leading to Hero's denunciation. Except for Dogberry's marvellous stupidity in the scene that just precedes the denunciation, Leonato would learn the truth that would prevent shame and hurt to Hero and himself. The scene begins auspiciously:

LEONATO What would you with me, honest neighbour?
DOGBERRY Marry, sir, I would have some confidence with you that decerns you nearly.
LEONATO Brief, I pray you, for you see it is a busy time with me.

III. 5. 1–6

But Dogberry is tedious and irrelevant, and the facts that would spare Hero lie fallow in his mind. When he can bear no more of the constable's digressive philosophizing – 'Well, God's a good man; an two men ride of a horse, one must ride behind' – Leonato ends the interview and directs Dogberry himself to examine his pair of 'aspicious persons'.

The race to spare Hero is thus lost; but though we are now denied hope that truth will out soon enough to prevent Claudio's denuncia-tion, yet nothing has shaken our confidence that it will come out in due time: Dogberry will never quite lose the scent. The last words of the scene are reassuring:

⟶y We are now to examination these men.
        And we must do it wisely.

⟶rry We will spare for no wit, I warrant you. Here's that shall
⟶e some of them to a non-come; only get the learned writer to set
down our excommunication, and meet me at the gaol.   III. 5. 64–9

Though the significance of what he discovers may never penetrate
his own insulated mind, yet Dogberry will obey Leonato's instruc-
tion: 'Take their examination yourself and bring it me'. It will all
eventually be set in writing, too, for Dogberry dispatches Verges to
bring one Francis Seacole, with his pen and inkhorn.

These comforts, strategically provided just before the entrance of
Hero, Claudio, and others for the wedding, hang overhead throughout the action of the most poignant scene in Shakespearian comedy,
that of Hero's denunciation at the altar. The bundle of awarenesses
given us to carry during this action is heavy, yet each item of the
burden contributes to the multiple and conflicting effects which the
scene is calculated to produce. At the opening, with every principal
person in view, we hold simultaneously comforting and dis-
comforting advantages over all. On the bottommost level of
awareness stand Hero and Leonato, ignorant that Don John's plot
has blackened Hero's name, that even now Claudio is framing the
words of Hero's denunciation, and, of course, that just now, also,
Dogberry's 'excommunication' is drawing out the facts that will
clear Hero's name. Our perception of their condition demands pity
– indeed, because Hero is Hero, anguish. However she may compare
with the great heroines of the comedies, Portia, Rosalind, and Viola,
Hero is a gentle girl, modest and tender, composed of such fine
sensibilities that Claudio's brutal condemnation must crush her
utterly. The more forceful heroines of other comedies, circumspect
and aggressive, would weaken the scene. A Portia or a Rosalind
would never do: supposing that either could be caught in such a
situation in the first place, we would have scant need of anguish on
her account – being sure that she would shatter the predicament like
glass, free herself, and leave Claudio's coxcomb bloody. Leonato,
like Hero, is right for the situation. He is a doting father, an open-
hearted and trusting friend; Borachio's boast that his plot will kill
Leonato is believable. Standing on the lowest level of awareness,

then, quite oblivious to the facts of their terrible situation, Hero and Leonato invite our pity – even while we know that joy lies just beyond, once Francis Seacole's pen has recorded the 'excommunication'.

On the level next above stand Claudio and Don Pedro, who know what Claudio intends but do not know either that their opinion of Hero is false or that it will shortly be corrected. Yet though they hold advantage over Hero in knowing what they mean to do at the altar, both are inferior to her in another way: their opinion of her character is false, and hers is true; once Claudio's accusation has been made, and she knows what is thought of her, it is she who holds the real advantage – albeit without satisfaction. The most insufferable of Shakespeare's heroes of comedy, combining the hero's usual oblivion with priggish egocentricity, Claudio, too, is perfectly right for his role here: one sees why Shakespeare made him thus. The eagerness which once showed in his anticipation of the moment when he would shame Hero becomes passionate as the moment nears. He therefore deserves the backlashes which, in our view, slash himself more sharply than those he intends to hurt. Shakespeare makes his 'knowing' words betray his terrible ignorance; they strike flashes of irony that engulf the speaker:

FRIAR If either of you know any inward impediment why you should not be conjoined, I charge you, on your souls, to utter it.

CLAUDIO Know you any, Hero?

HERO None, my lord.

FRIAR Know you any, count?

LEONATO I dare make his answer, none.

CLAUDIO O, what men dare do! What men may do! What men daily do, not knowing what they do!   IV. I. 12–21

A frequent way of Shakespeare's is to make a person speak at length in ignorance of the reality around him, erroneously denouncing the subjects of their wrath: thus Othello, coming to the murder of Desdemona; Capulet, raging at Juliet for her refusal to marry Paris; Posthumus Leonatus, condemning all womankind because Iachimo's false report has made him believe Imogen untrue; Leontes, excoriating Hermione because his own idiotic imagination

...sed her. These utterances made in ignorance most often
...d of us more pity than anger, for though they speak fiercely,
...men have no joy in their denunciations. They are themselves
deeply hurt. Even while he speaks, Othello so loves Desdemona
that his emotion almost persuades Justice to break her sword. But
Claudio, in his great moment, seems calculated to kindle only our
anger, for his denunciation of Hero has an exuberance that borders
sadism:

> There, Leonato, take her back again.
> Give not this rotten orange to your friend:
> She's but the sign and semblance of her honour.
> Behold how like a maid she blushes here!
> O, what authority and show of truth
> Can cunning sin cover itself withal!
> Comes not that blood as modest evidence
> To witness simple virtue? Would you not swear,
> All you that see her, that she were a maid,
> By these exterior shows? But she is none.
> She knows the heat of a luxurious bed;
> Her blush is guiltiness, not modesty.   IV. I. 32–43

Spoken to Rosalind, these words would meet replies that would
blast the speaker; spoken, with other cruel ones, to Hero, they
draw only a faint, solicitous question: 'Is my lord well, that he doth
speak so wide?' Though we are made to remember that Claudio
speaks in ignorance, the excessiveness of his outburst destroys the
mitigating effect of our awareness: ignorance cannot excuse so
much zeal. When the evidence of his conduct both before and after
the denunciation is added to his exhibition, the dominant impression left by Claudio is of one unworthy even of such a Hero as
he thinks her to be.

Present throughout the scene, Beatrice and Benedick are hardly
more than bystanders; yet their presence contributes to the complex
total effect, because they steadily remind us of the way of the
Messinan world. Further, their presence tempers the mood of this
bitter scene: we cannot observe them without being aware, at one
depth of consciousness, of their own recent gulling and of their
agitated states of mind even now, while this terrible scene goes on.

Seen out of a corner of the mind's eye, they add a touch of high comedy to the moment of heartbreak.

Also significantly present is Don John, the best reminder of the greatest advantage we hold during this action. Don John stands above Hero and Leonato, Beatrice and Benedick, Claudio and Don Pedro in his knowledge of the facts; indeed, his vantage-point is just under our own. He knows at the outset, as Hero and Leonato do not, what Claudio intends, and knows, as Claudio and Don Pedro do not, that they were abused by false evidence. But he does not know, as we do, that his accomplices have been caught and that even now the learned Seacole should be transcribing their 'excommunication'. This was the fact that Shakespeare fixed in our minds immediately before the church scene began, and, because it is comforting, it is the most precious fact in our possession during the action. For Hero and Leonato, momentarily stricken, the truth is better than it appears; for Don John, momentarily triumphant, most ignorant of what he is most assured, it is worse: in the comedies this is a regular formula, the pattern of which is always open to the view from our vantage-point. In the tragedies, conversely, the truth during climactic scenes usually favours villainy, and for heroes, heroines, and other innocents it is worse than they suspect. The climactic scene of *Much Ado About Nothing*, one of the most moving in the comedies, is true at last to its comic kind, for the razor's edge of anguish is blunted by our assurance that all will be well.

The climactic incident ends with Hero's swooning and the callous departure of Claudio, Don Pedro, and Don John. At once, even now, the prevailing spirit of the Messinan world reasserts itself. First Beatrice insists that her cousin has been belied; next the Friar, reading the innocence of Hero's face, risks his reputation for wisdom on the claim that she lies 'Under some biting error'. 'The practice of it lives in John the Bastard,' says Benedick, 'whose spirits toil in frame of villainies.' In the world of *Much Ado* the mere word 'practice' is a cue: abruptly all who have just been gulled turn gullers. It is the Friar – surely akin to Romeo's ghostly father, an unhappy practiser – who now proposes the seventh major deceptive device of the play:

> Your daughter here the princes left for dead.
> Let her awhile be secretly kept in,
> And publish it that she is dead indeed.
> Maintain a mourning ostentation
> And on your family's old monument
> Hang mournful epitaphs, and do all rites
> That appertain unto a burial.   IV. I. 204–10

The purpose of this practice is to 'Change slander to remorse'. Not knowing Claudio as well as we do, the Friar anticipates that Hero's reputed death will grieve him:

> Then shall he mourn
> If ever love had interest in his liver,
> And wish he had not so accused her,
> No, though he thought his accusation true.   IV. I. 232–5

The Friar, Hero, Leonato, Beatrice, and Benedick thus become proprietors of a new practice just before the most recent old one, that of Don John and his henchmen, is due to be exposed by Francis Seacole's transcription. By the time the one is finished, the next will be full-blown – and still the next preparing: such is the action of *Much Ado*, propelled by Messina's addiction to practising.

The closing scene of Act IV gives final confirmation to our assurance that all will be well, for in it Dogberry completes his 'excommunication'. It is given to Bottom alone of mortals to see and converse with fairies; yet he finds nothing wonderful in his association with them, nor can he report his experience afterwards: 'Man is but an ass, if he go about to expound this dream.' It is given to Dogberry to bring to light the dark plot of Don John. 'What your wisdoms could not discover,' says Borachio to Don Pedro and Claudio, 'these shallow fools have brought to light.' The significance of his accomplishment never quite penetrates the consciousness of Dogberry: 'Flat burglary as ever was committed' is his conclusion, and his final wrath is spent on Conrade for calling him an ass: 'O, that I had been writ down an ass.'

At the opening of Act V three large facts, the residue of practices, occupy our minds: that Hero was slandered; that Dogberry is on the way to Leonato's with the truth; that Hero, reported dead, is living. Two secondary facts reside with these: that Benedick and

AWARENESS AND UNAWARENESS

Beatrice were victimized by practices; and that Beatrice has bound Benedick, on his love for her, to kill Claudio. Leonato's ignorance of the first two facts is exploited first, in his long lament for Hero's dishonour. But the centre of attention is Claudio, whose reactions to three moments which the dramatist asks us to anticipate follow in quick succession. These are the moments in which he learns of Hero's 'death', in which he learns of her innocence, and in which he learns of her survival. The most powerful effects of Shakespeare's exploitation of discrepant awarenesses most commonly occur, first, at the time a participant, acting in ignorance, commits a wrong against another and, second, at the time he learns what he has done. In the scene of denunciation at the altar we have already tasted the first of these fruits. Claudio's successive reactions during Act V together represent the second, and the taste is sour.

The first of these moments, when Claudio learns of Hero's 'death', passes almost without notice. Leonato confronts him with the news, and this is the moment at which Claudio, by the Friar's reckoning, should begin to mourn Hero. But the Friar mistook his man: Claudio is merely self-defensive. With the entrance of Benedick only a moment after he has learned of Hero's death, he is ready with an ill-timed jest: 'We had like to have had our two noses snapp'd off by two old men without teeth.' Whatever is on his mind, it is not Hero. He speaks no word of her, but complains of boredom – 'high-proof melancholy' – and challenges Benedick to a duel of wits. The fact that, in our consciousness, Hero is not really dead cannot mitigate the fault of Claudio's conduct here: she is dead to him, and he should weep for her. That he does not do so is damning. 'Well, I will meet you,' he tells Benedick, who has accused him of killing Hero and challenged him to fight, 'so I may have good cheer.' By sustained and conspicuous representation of his indifference, Shakespeare exhibits the measure of the man. That the dramatist's exposure of Claudio's insufferableness was intentional is evinced by the speech given the Friar, predicting Claudio's reaction to Hero's death, and in effect advising us how a worthy human being should act in the circumstances: 'Then shall he mourn | If ever love had interest in his liver, | And wish he had not so accused her, | No, though he thought his accusation true.'

215

Claudio's actual reaction, quite contradicting this expectation, is damning.

In the second anticipated moment, when he learns that Hero died innocent, the hero's reaction approximates 'Ah! Then she was worthy of me after all!' Thus he speaks:

> Sweet Hero! now thy image doth appear
> In the rare semblance that I lov'd it first.   v. 1. 259–60

Borachio, outright villain, confessing his guilt to Don Pedro, concludes with: 'The lady is dead upon mine and my master's false accusation; and, briefly, I desire nothing but the reward of a villain.' Not to be outfaced, Claudio says to Leonato:

> Impose me to what penance your invention
> Can lay upon my sin.   v. 1. 283–4

– but he adds, defensively, 'yet sinn'd I not | But in mistaking.' On this cause, Othello kills himself; Claudio, no Othello, gladly grasps Leonato's offer of a 'niece' to replace Hero: 'I do embrace your offer; and dispose | For henceforth of poor Claudio.' Leonato, in making the offer, makes a point of saying that this child of his brother 'alone is heir to both of us' – a fact which helps Claudio to bear his penance heroically, with only the suggestion of a whimper: 'poor Claudio.'

Before the final moment arrives, when Claudio discovers Leonato's 'niece' to be Hero herself, a brief scene represents his mourning at the 'tomb' of Hero. It is noteworthy that this visit was not Claudio's idea, but Leonato's. Earlier, when Claudio asked Leonato to impose some penance, the father replied:

> . . . if your love
> Can labour aught in sad invention,
> Hang her an epitaph upon her tomb
> And sing it to her bones, sing it tonight.   v. 1. 292–5

The formal rite accomplished, Claudio and Don Pedro summarily withdraw with no comment but Claudio's expression of hope that his next matrimonial venture will turn out better.

Meanwhile Leonato's household prepares to work a final practice on the visitors; says Leonato:

> Well, daughter, and you gentlewomen all,
> Withdraw into a chamber by yourselves,
> And when I send for you, come hither mask'd.
> The Prince and Claudio promis'd by this hour
> To visit me. You know your office, brother.
> You must be father to your brother's daughter,
> And give her to young Claudio.   v. 4. 10–16

Here, as usual, the dramatist has not trusted us to guess: we must be told plainly that the 'niece' earlier promised Claudio is Hero herself; the surprise is to be Claudio's, not ours. We are required, in advance of every action, to understand its true nature, and we are not allowed to disregard the advantage we hold. Clear in our facts, then, we are able to observe Claudio objectively as the great moment of his reaction to the final truth approaches. Though he has just returned from the mourning rite at Hero's tomb, his sensibilities remain undisturbed beneath the callous: 'I'll hold my mind, were she an Ethiope,' he declares valiantly – and then he jests at Benedick:

> I think he thinks upon the savage bull.
> Tush, fear not, man; we'll tip thy horns with gold
> And all Europa shall rejoice at thee,
> As once Europa did at lusty Jove,
> When he would play the noble beast in love.   v. 4. 43–7

His greeting of the veiled bride is of the same character: 'here comes other reck'nings.' When Hero is unveiled, the sum of his reaction is contained in 'Another Hero!' Shakespeare gives him no more words on the matter, either of love, joy, or apology; his only remaining remarks are directed at Benedick and Beatrice. Viewed from our Olympian height, Claudio's conduct during his journey through several stages of ignorance has hardly appeared heroic. Believing Hero false, he was bestial; believing her dead, he gave her no more thought; learning that she had been true, but still supposing her dead, he compromised his formal expressions of grief with protestations that he should not be blamed; and finally, learning that she is both living and innocent, he is relieved to find that the face behind the veil is not an Ethiope's.

It is the affair of Beatrice and Benedick, though suspended and almost unexploited for two acts, that best sustains the comic spirit during this period and finally lifts it for a joyful close. One or the other has been present in almost every scene, serving the business of Hero and Claudio; though there has been little comment on the condition in which their gulling has left them, their presence alone reminds us that it continues. The fact of their error makes a gay backdrop for anguished scenes. Awareness of their state brings warmth and mirth even to those moments which demand grief and anger for the main action. In preserving the climate of comedy, thus, the subordinate action indispensably serves the central one. Unlike Claudio, both Benedick and Beatrice shine as gloriously in their ignorance as in their awareness. Each was won to love the other through a humane and noble sympathy which was not dimmed but made more luminous by error. Theirs is the final misapprehension to be cleared away, and when they perceive how they have been gulled, the revelation makes no difference in their love: 'Peace!' cries Benedick as he kisses his bride, 'I will stop your mouth.'

from *Shakespeare's Comedies* by Bertrand Evans, 1960

TWENTY-THREE

Much Ado About Nothing in the Theatre

SHAKESPEARE'S comedy of *Much Ado About Nothing* was written, as its Beatrice was born, under a dancing star. But its wit must not be uttered self-consciously, its rhythms blurred in romping, its festival terms disordered. Then it can seem to be much ado about nothing indeed; and I have met one or two productions that have sent me sadly from a theatre. No one, I feel, is likely to come sad away from the Phoenix. This Gielgud revival of *Much Ado* shines. Here, in production at least, we can find in the West End something of the riches of the Stratford-upon-Avon Memorial Theatre, news from Warwickshire. John Gielgud contrives to make the part of Benedick his own. We wonder again why so few front-rank actors have lately essayed it in London.

What delights me about this *Much Ado* is its infallible sense of style. Style is a word misused. Some producers interpret it as affectation, but the Phoenix revival has the grace, the suppleness, the rhythm that the high comedy needs, without ever causing us to be aware that its producer has wrestled for effect. Gielgud, as an actor, has this style. He does not stab and bang at Benedick. He speaks the prose with a silken rhythm – my third return to a word that in this context is inescapable – and he does not let the man dwindle. It is so easy to turn Benedick to a figure of farce, blundering through. There is no hint of that at the Phoenix, where he is always a man to be respected, the Prince's friend, not the Prince's jester. Visitors should observe two passages. The first is the Beatrice–Benedick colloquy at the end of the church scene: here I must say in haste that Diana Wynyard's golden Beatrice is a match for her partner. In the middle of the dialogue that begins, 'Lady Beatrice, have you wept all this while?' we have the famous exchange:

BENEDICK Come bid me do any thing for thee.
BEATRICE Kill Claudio.
BENEDICK Ha! not for the wide world.   IV. I. 286–8

Laughter in the audience on Benedick's answer is fatal. The genuine emotion of the scene is dispersed. The man stiffens to a puppet of comedy. Beatrice will have to fight to win back the house for her speech: 'Is a' not approved in the height a villain? . . .' Time and again I have heard the fatal laugh. Occasionally it has not been the actor's fault, but it is a very dangerous moment. If a Benedick has been presented insincerely; if an actor has shown him to us from the outside looking in, as a figure of artificial comedy, the laugh is certain: the true implications of the line are lost.

I hope all who go to the Phoenix will mark how the passage is treated; how it is lifted gradually to that 'Bid me do anything for thee' from a loyal lover; how Beatrice pauses for a moment in a charged silence; how the actress holds this before she replies 'Kill Claudio' (words forced from her); and how Benedick's 'Not for the wide world' is quick, low-toned, the almost incredulous exclamation of a man who has not realized how friendship must struggle with love and honour. Once past this line, and the scene moves on with an urgent sincerity; the serious heart of the comedy of wit-cracking, the Merry War's grave interlude. Someone said to me in the interval, 'I don't see that anyone could have got a laugh on that line'. It was an indirect tribute to Gielgud's playing.

Ellen Terry and Henry Irving, during a *Much Ado* revival, had one of their few disagreements. It was in 1882 at the Lyceum. That radiant Beatrice had discovered earlier – I quote from Laurence Irving's biography – that the 'slow, deliberate Benedick forced her to modify the pace and timing of her performance'. She rebelled further when she found that Irving proposed to interpolate a traditional gag at the end of the church scene. The lines, as Shakespeare wrote them, are:

BENEDICK Think you in your soul the Count Claudio hath wronged Hero?
BEATRICE Yea, as sure as I have a thought or a soul.

BENEDICK Enough, I am engaged, I will challenge him. I will kiss your hand, so I leave you. By this hand, Claudio shall render me a dear account. As you hear of me, so think of me. Go comfort your cousin. I must say she is dead: and so, farewell.   IV. I. 325-32

John Gielgud's performance is so clear and assured that the speech brings the scene to a natural close. But some old-school players before Irving's day, and (at the Lyceum) Irving himself, considered that there should be something more vigorous, some crack of the theatrical whip. It had become the custom, as Laurence Irving reminds us, for Beatrice to repeat, 'Benedick, kill Claudio!' and for Benedick, on his exit, to cry, 'As sure as I'm alive I will!' Ellen Terry knew that this was hopelessly cheap and inartistic. Irving stayed obdurate, and he won. 'No critics', the biographer adds, 'detected Irving's fall from grace. No doubt his delivery of the offending line was so forceful that Shakespeare himself might have been persuaded he had written it.'

Consider the church scenes at Irving's Lyceum and at Gielgud's Phoenix. At the Lyceum there was all the blaze of Telbin's set, its 'solid structure blending with painted perspectives lit with such subtlety as to suggest an infinity of pillared transepts and vaulted chapels'; its built-up pillars, iron-work gates, gold lamps, stained-glass windows, and statues of saints. At the Phoenix we have the austerity of Mariano Andreu's folding-screen set which gives the illusion with a minimum of fuss: an undistracting background for the players, and one that I find more helpful than the Andreu garden set of the first and last acts, with its niched statues, though this has grown on me with the years. Besides the church scene I noticed Gielgud's handling of the first scene of the fifth act, when Don Pedro and Claudio, after their awkward meeting with the old men, move on relieved to banter Benedick. Often this has jarred in revivals where Benedick has not established himself as more than a puppet of comedy. The scene becomes a disquieting huddle of jests, especially if Claudio has reverted entirely to the wit-snapper of the earlier acts.

At the Phoenix this is not produced for comedy. Claudio (Robert Hardy, transforming a dire part) keeps a worried eye upon Benedick. Don Pedro, too, knows that something is wrong, though he seeks to carry off the meeting with a high hand. Benedick challenges Claudio in earnest; it is no time for brittle wit. In a moment Dogberry and the Watch will come, Conrade and Borachio will confess, the whole miserable Don John plot is exposed, and Claudio is ready to cry:

> Sweet Hero, now thy image doth appear
> In the rare semblance that I loved it first.　　v. 1. 237–8

The plot of *Much Ado* does have its effect in this revival. The players from the first are human beings. Benedick and Beatrice, taking the Merry War with a high-noon gaiety, are always credible, alive, not a dramatist's marionettes in the sunlight of Messina. Visitors to the Phoenix may quarrel with Shaw's estimate of Benedick and Beatrice: one of those occasions – *The Importance of Being Earnest* was another – when the great critic nodded. I have spoken of John Gielgud and Diana Wynyard: let me note again the extreme grace of these performances. When Gielgud lingered on the word 'perturbation', some of us went to the other use of the word in Prince Hal's 'O polished perturbation! golden care!' My only troubles are the loss of the lapwing-movement in the Beatrice, and Benedick's failure to suggest a soldier from the wars returning. Sir Lewis Casson has a dignified vigour as Leonato; and that poised young actor, Paul Scofield, seizes the mind when he gazes out towards us at Don Pedro's lines:

> The wolves have preyed; and look, the gentle day,
> Before the wheels of Phoebus, round about
> Dapples the drowsy east with spots of grey.　　v. 3. 25–7

I am less happy about George Rose's Dogberry, who looks like the Duchess in *Alice*, and who labours the humour; or, surprisingly, about the pale Hero of Dorothy Tutin. For the rest, we must welcome *Much Ado*, Stratford's favourite comedy, at last done worthily again on the London stage where it is met so seldom. A star dances; under it a play is reborn.

from *A Play Tonight* by J. C. Trewin, 1952

Suggestions for Further Reading

M. C. BRADBROOK: *Shakespeare and Elizabethan Poetry*, x. 3. A firmly Elizabethan interpretation. What worries us in Claudio's behaviour would not have troubled the contemporary audience.

BARBARA EVERETT: '*Much Ado About Nothing*' (*Critical Quarterly*, Winter 1961). Within the framework of comedy the clash between the man's and the woman's world is treated seriously – and 'the woman's world dominates'.

FRANCIS FERGUSSON: 'Two Comedies (*The Comedy of Errors* and *Much Ado*)'. Included in the section on *The Comedy of Errors*, earlier in this volume.

G. K. HUNTER: *Shakespeare: The Late Comedies* (British Council pamphlet, 'Writers and Their Work'). A sensitive and scholarly study.

JOHN PALMER: 'Beatrice and Benedick' (*Comic Characters of Shakespeare*). Firmly anti-Claudio. Palmer calls him a young sprig, and his behaviour insupportable. Shakespeare 'simply uses him to make a man of Benedick'. Beatrice and Benedick are discussed as examples of comedy of manners, and compared with Congreve.

D. L. STEVENSON: *The Love Game Comedy*. Chapter XII discusses Comedy of Courtship in *Much Ado About Nothing*: Beatrice and Benedick offer an ironic acknowledgement of the paradoxical nature of love. In the Claudio story the complementary half of romance is 'desperate fact': it hovers on the edge of tragedy, and anticipates *Troilus and Cressida*.

GRAHAM STOREY: '*Much Ado About Nothing*' (*Talking of Shakespeare*, edited by John Garrett).

MARK VAN DOREN: *Shakespeare*. A sensitive commentary on the language of Beatrice and Benedick. Raises – but perhaps does not answer – the question whether the two stories sit uneasily together. Van Doren suggests that, by their mere juxtaposition, each keeps the love of the other from becoming lopsided. 'Beatrice and Benedick draw a clear circle of wit about the play to keep its tragedy in place'.

AS YOU LIKE IT

TWENTY-FOUR

The Alliance of Seriousness and Levity
in *As You Like It*

> In a true piece of Wit all things must be
> Yet all things there agree.
>
> Cowley, quoted by T. S. Eliot in *Andrew Marvell*
>
> Then is there mirth in heaven
> When earthly things made even
> Atone together. *As You Like It*

SHAKESPEARE'S next venture in comedy after *The Merchant of Venice* was probably in the Henry IV plays, which were probably written in 1597–8. Thus the Falstaff comedy comes right in the middle of the period, from about 1594 to 1600 or 1601, when Shakespeare produced festive comedy. *Much Ado About Nothing*, *As You Like It*, and *Twelfth Night* were written at the close of the period, *Twelfth Night* perhaps after *Hamlet*. *The Merry Wives of Windsor*, where Shakespeare's creative powers were less fully engaged, was produced sometime between 1598 and 1602, and it is not impossible that *All's Well That Ends Well* and even perhaps *Measure for Measure* were produced around the turn of the century, despite that difference in tone that has led to their being grouped with *Hamlet* and *Troilus and Cressida*. I shall deal only with *As You Like It* and *Twelfth Night*; they are the two last festive plays, masterpieces that include and extend almost all the resources of the form whose development we have been following. What I would have to say about *Much Ado About Nothing* can largely be inferred from the discussion of the other festive plays. To consider the various other sorts of comedy which Shakespeare produced around the inception of the period when his main concern became tragedy would require another, different frame of reference.

As You Like It is very similar in the way it moves to *A Midsummer Night's Dream* and *Love's Labour's Lost*, despite the fact that its plot is taken over almost entirely from Lodge's *Rosalynde*. As I have suggested in the introductory chapter, the reality we feel about the experience of love in the play, reality which is not in the pleasant little prose romance, comes from presenting what was sentimental extremity as impulsive extravagance and so leaving judgement free to mock what the heart embraces. The Forest of Arden, like the Wood outside Athens, is a region defined by an attitude of liberty from ordinary limitations, a festive place where the folly of romance can have its day. The first half of *As You Like It*, beginning with tyrant brother and tyrant Duke and moving out into the forest, is chiefly concerned with establishing this sense of freedom; the traditional contrast of court and country is developed in a way that is shaped by the contrast between everyday and holiday, as that antithesis has become part of Shakespeare's art and sensibility. Once we are securely in the golden world where the good Duke and 'a many merry men . . . fleet the time carelessly', the pastoral motif as such drops into the background; Rosalind finds Orlando's verses in the second scene of Act III, and the rest of the play deals with love. This second movement is like a musical theme with imitative variations, developing much more tightly the sort of construction which played off Costard's and Armado's amorous affairs against those of the nobles in Navarre, and which set Bottom's imagination in juxtaposition with other shaping fantasies. The love affairs of Silvius and Phebe, Touchstone and Audrey, Orlando and Rosalind succeed one another in the easygoing sequence of scenes, while the dramatist deftly plays each off against the others.

THE LIBERTY OF ARDEN

The thing that asks for explanation about the Forest of Arden is how this version of pastoral can feel so free when the Duke and his company are so high-minded. Partly the feeling of freedom comes from release from the tension established in the first act at the jealous court:

> Now go we in content
> To liberty, and not to banishment.   I. 3. 139–40

Several brief court scenes serve to keep this contrast alive. So does
Orlando's entrance, sword in hand, to interrupt the Duke's gracious
banquet by his threatening demand for food. Such behaviour on his
part is quite out of character (in Lodge he is most courteous);
but his brandishing entrance gives Shakespeare occasion to resolve
the attitude of struggle once again, this time by a lyric invocation of
'what 'tis to pity and be pitied' (II. 7. 117).

But the liberty we enjoy in Arden, though it includes relief from
anxiety in brotherliness confirmed 'at good men's feasts', is somehow easier than brotherliness usually is. The easiness comes from a
witty redefinition of the human situation which makes conflict seem
for the moment superfluous. Early in the play, when Celia and
Rosalind are talking of ways of being merry by devising sports,
Celia's proposal is 'Let us sit and mock the good housewife Fortune
from her wheel' I. 2. 34–5). The two go on with a 'chase' of wit that
goes 'from Fortune's office to Nature's' (I. 2. 43), whirling the two
goddesses through many variations; distinctions between them
were running in Shakespeare's mind. In Act II, the witty poetry
which establishes the greenwood mood of freedom repeatedly
mocks Fortune from her wheel by an act of mind which goes from
Fortune to Nature:

> A fool, a fool! I met a fool i'the'forest . . .
> Who laid him down and bask'd him in the sun
> And rail'd on Lady Fortune in good terms . . .
> 'Good morrow, fool,' quoth I. 'No, sir,' quoth he,
> 'Call me not fool till heaven hath sent me fortune.'
> And then he drew a dial from his poke,
> And looking on it with lack-lustre eye,
> Says very wisely, 'It is ten o'clock.
> Thus we may see,' quoth he, 'how the world wags.
> 'Tis but an hour ago since it was nine,
> And after one more hour 'twill be eleven;
> And so, from hour to hour, we ripe and ripe,
> And then, from hour to hour, we rot and rot;
> And thereby hangs a tale.'   II. 7. 12–28

Why does Jaques, in his stylish way, say that his lungs 'began to crow like chanticleer' to hear the fool 'thus moral on the time', when the moral concludes in 'rot and rot'? Why do we, who are not 'melancholy', feel such large and free delight? Because the fool 'finds', with wonderfully bland wit, that nothing whatever happens under the aegis of Fortune. ('Fortune reigns in gifts of the world', said Rosalind in Act I, Scene 2 (line 44).) The almost tautological inevitability of nine, ten, eleven, says that all we do is ripe and ripe and rot and rot. And so there is no reason not to bask in the sun and 'lose and neglect the creeping hours of time' (II. 7. 112). As I observed in the introductory chapter, Touchstone's 'deep contemplative' moral makes the same statement as the spring song towards the close of the play: 'How that a life was but a flower'. When they draw the moral, the lover and his lass are only thinking of the 'spring time' as they take 'the present time' when 'love is crowned with the prime'. (The refrain mocks them a little for their obliviousness, by its tinkling 'the only pretty ring time'.) But Touchstone's festive gesture is *not* oblivious.

The extraordinary thing about the poised liberty of the second act is that the reduction of life to the natural and seasonal and physical works all the more convincingly as a festive release by including a recognition that the physical can be unpleasant. The good Duke, in his opening speech, can 'translate the stubbornness of fortune' into a benefit: he does it by the witty shift which makes the 'icy fang | And churlish chiding of the winter's wind' into 'counsellors | That feelingly persuade me what I am' (II. 1. 6–11). The two songs make the same gesture of welcoming physical pain in place of moral pain:

> Come hither, come hither, come hither!
>   Here shall he see
>   No enemy
> But winter and rough weather.   II. 5. 5–8

They are patterned on holiday drinking songs, as we have seen already in considering the Christmas refrain, 'Heigh-ho, sing heigh-ho, unto the green holly', and they convey the free solidarity of a group who, since they relax in physical pleasures together, need not fear the fact that 'Most friendship is feigning, most loving mere folly'.

Jaques's speech on the seven ages of man, which comes at the end of Act II, just before 'Blow, Blow, thou winter wind', is another version of the liberating talk about time; it expands Touchstone's 'And thereby hangs a tale'. The simplification, 'All the world's a stage', has such imaginative reach that we are as much astonished as amused, as with Touchstone's summary ripe and rot. But simplification it is, nevertheless; quotations (and recitations) often represent it as though it were dramatist Shakespeare's 'philosophy', his last word, or one of them, about what life really comes to. To take it this way is sentimental, puts a part in place of the whole. For it only is *one* aspect of the truth that the roles we play in life are settled by the cycle of growth and decline. To face this part of the truth, to insist on it, brings the kind of relief that goes with accepting folly – indeed this speech is praise of folly, superbly generalized, praise of the folly of living in time (or is it festive abuse? the poise is such that relish and mockery are indistinguishable). Sentimental readings ignore the wit that keeps reducing social roles to caricatures and suggesting that meanings really are only physical relations beyond the control of mind or spirit:

> Then a soldier . . .
> Seeking the bubble reputation
> Even in the cannon's mouth. And then the justice,
> In fair round belly with good capon lin'd . . .
>
> II. 7. 149–54

Looking back at time and society in this way, we have a detachment and sense of mastery similar to that established by Titania and Oberon's outside view of 'the human mortals' and their weather.

COUNTERSTATEMENTS

That Touchstone and Jaques should at moments turn and mock pastoral contentment is consistent with the way it is presented; their mockery makes explicit the partiality, the displacement of normal emphasis, which is implicit in the witty advocacy of it.

If it do come to pass
That any man turn ass,
Leaving his wealth and ease
A stubborn will to please....   II. 5. 52–5

The folly of going to Arden has something about it of Christian humility, brotherliness and unworldliness ('Consider the lilies of the field . . .'), but one can also turn it upside down by 'a Greek invocation to call fools into a circle' and find it stubbornness. Touchstone brings out another kind of latent irony about pastoral joys when he plays the role of a discontented exile from the court:

CORIN And how like you this shepherd's life, Master Touchstone?
TOUCHSTONE Truly, shepherd, in respect of itself, it is a good life; but in respect that it is a shepherd's life, it is naught. In respect that it is solitary, I like it very well; but in respect that it is private, it is a very vile life. Now in respect it is in the fields, it pleaseth me well; but in respect it is not in the court, it is tedious. As it is a spare life, look you, it fits my humour well; but as there is no more plenty in it, it goes much against my stomach.   III. 2. 12–22

Under the apparent nonsense of his self-contradictions, Touchstone mocks the contradictory nature of the desires ideally resolved by pastoral life, to be at once at court and in the fields, to enjoy both the fat advantages of rank and the spare advantages of the mean and sure estate. The humour goes to the heart of the pastoral convention and shows how very clearly Shakespeare understood it.

The fact that he created both Jaques and Touchstone out of whole cloth, adding them to the story as it appears in Lodge's *Rosalynde*, is an index to what he did in dramatizing the prose romance. Lodge, though he has a light touch, treats the idyllic material at face value. He never makes fun of its assumptions, but stays safely within the convention, because he has no securely grounded attitude towards it, not being sure of its relation to reality. Shakespeare scarcely changes the story at all, but where in Lodge it is presented in the flat, he brings alive the dimension of its relation to life as a whole. The control of this dimension makes his version solid as well as delicate.

Although both Jaques and Touchstone are connected with the

action well enough at the level of plot, their real position is generally mediate between the audience and something in the play, the same position Nashe assigns to the court fool, Will Summers, in *Summer's Last Will and Testament*. Once Jaques stands almost outside the play, when he responds to Orlando's romantic greeting: 'Good day and happiness, dear Rosalind!' with 'Nay then, God b'wi'you, and you talk in blank verse!' (IV. I. 31). Jaques's factitious melancholy, which critics have made too much of as a 'psychology', serves primarily to set him at odds both with society and with Arden and so motivate contemplative mockery. Touchstone is put outside by his special status as a fool. As a fool, incapable, at least for professional purposes, of doing anything right, he is beyond the pale of normal achievements. In anything he tries to do he is comically disabled, as, for example, in falling in love. All he achieves is a burlesque of love. So he has none of the illusions of those who try to be ideal, and is in a position to make a business of being dryly objective. 'Call me not fool till heaven hath sent me fortune'. Heaven sends him Audrey instead, 'an ill-favour'd thing, sir, but mine own' (V. 4. 60) – not a mistress to generate illusions. In *As You Like It* the court fool for the first time takes over the work of comic commentary and burlesque from the clown of the earlier plays; in Jaques's praise of Touchstone and the corrective virtues of fooling, Shakespeare can be heard crowing with delight at his discovery. The figure of the jester, with his recognized social role and rich traditional meaning, enabled the dramatist to embody in a character and his relations with other characters the comedy's purpose of maintaining objectivity.

The satirist presents life as it is and ridicules it because it is not ideal, as we would like it to be and as it should be. Shakespeare goes the other way about: he represents or evokes ideal life, and then makes fun of it because it does not square with life as it ordinarily is. If we look for social satire in *As You Like It*, all we find are a few set pieces about such stock figures as the traveller and the duellist. And these figures seem to be described rather to enjoy their extravagance than to rebuke their folly. Jaques, in response to a topical interest at the time when the play appeared, talks a good deal about satire, and proposes to 'cleanse the foul body of th'infected world' (II. 7. 60) with the fool's medicine of ridicule. But neither Jaques, the amateur fool, nor Touchstone, the professional, ever really gets around to doing the satirist's work of ridiculing life as it is, 'deeds, and language, such as men do use'. After all, they are in Arden, not in Jonson's London: the infected body of the world is far away, out of range. What they make fun of instead is what they can find in Arden – pastoral innocence and romantic love, life as it might be, lived 'in a holiday humour'. Similar comic presentation of what is not ideal in man is characteristic of medieval fool humour, where the humorist, by his gift of long ears to the long-robed dignitaries, makes the point that, despite their pageant perfection, they are human too, that 'stultorum numerus infinitus est'. Such humour is very different from modern satire, for its basic affirmation is not man's possible perfection but his certain imperfection. It was a function of the pervasively formal and ideal cast of medieval culture, where what should be was more present to the mind than what is: the humorists' natural recourse was to burlesque the pageant of perfection, presenting it as a procession of fools, in crowns, mitres, caps, and gowns. Shakespeare's point of view was not medieval. But his clown and fool comedy is a response, a counter-movement, to artistic idealization, as medieval burlesque was a response to the ingrained idealism of the culture.

'ALL NATURE IN LOVE MORTAL IN FOLLY'

I have quoted already in the Introduction a riddling comment of Touchstone which moves from acknowledging mortality to accepting the folly of love:

We that are true lovers run into strange capers; but as all is mortal in nature, so is all nature in love mortal in folly.   II. 4. 53–6

The lovers who in the second half of the play present 'nature in love' each exhibit a kind of folly. In each there is a different version of the incongruity between reality and the illusions (in poetry, the hyperboles) which love generates and by which it is expressed. The comic variations are centred around the seriously-felt love of

Rosalind and Orlando. The final effect is to enhance the reality of this love by making it independent of illusions, whose incongruity with life is recognized and laughed off. We can see this at closer range by examining each affair in turn.

All-suffering Silvius and his tyrannical little Phebe are a bit of Lodge's version taken over, outwardly intact, and set in a wholly new perspective. A 'courting eglogue' between them, in the mode of Lodge, is exhibited almost as a formal spectacle, with Corin for presenter and Rosalind and Celia for audience. It is announced as

> a pageant truly play'd
> Between the pale complexion of true love
> And the red glow of scorn and proud disdain.
>
> III. 4. 55–7

What we then watch is played 'truly' – according to the best current convention: Silvius, employing a familiar gambit, asks for pity; Phebe refuses to believe in love's invisible wound, with exactly the literal-mindedness about hyperbole which the sonneteers imputed to their mistresses. In Lodge's version, the unqualified Petrarchan sentiments of the pair are presented as valid and admirable. Shakespeare lets us feel the charm of the form; but then he has Rosalind break up their pretty pageant. She reminds them that they are nature's creatures, and that love's purposes are contradicted by too absolute a cultivation of romantic liking or loathing: 'I must tell you friendly in your ear, | Sell when you can! you are not for all markets' (III. 5. 59–60). Her exaggerated downrightness humorously underscores the exaggerations of conventional sentiment. And Shakespeare's treatment breaks down Phebe's stereotyped attitudes to a human reality: he lightly suggests an adolescent perversity underlying her resistance to love. The imagery she uses in disputing with Silvius is masterfully squeamish, at once preoccupied with touch and shrinking from it:

> 'Tis pretty, sure, and very probable
> That eyes, which are the frail'st and softest things,
> Who shut their coward gates on atomies,
> Should be call'd tyrants, butchers, murtherers!
> . . . lean but upon a rush,

The cicatrice and capable impressure
Thy palm some moment keeps; but now mine eyes,
Which I have darted at thee, hurt thee not.... III. 5. 11–25

Rosalind, before whom this resistance melts, appears in her boy's disguise 'like a ripe sister', and the qualities Phebe picks out to praise are feminine. She has, in effect, a girlish crush on the femininity which shows through Rosalind's disguise; the aberrant affection is happily got over when Rosalind reveals her identity and makes it manifest that Phebe has been loving a woman. 'Nature to her bias drew in that' is the comment in *Twelfth Night* when Olivia is fortunately extricated from a similar mistaken affection.

Touchstone's affair with Audrey complements the spectacle of exaggerated sentiment by showing love reduced to its lowest common denominator, without any sentiment at all. The fool is detached, objective and resigned when the true-blue lover should be

All made of passion, and all made of wishes,
All adoration, duty, and observance.   V. 2. 101–2

He explains to Jaques his reluctant reasons for getting married:

JAQUES Will you be married, motley?
TOUCHSTONE As the ox hath his bow, sir, the horse his curb, and the
    falcon her bells, so man hath his desires; and as pigeons bill, so
    wedlock would be nibbling.   III. 3. 79–83

This reverses the relation between desire and its object, as experienced by the other lovers. They are first overwhelmed by the beauty of their mistresses, then impelled by that beauty to desire them. With Touchstone, matters go the other way about: he discovers that man has his troublesome desires, as the horse his curb; then he decides to cope with the situation by marrying Audrey:

Come, sweet Audrey.
We must be married, or we must live in bawdry.

III. 3. 98–9

Like all the motives which Touchstone acknowledges, this priority of desire to attraction is degrading and humiliating. One of the hall-marks of chivalric and Petrarchan idealism is, of course, the high valuation of the lover's mistress, the assumption that his desire springs entirely from her beauty. This attitude of the poets has contributed to that progressively-increasing respect for women so fruitful in modern culture. But to assume that only one girl will do is, after all, an extreme, an ideal attitude: the other half of the truth, which lies in wait to mock sublimity, is instinct – the need of a woman, even if she be an Audrey, because 'as pigeons bill, so wedlock would be nibbling'. As Touchstone put it on another occasion:

> If the cat will after kind,
> So be sure will Rosalinde.   III. 109–10

The result of including in Touchstone a representative of what in love is unromantic is not, however, to undercut the play's romance: on the contrary, the fool's cynicism, or one-sided realism, forestalls the cynicism with which the audience might greet a play where his sort of realism had been ignored. We have a sympathy for his downright point of view, not only in connexion with love but also in his acknowledgement of the vain and self-gratifying desires excluded by pastoral humility; he embodies the part of ourselves which resists the play's reigning idealism. But he does not do so in a fashion to set himself up in opposition to the play. Romantic commentators construed him as 'Hamlet in motley', a devastating critic. They forgot, characteristically, that he is ridiculous: he makes his attitudes preposterous when he values rank and comfort above humility, or follows biology rather than beauty. In laughing at him, we reject the tendency in ourselves which he for the moment represents. The net effect of the fool's part is thus to consolidate the hold of the serious themes by exorcizing opposition. The final Shakespearian touch is to make the fool aware that in humiliating himself he is performing a public service. He goes through his part with an irony founded on the fact (and it is a fact) that he is only making manifest the folly which others, including the audience, hide from themselves.

Romantic participation in love and humorous detachment from its follies, the two polar attitudes which are balanced against each other in the action as a whole meet and are reconciled in Rosalind's personality. Because she remains always aware of love's illusions while she herself is swept along by its deepest currents, she possesses as an attribute of character the power of combining wholehearted feeling and undistorted judgement which gives the play its value. She plays the mocking reveller's role which Berowne played in *Love's Labour's Lost*, with the advantage of disguise. Shakespeare exploits her disguise to permit her to furnish the humorous commentary on her own ardent love affair, thus keeping comic and serious actions going at the same time. In her pretended role of saucy shepherd youth, she can mock at romance and burlesque its gestures while playing the game of putting Orlando through his paces as a suitor, to 'cure' him of love. But for the audience, her disguise is transparent, and through it they see the very ardour which she mocks. When, for example, she stages a gaily overdone take-off of the conventional impatience of the lover, her own real impatience comes through the burlesque; yet the fact that she makes fun of exaggerations of the feeling conveys an awareness that it has limits, that there is a difference between romantic hyperbole and human nature:

ORLANDO For these two hours, Rosalind, I will leave thee.
ROSALIND Alas, dear love, I cannot lack thee two hours!
ORLANDO I must attend the Duke at dinner. By two o'clock I will be with thee again.
ROSALIND Ay, go your ways, go your ways! I knew what you would prove. My friends told me as much, and I thought no less. That flattering tongue of yours won me. 'Tis but one cast away, and so, come death! Two o'clock is your hour?   IV. I. 181–90

One effect of this indirect, humorous method of conveying feeling is that Rosalind is not committed to the conventional language and attitudes of love, loaded as these inevitably are with sentimentality. Silvius and Phebe are her foils in this: they take their conventional language and their conventional feelings perfectly seriously, with nothing in reserve. As a result they seem naïve and rather trivial. They are no more than what they say, until Rosalind comes forward to realize their personalities for the audience by suggesting what they humanly are beneath what they romantically think themselves. By contrast, the heroine in expressing her own love conveys by her humorous tone a valuation of her sentiments, and so realizes her own personality for herself, without being indebted to another for the favour. She uses the convention where Phebe, being unaware of its exaggerations, abuses it, and Silvius, equally naïve about hyperbole, lets it abuse him. This control of tone is one of the great contributions of Shakespeare's comedy to his dramatic art as a whole. The discipline of comedy in controlling the humorous potentialities of a remark enables the dramatist to express the relation of a speaker to his lines, including the relation of naïveté. The focus of attention is not on the outward action of saying something but on the shifting, uncrystallized life which motivates what is said.

The particular feeling of headlong delight in Rosalind's encounters with Orlando goes with the prose of these scenes, a medium which can put imaginative effects of a very high order to the service of humour and wit. The comic prose of this period is first developed to its full range in Falstaff's part, and steals the show for Benedick and Beatrice in *Much Ado About Nothing*. It combines the extravagant linguistic reach of the early clowns' prose with the sophisticated wit which in the earlier plays was usually cast, less flexibly, in verse. High patterned, it is built up of balanced and serial clauses, with everything linked together by alliteration and kicked along by puns. Yet it avoids a stilted, Euphuistic effect because regular patterns are set going only to be broken to underscore humour by asymmetry. The speaker can rock back and forth on antitheses, or climb 'a pair of stairs' (v. 2. 42) to a climax, then slow down meaningly, or stop dead, and so punctuate a pithy reduction, bizarre exaggeration or broad allusion. T. S. Eliot has observed that we often forget that it was Shakespeare who wrote the greatest prose in the language. Some of it is in *As You Like It*. His control permits him to convey the constant shifting of attitude and point of view which expresses Rosalind's excitement and her poise. Such writing, like the brushwork and line of great painters, is in one sense everything. But the whole design supports each stroke, as each stroke supports the whole design.

The expression of Rosalind's attitude towards being in love, in the great scene of disguised wooing, fulfils the whole movement of the play. The climax comes when Rosalind is able, in the midst of her golden moment, to look beyond it and mock its illusions, including the master illusion that love is an ultimate and final experience, a matter of life and death. Ideally, love should be final, and Orlando is romantically convinced that his is so, that he would die if Rosalind refused him. But Rosalind humorously corrects him, from behind her page's disguise:

> ... Am I not your Rosalind?

ORLANDO I take some joy to say you are, because I would be talking of her.

ROSALIND Well, in her person, I say I will not have you.

ORLANDO Then, in mine own person, I die.

ROSALIND No, faith, die by attorney. The poor world is almost six thousand years old, and in all this time there was not any man died in his own person, videlicet, in a love cause. Troilus had his brains dash'd out with a Grecian club; yet he did what he could to die before, and he is one of the patterns of love. Leander, he would have liv'd many a fair year though Hero had turn'd nun, if it had not been for a hot midsummer night; for (good youth) he went but forth to wash him in the Hellespont, and being taken with the cramp, was drown'd; and the foolish chroniclers of that age found it was 'Hero of Sestos'. But these are all lies. Men have died from time to time, and worms have eaten them, but not for love.

ORLANDO I would not have my right Rosalind of this mind, for I protest her frown might kill me.

ROSALIND By this hand, it will not kill a fly!   IV. I. 90–108

A note almost of sadness comes through Rosalind's mockery towards the end. It is not sorrow that men die from time to time, but that they do not die for love, that love is not so final as romance would have it. For a moment we experience as pathos the tension between feeling and judgement which is behind all laughter. The same pathos of objectivity is expressed by Chaucer in the sad smile of Pandarus as he contemplates the illusions of Troilus's love. But in *As You Like It* the mood is dominant only in the moment when the last resistance of feeling to judgement is being surmounted: the illusions thrown up by feeling are mastered by laughter and so love is reconciled with judgement. This resolution is complete by the close of the wooing scene. As Rosalind rides the crest of a wave of happy fulfilment (for Orlando's behaviour to the pretended Rosalind has made it perfectly plain that he loves the real one) we find her describing with delight, almost in triumph, not the virtues of marriage, but its fallibility:

> Say 'a day' without the 'ever'. No, no, Orlando! Men are April when they woo, December when they wed. Maids are May when they are maids, but the sky changes when they are wives.   IV. I. 146–50

Ordinarily, these would be strange sentiments to proclaim with joy at such a time. But as Rosalind says them, they clinch the achievement of the humour's purpose. (The wry, retarding change from the expected cadence at 'but the sky changes' is one of those brush strokes that fulfil the large design.) Love has been made independent of illusions without becoming any the less intense; it is therefore inoculated against life's unromantic contradictions. To emphasize by humour the limitations of the experience has become a way of asserting its reality. The scenes which follow move rapidly and deftly to complete the consummation of the love affairs on the level of plot. The treatment becomes more and more frankly artificial, to end with a masque. But the lack of realism in presentation does not matter, because a much more important realism in our attitude towards the substance of romance has been achieved already by the action of the comedy.

In writing of Marvell and the metaphysical poets, T. S. Eliot spoke of an 'alliance of levity and seriousness (by which the seriousness is intensified)'. What he has said about the contribution of wit to this poetry is strikingly applicable to the function of Shakespeare's comedy in *As You Like It*: that wit conveys 'a recognition, implicit in the expression of every experience, of other kinds of experience which are possible'. The likeness does not consist simply in the fact that the wit of certain of Shakespeare's characters at times is like the wit of the metaphysicals. The crucial similarity is in the way the humour functions in the play as a whole to implement a wider awareness, maintaining proportion where less disciplined and coherent art falsifies by presenting a part as though it were the whole. The dramatic form is very different from the lyric: Shakespeare does not have or need the sustained, inclusive poise of metaphysical poetry when, at its rare best, it fulfils Cowley's ideal:

In a true piece of Wit all things must be
Yet all things there agree.

The dramatist tends to show us one thing at a time, and to realize that one thing, in its moment, to the full; his characters go to extremes, comical as well as serious; and no character, not even a Rosalind, is in a position to see all around the play and so be completely poised, for if this were so the play would cease to be dramatic. Shakespeare, moreover, has an Elizabethan delight in extremes for their own sake, beyond the requirements of his form and sometimes damaging to it, an expansiveness which was subordinated later by the seventeenth century's conscious need for coherence. But his extremes, where his art is at its best, are balanced in the whole work. He uses his broad-stroked, wide-swung comedy for the same end that the seventeenth-century poets achieved by their wire-drawn wit. In Silvius and Phebe he exhibits the ridiculous (and perverse) possibilities of that exaggerated romanticism which the metaphysicals so often mocked in their serious love poems. In Touchstone he includes a representative of just those aspects of love which are not romantic, hypostatizing as a character what in direct lyric expression would be an irony:

Love's not so pure and abstract as they use
To say who have no mistress but their muse.

Donne, *Love's Growth*

By Rosalind's mockery a sense of love's limitations is kept alive at the very moments when we most feel its power:

But at my back I always hear
Time's winged chariot hurrying near.

Marvell, *To his Coy Mistress*

The fundamental common characteristic is that the humour is not directed at 'some outside sentimentality or stupidity', but is an agency for achieving proportion of judgement and feeling about a seriously felt experience.

As You Like It seems to me the most perfect expression Shakespeare or anyone else achieved of a poise which was possible because a traditional way of living connected different kinds of experience to each other. The play articulates fully the feeling for the rhythms of life which we have seen supporting Nashe's strong but imperfect art in his seasonal pageant. Talboys Dimoke and his friends had a similar sense of times and places when they let holiday lead them to making merry with the Earl of Lincoln; by contrast, the Puritan and/or time-serving partisans of Lincoln could not or would not recognize that holiday gave a licence and also set a limit. An inclusive poise such as Shakespeare exhibits in Rosalind was not, doubtless, easy to achieve in any age; no culture was ever so 'organic' that it would do men's living for them. What Yeats called Unity of Being became more and more difficult as the Renaissance progressed; indeed, the increasing difficulty of poise must have been a cause of the period's increasing power to express conflict and order it in art. We have seen this from our special standpoint in the fact that the everyday–holiday antithesis was most fully expressed in art when the keeping of holidays was declining.

The humorous recognition, in *As You Like It* and other products of this tradition, of the limits of nature's moment, reflects not only the growing consciousness necessary to enjoy holiday attitudes with poise, but also the fact that in English Christian culture saturnalia was never fully enfranchised. Saturnalian customs existed along with the courtly tradition of romantic love and an ambient disillusion about nature stemming from Christianity. In dramatizing love's intensity as the release of a festive moment, Shakespeare keeps that part of the romantic tradition which makes love an experience of the whole personality, even though he ridicules the wishful absolutes of doctrinaire romantic love. He does not found his comedy on the sort of saturnalian simplification which equates love with sensual gratification. He includes spokesmen for this sort of release in reduction; but they are never given an unqualified predominance, though they contribute to the atmosphere of liberty within which the aristocratic lovers find love. It is the latter who hold the balance near the centre. And what gives the predominance to figures like Berowne, Benedick and Beatrice, or Rosalind, is that they enter nature's whirl consciously, with humour that recognizes it as only part of life and places their own extravagance by moving back and forth between holiday and everyday perspectives. Aristophanes provides a revealing contrast here. His comedies present experience entirely polarized by saturnalia; there is little *within* the play to qualify that perspective. Instead, an irony attaches to the whole performance which went with the accepted place of comedy in the Dionysia. Because no such clear-cut role for saturnalia or saturnalian comedy existed within Shakespeare's culture, the play itself had to place that pole of life in relation to life as a whole. Shakespeare had the art to make this necessity into an opportunity for a fuller expression, a more inclusive consciousness.

Chapter IX of *Shakespeare's Festive Comedy* by C. L. Barber, 1959

TWENTY-FIVE

As You Like It

As its title declares, this is a play to please all tastes. It is the last play in the world to be solemn over, and there is more than a touch of absurdity in delivering a lecture, particularly on a lovely summer morning, on this radiant blend of fantasy, romance, wit and humour. The play itself provides its own ironic comment on anyone who attempts to speak about it: 'You have said; but whether wisely or no, let the forest judge'.

For the simple, it provides the stock ingredients of romance: a handsome, well-mannered young hero, the youngest of three brothers, two disguised princesses to be wooed and wed, and a banished, virtuous Duke to be restored to his rightful throne. For the more sophisticated, it propounds, in the manner of the old courtly literary form of the *débat*, a question which is left to us to answer: is it better to live in the court or the country? 'How like you this shepherd's life, Master Touchstone?', asks Corin, and receives a fool's answer: 'Truly, shepherd, in respect of itself, it is a good life; but in respect that it is a shepherd's life, it is naught. In respect that it is solitary, I like it very well; but in respect that it is private, it is a very vile life'. Whose society would you prefer, Le Beau's or Audrey's? Would you rather be gossiped at in the court or gawped at in the country? The play has also the age-old appeal of the pastoral, and in different forms. The pastoral romance of princesses playing at being a shepherd boy and his sister is combined with the pastoral love-eclogue in the wooing of Phebe, with the burlesque of this in the wooing of Audrey, and with the tradition of the moral eclogue, in which the shepherd is the wise man, in Corin. For the learned and literary this is one of Shakespeare's most allusive plays, uniting old traditions and playing with them lightly. Then there are the songs – the forest is full of music – and there is spectacle: a wrestling match to delight lovers of sport, the procession with the deer, which goes back to old country rituals and folk plays, and finally the masque of Hymen, to end the whole with courtly grace and dignity. This is an image of civility and true society, for Hymen is a god of cities, as Milton knew:

> There let *Hymen* oft appear
> In Saffron robe, with Taper clear,
> And pomp, and feast, and revelry,
> With mask, and antique Pageantry. *L'Allegro*, 125–8

The only thing the play may be said to lack, when compared with Shakespeare's other comedies, is broad humour, the humour of gross clowns. William makes only a brief appearance. The absence of clowning may be due to a historic reason, the loss of Kempe, the company's funny man. But if this was the original reason for the absence of pure clowning, Shakespeare has turned necessity to glorious gain and made a play in which cruder humours would be out of place. *As You Like It* is the most refined and exquisite of the comedies, the one which is most consistently played over by a delighted intelligence. It is Shakespeare's most Mozartian comedy.

The basic story is a folk-tale. The ultimate sources for the plots of Shakespeare's greatest tragedy and his most unflawed comedy are stories of the same kind. The tale of the old king who had three daughters, of whom the elder two were wicked and the youngest was good, belongs to the same primitive world of the imagination as the tale of the knight who had three sons, the eldest of whom was wicked and robbed the youngest, who was gallant and good, of his inheritance. The youngest son triumphed, like Jack the Giant-Killer, over a strong man, a wrestler, joined a band of outlaws in the forest, became their king, and with the aid of an old servant of his father, the wily Adam Spencer, in the end had his revenge on his brother and got his rights. Lodge retained some traces of the boisterous elements of this old story; but Shakespeare omitted them. His Orlando is no bully, threatening and blustering and breaking down the doors to feast with his boon companions in his brother's house. He is brave enough and quick-tempered; but he is above all gentle. On this simple story Lodge grafted a pastoral romance in his *Rosalynde*. He made the leader of the outlaws a banished Duke, and gave both exiled Duke and tyrant usurper only daughters, as fast friends as their fathers are sworn enemies. The wrestling match takes place at the tyrant's court and is followed by the banishment of Rosalynde and the flight of the two girls to the forest, disguised as shepherd and shepherdess. There the shepherd boy is wooed by the gallant hero, and arouses a passion of love-sickness in a shepherdess who scorns her faithful lover. The repentance of the wicked brother and his flight to the forest provide the necessary partner for the tyrant's good daughter, and all ends happily with marriages and the restoration of the good Duke. Shakespeare added virtually nothing to the plot of Lodge's novel. There is no comedy in which, in one sense, he invents so little. He made the two Dukes into brothers. Just as in *King Lear* he put together two stories of good and unkind children, so here he gives us two examples of a brother's unkindness. This adds to the fairy-tale flavour of the plot, because it turns the usurping Duke into a wicked uncle. But if he invents no incidents, he leaves out a good deal. Besides omitting the blusterings of Rosader (Orlando), he leaves out a final battle and the death in battle of the usurping Duke, preferring to have him converted off stage by a chance meeting with a convenient and persuasive hermit. In the same way he handles very cursorily the repentance of the wicked brother and his good fortune in love. In Lodge's story, the villain is cast into prison by the tyrant who covets his estates. In prison he repents, and it is as a penitent that he arrives in the forest. Shakespeare also omits the incident of the attack on Ganymede and Aliena by robbers, in which Rosader is overpowered and wounded and Saladyne (Oliver) comes to the rescue and drives off the assailants. As has often been pointed out, this is both a proof of the genuineness of his repentance and a reason, which many critics of the play have felt the want of, for Celia's falling in love. Maidens naturally fall in love with brave young men who rescue them. But Shakespeare needs to find no 'reasons for loving' in this play in which a dead shepherd's saw is quoted as a word of truth: 'Whoever lov'd that lov'd not at first sight'. He has far too much other business in hand at the centre and heart of his play to find time for mere exciting incidents. He stripped Lodge's plot down to the bare bones, using it as a kind of frame, and created no sub-plot of his own. But he added four characters. Jaques, the philosopher, bears the same name as the middle son of Sir Rowland de Boys – the one whom Oliver kept at his books – who does not appear in the play until he turns up casually at the end as a messenger. It seems possible that the melancholy Jaques began as this middle son and that his melancholy was in origin a scholar's melancholy. If so, the character changed as it developed, and by the time that Shakespeare had fully conceived his cynical spectator he must have realized that he could not be kin to Oliver and Orlando. The born solitary must have no family: Jaques seems the quintessential only child. To balance Jaques, as another kind of commentator, we are given Touchstone, critic and parodist of love and lovers and of court and courtiers. And, to make up the full consort of pairs to be mated, Shakespeare invented two rustic lovers, William and Audrey, dumb yokel and sluttish goat-girl. These additional characters add nothing at all to the story. If you were to tell it you would leave them out. They show us that story was not Shakespeare's concern in this play; its soul is not to be looked for there. If you were to go to *As You Like It* for the story you would, in Jonson's phrase, 'hang yourself'.

In an essay called 'The Basis of Shakespearean Comedy' Professor Nevill Coghill attempted to 'establish certain things concerning the nature of comic form, as it was understood at Shakespeare's time'. He pointed out that there were two conceptions of comedy current in the sixteenth century, both going back to grammarians of the fourth century, but radically opposed to each other. By the one definition a comedy was a story beginning in sadness and ending in happiness. By the other it was, in Sidney's words, 'an imitation of the common errors of our life' represented 'in the most ridiculous and scornefull sort that may be; so that it is impossible that any beholder can be content to be such a one'. Shakespeare, he declared, accepted the first; Jonson, the second. But although *As You Like It*, like *A Midsummer Night's Dream*, certainly begins in sadness and ends with happiness, I do not feel, when we have said this, that we have gone very far towards defining the play's nature, and I do not think that the plot in either of these two lovely plays, or in the enchanting early comedy *Love's Labour's Lost*, which indeed has hardly any plot at all, can be regarded as the 'soul' or animating force of Shakespeare's most original and characteristic comedies. Professor Coghill's formula fits plays which we feel rather uneasy about, *The Merchant of Venice* and *Measure for Measure*. It is precisely the stress on the plot which makes us think of these as being more properly described as tragi-comedies than comedies. Neither of them is a play which we would choose as a norm of Shakespeare's genius in comedy. In *As You Like It* the plot is handled in the most perfunctory way. Shakespeare crams his first act with incident in order to get everyone to the forest as soon as he possibly can and, when he is ready, he ends it all as quickly as possible. A few lines dispose of Duke Frederick, and leave the road back to his throne empty for Duke Senior. As for the other victim of a wicked brother, it is far more important that Orlando should marry Rosalind than that he should be restored to his rights.

Mrs Suzanne Langer, in her brilliant and suggestive book *Feeling and Form*, has called comedy an image of life triumphing over chance. She declares that the essence of comedy is that it embodies in symbolic form our sense of happiness in feeling that we can meet and master the changes and chances of life as it confronts us. This seems to me to provide a good description of what we mean by 'pure comedy', as distinct from the corrective or satirical comedy of Jonson. The great symbol of pure comedy is marriage by which the world is renewed, and its endings are always instinct with a sense of fresh beginnings. Its rhythm is the rhythm of the life of mankind, which goes on and renews itself as the life of nature does. The rhythm of tragedy, on the other hand, is the rhythm of the individual life which comes to a close, and its great symbol is death. The one inescapable fact about every human being is that he must die. No skill in living, no sense of life, no inborn grace or acquired wisdom can avert this individual doom. A tragedy, which is played out under the shadow of an inevitable end, is an image of the life pattern of every one of us. A comedy, which contrives an end which is not implicit in its beginning, and which is, in itself, a fresh beginning, is an image of the flow of human life. The young wed, so that they may become in turn the older generation, whose children will wed, and so on, as long as the world lasts. Comedy pictures what

Rosalind calls 'the full stream of the world'. At the close of a
tragedy we look back over a course which has been run: 'the rest
is silence'. The end of a comedy declares that life goes on: 'Here
we are all over again.' Tragic plots must have a logic which leads to
an inescapable conclusion. Comic plots are made up of changes,
chances and surprises. Coincidences can destroy tragic feeling: they
heighten comic feeling. It is absurd to complain in poetic comedy of
improbable encounters and characters arriving pat on their cue, of
sudden changes of mind and mood by which an enemy becomes a
friend. Puck, who creates and presides over the central comedy of
A Midsummer Night's Dream, speaks for all comic writers and
lovers of true comedy when he says:

> And those things do best please me
> That befall preposterously.
> *A Midsummer Night's Dream*, III. 2. 120–21

This aspect of life, as continually changing and presenting fresh
opportunities for happiness and laughter, poetic comedy idealizes
and presents to us by means of fantasy. Fantasy is the natural
instrument of comedy, in which plot, which is the 'soul' of tragedy,
is of secondary importance, an excuse for something else. After
viewing a tragedy we have an 'acquist of true experience' from a
'great event'. There are no 'events' in comedy; there are only
'happenings'. Events are irreversible and comedy is not concerned
with the irreversible, which is why it must always shun the presentation of death. In adapting Lodge's story Shakespeare did not allow
Charles the wrestler to kill the Franklin's sons. Although they are
expected to die, we may hope they will recover from their broken
ribs. And he rejected also Lodge's ending in which the wicked
Duke was killed in battle, preferring his improbable conversion by
a hermit. But why should we complain of its improbability? It is
only in tragedy that second chances are not given. Comedy is full
of purposes mistook, not 'falling on the inventor's head' but
luckily misfiring altogether. In comedy, as often happens in life,
people are mercifully saved from being as wicked as they meant to
be.

Generalization about the essential distinctions between tragedy and comedy is called in question, when we turn to Shakespeare, by the inclusiveness of his vision of life. In the great majority of his plays the elements are mixed. But just as he wrote one masterpiece which is purely tragic, dominated by the conception of Fate, in *Macbeth*, so he wrote some plays which embody a purely comic vision. Within the general formula that 'a comedy is a play with a happy ending', which can, of course, include tragi-comedies, he wrote some plays in which the story is a mere frame and the essence of the play lies in the presentation of an image of human life, not as an arena for heroic endeavour but as a place of encounters.

Tragedy is presided over by time, which urges the hero onwards to fulfil his destiny. In Shakespeare's comedies time goes by fits and starts. It is not so much a movement onwards as a space in which to work things out: a midsummer night, a space too short for us to feel time's movement, or the unmeasured time of *As You Like It* or *Twelfth Night*. The comedies are dominated by a sense of place rather than of time. In Shakespeare's earliest comedy it is not a very romantic place: the city of Ephesus. Still, it is a place where two pairs of twins are accidentally reunited, and their old father, in danger of death at the beginning, is united to his long-lost wife at the close. The substance of the play is the comic plot of mistakings, played out in a single place on a single day. The tragi-comedy story of original loss and final restoration provides a frame. In what is probably his second comedy, *The Two Gentlemen of Verona*, Shakespeare tried quite different method. The play is a dramatiza-tion of a *novella*, and it contains no comic place of encounters where time seems to stand still. The story begins in Verona, passes to Milan, and ends in a forest between the two cities. None of these places exerts any hold upon our imaginations. The story simply moves forward through them. In *Love's Labour's Lost*, by contrast, Shakespeare went as far as possible in the other direction. The whole play is a kind of ballet of lovers and fantastics, danced out in the King of Navarre's park. Near-by is a village where Holofernes is the school-master, Nathaniel the curate, and Dull the constable. In this play we are given, as a foil to the lords and ladies, not comic servants parasitic on their masters, but a little comic world, society in miniature, going about its daily business while the lovers are engaged in the discovery of theirs. Shakespeare dispensed with the tragi-comic frame altogether here. There is no sorrow at the beginning, only youthful male fatuity; and the 'putting right' at the close lies in the chastening of the lords by the ladies. The picture of the course of life as it appears to the comic vision, with young men falling in love and young women testing their suitors, and other men 'labouring in their vocations' to keep the world turning and to impress their fellows, is the whole matter of the play. Much more magical than the sunlit park of the King of Navarre is the wood near Athens where Puck plays the part of chance. Shakespeare reverted here to the structural pattern of his earliest comedy, beginning with the cruel fury of Egeus against his daughter, the rivalry of Lysander and Demetrius and the unhappiness of the scorned Helena, and ending with Theseus's over-riding of the father's will and the proper pairing of the four lovers. But here he not only set his comic plot of mistakings within a frame of sorrow turning to joy, he also set his comic place of encounters apart from the real world, the palace where the play begins and ends. All the centre of the play takes place in the moonlit wood where lovers immortal and mortal quarrel, change partners, are blinded, and have their eyes purged.

Having created a masterpiece, Shakespeare, who never repeated a success, went back in his next play to tragi-comedy, allowing the threat of terrible disaster to grow through the play up to a great dramatic fourth act. *The Merchant of Venice* has what *The Two Gentlemen of Verona* lacks, an enchanted place. Belmont, where Bassanio goes to find his bride, and where Lorenzo flees with Jessica, and from which Portia descends like a goddess to solve the troubles of Venice, is a place apart, 'above the smoke and stir'. But it is not, like the wood near Athens, a place where the changes and chances of our mortal life are seen mirrored. It stands too sharply over against Venice, a place of refuge rather than a place of discovery. *Much Ado About Nothing* reverts to the single place of *The Comedy of Errors* and *Love's Labour's Lost*; and its tragi-comic plot, which also comes to a climax in a dramatic scene in the fourth act, is lightened not by a shift of scene but by its interweaving with a brilliant comic plot, and by all kinds of indications that all will soon be well again. The trouble comes in the middle of this play: at the beginning, as at the end, all is revelry and happiness. A sense of holiday, of time off from the world's business, reigns in Messina. The wars are over, peace has broken out, and Don Pedro and the gentlemen have returned to where the ladies are waiting for them to take up again the game of love and wit. In the atmosphere created by the first act Don John's malice is a cloud no bigger than a man's hand. And although it grows as the play proceeds, the crisis of the fourth act is like a heavy summer thunder-shower which darkens the sky for a time but will, we know, soon pass. The brilliant lively city of Messina is a true place of mistakings and discoveries, like the park of the King of Navarre; but, also like the park of the King of Navarre, it lacks enchantment. It is too near the ordinary world to seem more than a partial image of human life. In *As You Like It* Shakespeare returned to the pattern of *A Midsummer Night's Dream*, beginning his play in sorrow and ending it with joy, and making his place of comic encounters a place set apart from the ordinary world.

The Forest of Arden ranks with the wood near Athens and Prospero's island as a place set apart, even though, unlike them, it is not ruled by magic. It is set over against the envious court ruled by a tyrant, and a home which is no home because it harbours hatred, not love. Seen from the court it appears untouched by the discontents of life, a place where 'they fleet the time carelessly, as they did in the golden age', the gay greenwood of Robin Hood. But, of course, it is no such Elysium. It contains some unamiable characters. Corin's master is churlish and Sir Oliver Martext is hardly sweet-natured; William is a dolt and Audrey graceless. Its weather, too, is by no means always sunny. It has a bitter winter. To Orlando, famished with hunger and supporting the fainting Adam, it is 'an uncouth forest' and a desert where the air is bleak. He is astonished to find civility among men who

in this desert inaccessible,
Under the shade of melancholy boughs,
Lose and neglect the creeping hours of time.

II. 7. 110–12

253

In fact Arden does not seem very attractive at first sight to the weary escapers from the tyranny of the world. Rosalind's 'Well, this is the forest of Arden' does not suggest any very great enthusiasm; and to Touchstone's 'Ay, now I am in Arden; the more fool I: when I was at home, I was in a better place: but travellers must be content', she can only reply 'Ay, be so, good Touchstone'. It is as if they all have to wake up after a good night's rest to find what a pleasant place they have come to. Arden is not a place for the young only. Silvius, for ever young and for ever loving, is balanced by Corin, the old shepherd, who reminds us of that other 'penalty of Adam' beside 'the seasons' difference': that man must labour to get himself food and clothing. Still, the labour is pleasant and a source of pride: 'I am a true labourer: I earn that I eat, get that I wear, owe no man hate, envy no man's happiness, glad of other men's good, content with my harm; and the greatest of my pride is to see my ewes graze and my lambs suck'. Arden is not a place where the laws of nature are abrogated and roses are without their thorns. If, in the world, Duke Frederick has usurped on Duke Senior, Duke Senior is aware that he has in his turn usurped upon the deer, the native burghers of the forest. If man does not slay and kill man, he kills the poor beasts. Life preys on life. Jaques, who can suck melancholy out of anything, points to the callousness that runs through nature itself as a mirror of the callousness of men. The herd abandons the wounded deer, as prosperous citizens pass with disdain the poor bankrupt, the failure. The race is to the swift. But this is Jaques's view. Orlando, demanding help for Adam, finds another image from nature:

> Then but forbear your food a little while,
> Whiles, like a doe, I go to find my fawn
> And give it food. There is an old poor man,
> Who after me hath many a weary step
> Limp'd in pure love: till he be first suffic'd,
> Oppress'd with two weak evils, age and hunger,
> I will not touch a bit.   II. 7. 127–33

The fact that they are both derived ultimately from folk-tale is not the only thing that relates *As You Like It* to *King Lear*. Adam's sombre line, 'And unregarded age in corners thrown', which

Quiller-Couch said might have come out of one of the greater sonnets, sums up the fate of Lear:

> Dear daughter, I confess that I am old;
> Age is unnecessary: on my knees I beg
> That you'll vouchsafe me raiment, bed, and food.
>
> *King Lear*, II. 4. 152–3

At times Arden seems a place where the same bitter lessons can be learnt as Lear has to learn in his place of exile, the blasted heath. Corin's natural philosophy, which includes the knowledge that 'the property of rain is to wet', is something which Lear has painfully to acquire:

> When the rain came to wet me once and the wind to make me chatter, when the thunder would not peace at my bidding, there I found 'em, there I smelt 'em out. Go to, they are not men o'their words: they told me I was everything: 'tis a lie, I am not ague-proof.
>
> *King Lear*, IV. 6. 101–5

He is echoing Duke Senior, who smiles at the 'icy fang and churlish chiding of the winter's wind', saying:

> This is no flattery: these are counsellors
> That feelingly persuade me what I am.
>
> *As You Like It*, II. 1. 10–11

Amiens's lovely melancholy song:

> Blow, blow, thou winter wind,
> Thou art not so unkind
> As man's ingratitude. . . .
>
> Freeze, freeze, thou bitter sky,
> That dost not bite so nigh
> As benefits forgot . . .   II. 7. 174–6, 184–6

is terribly echoed in Lear's outburst:

> Blow, winds, and crack your cheeks! rage! blow! . . .
> Rumble thy bellyful! Spit, fire! spout, rain!
> Nor rain, wind, thunder, fire, are my daughters:
> I tax not you, you elements, with unkindness;
> I never gave you kingdom, call'd you children. . . .
>
> *King Lear*, III. 2. 1, 14–17

And Jaques's reflection that 'All the world's a stage' becomes in Lear's mouth a cry of anguish:

> When we are born, we cry that we are come
> To this great stage of fools.   *King Lear*, IV. 6. 183–4

It is in Arden that Jaques presents his joyless picture of human life, passing from futility to futility and culminating in the nothingness of senility – 'sans everything'; and in Arden also a bitter judgement on human relations is lightly passed in the twice repeated 'Most Friendship is feigning, most loving mere folly'. But then one must add that hard on the heels of Jaques's melancholy conclusion Orlando enters with Adam in his arms, who, although he may be 'sans teeth' and at the end of his usefulness as a servant, has, beside his store of virtue and his peace of conscience, the love of his master. And the play is full of signal instances of persons who do not forget benefits: Adam, Celia, Touchstone – not to mention the lords who chose to leave the court and follow their banished master to the forest. In a recent number of the *Shakespeare Survey* Professor Harold Jenkins has pointed out how points of view put forward by one character find contradiction or correction by another, so that the whole play is a balance of sweet against sour, of the cynical against the idealistic, and life is shown as a mingling of hard fortune and good hap. The lords who have 'turned ass', 'leaving their wealth and ease a stubborn will to please', are happy in their gross folly, as Orlando is in a love-sickness which he does not wish to be cured of. What Jaques has left out of his picture of man's strange eventful pilgrimage is love and companionship, sweet society, the banquet under the boughs to which Duke Senior welcomes Orlando and Adam. Although life in Arden is not wholly idyllic, and this place set apart from the world is yet touched by the world's sorrows and can be mocked at by the worldly wise, the image of life which the forest presents is irradiated by the conviction that the gay and the gentle can endure the rubs of fortune and that this earth is a place where men can find happiness in themselves and in others.

The Forest of Arden is, as has often been pointed out, a place which all the exiles from the court, except one, are only too ready to leave at the close. As, when the short midsummer night is over, the lovers emerge from the wood, in their right minds and correctly paired, and return to the palace of Theseus; and, when Prospero's magic has worked the cure, the enchanted island is left to Caliban and Ariel, and its human visitors return to Naples and Milan; so the time of holiday comes to an end in Arden. The stately masque of Hymen marks the end of this interlude in the greenwood, and announces the return to a court purged of envy and baseness. Like other comic places, Arden is a place of discovery where the truth becomes clear and where each man finds himself and his true way. This discovery of truth in comedy is made through errors and mistakings. The trial and error by which we come to knowledge of ourselves and of our world is symbolized by the disguisings which are a recurrent element in all comedy, but are particularly common in Shakespeare's. Things have, as it were, to become worse before they become better, more confused and farther from the proper pattern. By misunderstandings men come to understand, and by lies and feignings they discover truth. If Rosalind, the princess, had attempted to 'cure' her lover Orlando, she might have succeeded. As Ganymede, playing Rosalind, she can try him to the limit in perfect safety, and discover that she cannot mock or flout him out of his 'mad humour of love to a living humour of madness', and drive him 'to forswear the full stream of the world, and to live in a nook merely monastic'. By playing with him in the disguise of a boy, she discovers when she can play no more. By love of a shadow, the mere image of a charming youth, Phebe discovers that it is better to love than to be loved and scorn one's lover. This discovery of truth by feigning, and of what is wisdom and what folly by debate, is the centre of *As You Like It*. It is a play of meetings and encounters, of conversations and sets of wit: Orlando versus Jaques, Touchstone versus Corin, Rosalind versus Jaques, Rosalind versus Phebe, and above all Rosalind versus Orlando. The truth discovered is, at one level, a very 'earthy truth': Benedick's discovery that, 'the world must be peopled'. The honest toil of Corin, the wise man of the forest, is mocked at by Touchstone as 'simple sin'. He brings 'the ewes and the rams together' and gets his living 'by the copulation of cattle'. The goddess Fortune seems similarly occupied in this play: 'As the ox hath his bow, the horse his curb, and the falcon her bells, so man hath his desires; and as pigeons bill, so wedlock would be nibbling'. Fortune acts the role of a kindly bawd. Touchstone's marriage to Audrey is a mere coupling. Rosalind's advice to Phebe is brutally frank: 'Sell when you can, you are not for all markets'. The words she uses to describe Oliver and Celia 'in the very wrath of love' are hardly delicate, and after her first meeting with Orlando she confesses to her cousin that her sighs are for her 'child's father'. Against the natural background of the life of the forest there can be no pretence that the love of men and women can 'forget the He and She'. But Rosalind's behaviour is at variance with her bold words. Orlando has to prove that he truly is, as he seems at first sight, the right husband for her, and show himself gentle, courteous, generous and brave, and a match for her in wit, though a poor poet. In this, the great coupling of the play, there is a marriage of true minds. The other couplings run the gamut downwards from it, until we reach Touchstone's image of 'a she-lamb of a twelvemonth' and 'a crooked-pated, old, cuckoldy ram', right at the bottom of the scale. As for the debate as to where happiness is to be found, the conclusion come to is again, like all wisdom, not very startling or original: that 'minds innocent and quiet' can find happiness in court or country:

> Happy is your Grace,
> That can translate the stubbornness of fortune
> Into so quiet and so sweet a style.   II. I. 18–20

And, on the contrary, those who wish to can 'suck melancholy' out of anything, 'as a weasel sucks eggs'.

In the pairing one figure is left out. 'I am for other than for dancing measures,' says Jaques. Leaving the hateful sight of revelling and pastime, he betakes himself to the Duke's abandoned cave, on his way to the house of penitents where Duke Frederick has gone. The two commentators of the play are nicely contrasted. Touchstone is the parodist, Jaques the cynic. The parodist must love what he parodies. We know this from literary parody. All the best parodies are written by those who understand, because they love, the thing they mock. Only poets who love and revere the epic can write mock-heroic and the finest parody of classical tragedy comes from Housman, a great scholar. In everything that Touchstone says and does gusto, high spirits and a zest for life ring out. Essentially comic, he can adapt himself to any situation in which he may find himself. Never at a loss, he is life's master. The essence of clowning is adaptability and improvisation. The clown is never baffled and is marked by his ability to place himself at once *en rapport* with his audience, to be all things to all men, to perform the part which is required at the moment. Touchstone sustains many different roles. After hearing Silvius's lament and Rosalind's echo of it, he becomes the maudlin lover of Jane Smile; with the simple shepherd Corin he becomes the cynical and worldly-wise man of the court; with Jaques he is a melancholy moralist, musing on the power of time and the decay of all things; with the pages he acts the lordly amateur of the arts, patronizing his musicians. It is right that he should parody the rest of the cast, and join the procession into Noah's ark with his Audrey. Jaques is his opposite. He is the cynic, the person who prefers the pleasures of superiority, cold-eyed and cold-hearted. The tyrannical Duke Frederick and the cruel Oliver can be converted; but not Jaques. He likes himself as he is. He does not wish to plunge into the stream, but prefers to stand on the bank and 'fish for fancies as they pass'. Sir Thomas Elyot said that dancing was an image of matrimony: 'In every daunse, of a most auncient custome, there daunseth together a man and a woman, holding eche other by the hande or the arme, which betokeneth concorde.' There are some who will not dance, however much they are piped to, any more than they will weep when there is mourning. 'In this theatre of man's life,' wrote Bacon, 'it is reserved only for God and angels to be lookers on.' Jaques arrogates to himself the divine role. He has opted out from the human condition.

It is characteristic of Shakespeare's comedies to include an element that is irreconcilable, which strikes a lightly discordant note, casts a slight shadow, and by its presence questions the completeness of the comic vision of life. In *Love's Labour's Lost* he dared to allow the news of a death to cloud the scene of revels at the close, and, through Rosaline's rebuke to Berowne, called up the image of a whole world of pain and weary suffering where 'Mirth cannot move a soul in agony'. The two comedies whose main action is motivated by hatred end with malice thwarted but not removed. In *The Merchant of Venice* and *Much Ado About Nothing*, Shakespeare asks us to accept the fact that the human race includes not only a good many fools and rogues but also some persons who are positively wicked, a fact which comedy usually ignores. They are prevented from doing the harm they wish to do. They are not cured of wishing to do harm. Shylock's baffled exit and Don John's flight to Messina leave the stage clear for lovers and well-wishers. The villains have to be left out of the party at the close. At the end of *Twelfth Night* the person who is left out is present. The impotent misery and fury of the humiliated Malvolio's last words, 'I'll be reveng'd on the whole pack of you', call in question the whole comic scheme by which, through misunderstandings and mistakes, people come to terms with themselves and their fellows. There are some who cannot be 'taught a lesson'. In Malvolio pride is not purged; it is fatally wounded and embittered. It is characteristic of the delicacy of temper of *As You Like It* that its solitary figure, its outsider, Jaques, does nothing whatever to harm anyone, and is perfectly satisfied with himself and happy in his melancholy. Even more, his melancholy is a source of pleasure and amusement to others. The Duke treats him as virtually a court entertainer, and he is a natural butt for Orlando and Rosalind. Anyone in the play can put him down and feel the better for doing so. All the same his presence casts a faint shadow. His criticism of the world has its sting drawn very early by the Duke's rebuke to him as a former libertine, discharging his filth upon the world, and he is to some extent discredited before he opens his mouth by the unpleasant implication of his name. But he cannot be wholly dismissed. A certain sour distaste for life is voided through him, something most of us feel at some time or other. If he were not there to give expression to it, we might be tempted to find the picture of life in the forest too sweet. His only action is to interfere in the marriage of Touchstone and Audrey; and this he merely postpones. His effect, whenever he appears, is to deflate: the effect does not last and cheerfulness soon breaks in again. Yet as there is a scale of love, so there is a scale of sadness in the play. It runs down from the Duke's compassionate words:

> Thou seest we are not all alone unhappy:
> This wide and universal theatre
> Presents more woeful pageants than the scene
> Wherein we play in . . .   II. 7. 136–9

through Rosalind's complaint 'O, how full of briers is this working-day world', to Jaques's studied refusal to find anything worthy of admiration or love.

One further element in the play I would not wish to stress, because though it is pervasive it is unobtrusive: the constant, natural and easy reference to the Christian ideal of loving-kindness, gentleness, pity and humility and to the sanctions which that ideal finds in the commands and promises of religion. In this fantasy world, in which the world of our experience is imaged, this element in experience finds a place with others, and the world is shown not only as a place where we may find happiness, but as a place where both happiness and sorrow may be hallowed. The number of religious references in *As You Like It* has often been commented on, and it is striking when we consider the play's main theme. Many are of little significance and it would be humourless to enlarge upon the significance of the 'old religious man' who converted Duke Frederick, or of Ganymede's 'old religious uncle'. But some are explicit and have a serious, unforced beauty: Orlando's appeal to outlawed men,

> If ever you have look'd on better days,
> If ever been where bells have knoll'd to church . . . .
> II. 7. 113–14

Adam's prayer,

> He that doth the ravens feed,
> Yea, providently caters for the sparrow,
> Be comfort to my age! . . .   II. 3. 43–5

and Corin's recognition, from St Paul, that we have to find the way to heaven by doing deeds of hospitality. These are all in character. But the God of Marriage, Hymen, speaks more solemnly than we expect and his opening words with their New Testament echo are more than conventional:

261

> Then is there mirth in heaven,
> When earthly things made even
> Atone together.   v. 4. 102–4

The appearance of the god to present daughter to father and to bless the brides and grooms turns the close into a solemnity, an image of the concord which reigns in Heaven and which Heaven blesses on earth. But this, like much else in the play, may be taken as you like it. There is no need to see any more in the god's appearance with the brides than a piece of pageantry which concludes the action with a graceful spectacle and sends the audience home contented with a very pretty play.

'*As You Like It*' by Helen Gardner, in *More Talking of Shakespeare*, edited by John Garrett, 1959

Suggestions for Further Reading

S. L. BETHELL: *Shakespeare and the Popular Dramatic Tradition*. This book, which discusses Shakespeare's use of the principle of multi-consciousness ('the audience's ability to respond spontaneously and unconsciously on more than one plane of attention at the same time'), has two interesting passages on *As You Like It*. In Chapter II (pages 35–8) it discusses the use of verse-technique to achieve distancing; and in Chapter V, Section 3 (pages 92–6), Touchstone.

M. C. BRADBROOK: *Shakespeare and Elizabethan Poetry*, XII. 2. Emphasizes the elements of pastoral, satire, courtesy literature, and the plays of Robin Hood. 'An appreciation of *As You Like It* might be called the last reward of Elizabethan studies'.

WILLIAM EMPSON: *Some Versions of Pastoral*, pages 136–8 (of the Chatto & Windus edition). Explores the pun in 'the truest poetry is the most faining' (feign=pretend and fain=desire).

G. K. HUNTER: *Shakespeare: The Late Comedies* (British Council pamphlet, 'Writers and Their Work').

HAROLD JENKINS: '*As You Like It*' (*Shakespeare Survey 8*). Points out how little action there is, and that the play is concerned with contrasting views of love and pastoral life, through 'piquant but seemingly casual juxtapositions'.

SIR ARTHUR QUILLER-COUCH: *Shakespeare's Workmanship*, Chapter VI. Here the always chatty Q is even more rambling than usual on this 'most adorable play of [his] boyhood'.

JAMES SMITH: '*As You Like It*' (*Scrutiny*, June 1940). A lopsided but fascinating study of the unromantic streak in the play, which Smith sees as anticipating the problem plays and the tragedies.

JANET SPENS: *An Essay on Shakespeare's Relation to Tradition*, I. 3. A simpler version of Barber's approach.

D. L. STEVENSON: *The Love Game Comedy*, Chapter XI. The interplay of romance and cynicism.

MARK VAN DOREN: *Shakespeare*. One of the most graceful essays in a graceful book. Is Shakespeare praising or satirizing the pastoral sentiment, the ideal life of Arden? 'The idea of the simple life has been smiled off the earth and yet here it still is smiling back at us from every bough of Arden'.

TWELFTH NIGHT

TWENTY-SIX

Amari Aliquid

TOWARDS the end of the period something happens. I do not pretend to know what it was; but I am content to fancy that it may have been the discovery that Shakespeare's friendship with his friend was not of a nature to endure. Or it may simply have been the consciousness of advancing age, and something missed in life. That *Julius Caesar* is grave is no more than we should expect from the nature of the theme, which compelled Shakespeare to

> bear it as our Roman actors do,
> With untired spirits and formal constancy.
>
> *Julius Caesar*, II. I. 226–7

But, to my sense, there is the counterpart of the same settled gravity in *Twelfth Night* – a silvery undertone of sadness, which makes it perhaps the loveliest of all Shakespeare's high comedies. Maybe, in this, my ear is super-subtle, and self-deceived; but the impression is unfailing. In *Twelfth Night* even 'fooling grows old': Feste is an older, sadder, wiser man than Touchstone; and he has outworn his favour. Though Malvolio alone bears him any ill-will, nobody cares for him. Since Malvolio grudges Feste his place, we accommodate ourselves to Malvolio's baffling: but, as such things are in life, it is a little excessive and leaves a wry taste in the mouth. Malvolio should have been more malevolent to deserve all his punishment. The songs are tinged with sadness.

> What is love? 'tis not hereafter;
> Present mirth hath present laughter;
>   What's to come is still unsure:
> In delay there lies no plenty;
> Then come kiss me, sweet and twenty,
>   Youth's a stuff will not endure.
>
> *Twelfth Night*, II. 3. 48 ff.

The old and antique song which brings the balm to the Duke's heart is by him deliberately contrasted with

> light airs and recollected terms
> Of these most brisk and giddy-paced times.   II. 4. 5–6

While Feste is being sought to sing it, the tune is played. Hearing it, Viola declares:

> It gives a very echo to the seat
> Where love is throned.   II. 4. 20–21

This emphasis on the song is sustained. We are made to feel that the quintessence of love is caught in it.

> Mark it, Cesario, it is old and plain;
> The spinsters and the knitters in the sun
> And the free maids that weave their thread with bones
> Do use to chant it: it is silly sooth,
> And dallies with the innocence of love,
> Like the old age.   II. 4. 43–9

Viola is but a girl; Sebastian but a boy: but ages are deceptive in *Twelfth Night*. This girl is older, if not in years, then in experience, than Beatrice or Rosalind or Portia. She has neither their high-spirited gaiety, nor the new-born innocence of Perdita or Miranda. A mood which seems to hover in the background of *The Merchant of Venice*, and is there thrust under by the bravery of youth and the ecstasy of love, now suffuses the whole of a comedy. The Duke in *Twelfth Night* is the counterpart of Antonio in the *Merchant*; but whereas in the tragi-comedy he fades into the background, in the comedy he subtly dominates the whole.

His is not the perfunctory and conventional lover's melancholy, of which Shakespeare had so often and so happily made fun. It is the Melancholy of Keats's ode, the sovereign goddess who

> Dwells with beauty, beauty that must die
> And joy whose hand is ever at his lips
> Bidding adieu.

It looks back on gaiety and confidence as belonging to the past. And *Twelfth Night* is, to my sense, the most perfect example of the way in which Shakespeare could make his mood over-ride his fable. Than the actual story of *Twelfth Night*, what could be happier? There are no disturbing villainies as there are in *Much Ado* and even in *As You Like It*. The plot is as innocent as that of the *Dream*. Yet the thing is sad: sad, partly with the weight of its own beauty, but sad also with a wistfulness to which Shakespeare could not help giving direct expression. The song the Duke loves – 'Come away, come away, death' – contains it in part; there is something of it in the ambiguous twist of Malvolio's taking down: but most of all it is contained in Feste, and in his singing. There is a strange aloofness in Feste: he is attached, as Dr Bradley has remarked, to nobody. He is woven in and out the play like a careless wraith. Nothing matters to him. If he is turned away, 'let summer bear it out'. His fooling has a different flavour from the fooling of any other fool. It is almost metaphysical in its aloofness. And – once more as Dr Bradley has remarked – it seems natural that he should be, as he is, more unblushing in his demands for money than any other of Shakespeare's fools. He has no illusion about his own precariousness. It sorts with this that at one moment he appears to be abrupt and careless of his reward – after singing 'Come away, death'. 'There's for thy pains,' says the Duke. 'No pains, sir, I take pleasure in singing,' says Feste. At all events, it is clear that he does take pleasure in singing – more truly than any other character in a play which begins and ends in music, and is saturated with it. For the others, music is the food of love, or languor, or mirth: for Feste it is an art – aloof, abstract, akin to himself. At the last, he is left on the stage alone – not unlike Firs at the end of *The Cherry Orchard* – as it were in anticipation of his end:

> And unregarded age in corners thrown.
>
> *As You Like It*, ii. 3. 42

There he stands and sings. Perhaps it was an old song, not of Shakespeare's making. But whether he made it, or merely put it there, just as magically as the final song in *Love's Labour* gathers up the hidden potentiality of that gay and clumsy and youthful play, so is the bitter-sweet of *Twelfth Night* caught into the first verse of Feste's song:

When that I was and a little tiny boy,
    With hey, ho, the wind and the rain,
A foolish thing was but a toy,
    For the rain it raineth every day.   v. 2. 375–8

It is almost nonsense, yet it seems like a perfect lament over the passing of innocence, the passing of all things. *Surgit amari aliquid medio de fonte leporum.*

*

The relation between *Twelfth Night* and *Hamlet* is real, but intangible: for in *Twelfth Night* there is no Shakespeare man. He is diffused in a mood, not concentrated in a character. And that is the appropriate ending to this period. When the new period begins, we have the Shakespeare man again – and this time in the form in which he has fascinated the imagination of the entire world. A Bastard, a Mercutio, a Benedick, a Hotspur, a Falstaff – these are too native and insular. Translated, they become but shadows of themselves. But Prince Hamlet is substantial for other minds than ours. More securely even than Faust he is a figure of the European consciousness.

from *Shakespeare*, pages 225–9, by J. Middleton Murry, 1936

TWENTY-SEVEN

The Psychology of *Twelfth Night*

... OF fantasy, in its less tragic forms, there is no better example than *Twelfth Night*. Orsino is sighing, not for love, but about it. Type of the perpetual adolescent, the man who will not grow up, he knows intuitively that, if ever he falls in love, he will have to do something about it. A shadow love is easier to deal with, and has the extra advantage of making him an object of pity. He therefore indulges in a protective fantasy, carefully choosing a lady who is inaccessible, and so will leave him undisturbed.

Olivia, the lady of his choice, is also avoiding love, but for a different reason. She knows well that, when it comes, it will shake her spirit to its depths. Her protective fantasy is a vow of mourning for her brother. She will 'cloistered walk', etc., for seven years, and keep herself from the thunderbolt.

The third victim of fantasy, Malvolio, is compensating himself by a dream of power and conquest for the position which, he knows well, is too low for his gifts and his serious intelligence. He is compensating himself too for the snubs from Sir Toby, to which that position exposes him. Did contemplation not make a rare turkey-cock of him, he could readily manage them all: but it is the quality of this kind of fantasy that others may perceive it, and the sober well-read man is brought to such a pass, he jets so under his advanced plumes, that Maria, quick-witted and practical, unerringly reads his mind. It is his bitterest humiliation that his fantasy has betrayed him to the 'idle, shallow creatures' whom he so despised.

The fantasies of Orsino and Olivia are dispelled less rudely. Olivia has fallen headlong in love with the disguised Viola, and is speedily brought to such a pitch that even her pride is gone. 'I do I know not what,' she complains. 'Ourselves we do not owe.' How rightly had she feared what love would do to her! The advent of the straight-forward, uncomplicated Sebastian introduces a strand of reality parallel to that which trips Malvolio. Finding himself wooed by a beautiful and wealthy woman, Sebastian scratches his head, embraces his good luck, and marries her. We do not see how Olivia accepts the transference: his character does not resemble Viola's: but probably his physical resemblance to 'Cesario' will do the trick, especially when Viola is once more dressed as a girl.

For Orsino, all falls out pat. He is offered love on a plate, without having to do anything about it. Still, Viola is not one to cosset fantasy. She will probably make a man of the sentimentalist, as surely as the wittiest piece of Eve's flesh in Illyria will make Sir Toby leave drinking. . . .

from 'Shakespeare and the Psychologists' by L. A. G. Strong, in *Talking of Shakespeare*, edited by John Garrett, 1954

TWENTY-EIGHT

The Atmosphere of *Twelfth Night*

... I HAVE always found the atmosphere of *Twelfth Night* a bit whiffy. I get the impression that Shakespeare wrote the play at a time when he was in no mood for comedy, but in a mood of puritanical aversion to all those pleasing illusions which men cherish and by which they lead their lives. The comic convention in which the play is set prevents him from giving direct expression to this mood, but the mood keeps disturbing, even spoiling, the comic feeling. One has a sense, and nowhere more strongly than in the songs, of there being inverted commas around the 'fun'.

There is a kind of comedy, *A Midsummer Night's Dream* and *The Importance of Being Earnest* are good examples, which take place in Eden, the place of pure play where suffering is unknown. In Eden, Love means the 'Fancy engendered in the eye'. The heart has no place there, for it is a world ruled by wish not by will. In *A Midsummer Night's Dream* it does not really matter who marries whom in the end, provided that the adventures of the lovers form a beautiful pattern; and Titania's fancy for Bottom is not a serious illusion in contrast to reality, but an episode in a dream.

To introduce will and real feeling into Eden turns it into an ugly place, for its native inhabitants cannot tell the difference between play and earnest, and in the presence of the earnest they appear frivolous in the bad sense. The trouble, to my mind, about *Twelfth Night* is that Viola and Antonio are strangers to the world which all the other characters inhabit. Viola's love for the Duke, and Antonio's love for Sebastian are much too strong and real.

Against their reality, the Duke, who up till the moment of recognition has thought himself in love with Olivia but then drops her like a hot potato and falls in love with Viola on the spot, and Sebastian, who accepts Olivia's proposal of marriage within two minutes of meeting her for the first time, appear contemptible, and it is impossible to believe that either will make a good husband. They give the impression of simply having abandoned one dream for another.

Taken by themselves, the songs in this play are among the most beautiful Shakespeare wrote and, read in an anthology, we hear them as the voice of Eden, as 'pure' poetry. But in the contexts in which Shakespeare places them, they sound shocking.

ACT II, SCENE 3

Song: O mistress mine, where are you roaming?
Audience: Sir Toby Belch, Sir Andrew Aguecheek.

Taken playfully, such lines as

> What's to come is still unsure:
> In delay there lies no plenty;
> Then come kiss me, sweet-and-twenty.
> Youth's a stuff will not endure . . .

are charming enough, but suppose one asks: 'For what kind of person would these lines be an expression of their true feelings?' True love certainly does not plead its cause by telling the beloved that love is transitory; and no young man, trying to seduce a girl, would mention her age. He takes her youth and his own for granted. Taken seriously, these lines are the voice of elderly lust, afraid of its own death. Shakespeare forces this awareness of our consciousness by making the audience to the song a couple of seedy old drunks.

ACT II, SCENE 4

Song: Come away, come away, death.
Audience: The Duke, Viola, courtiers.

Again, outside the pastures of Eden, no true lover talks of being slain by a fair, cruel maid, or weeps over his own grave. In real life, such reflections are the day-dreams of self-love, which is never faithful to others.

And again, Shakespeare has so placed the song as to make it seem an expression of the Duke's real character. Beside him sits the disguised Viola, for whom the Duke is not a playful fancy but a serious passion. It would be painful enough for her if the man she loved really loved another, but it is much worse to be made to see that he only loves himself, and it is this insight which at this point Viola has to endure. In the dialogue about the difference between man's love and woman's which follows on the song, Viola is, I think, being anything but playful when she says:

> We men may say more, swear more; but indeed,
> Our vows are more than will; for still we prove
> Much in our vows, but little in our love. . . .

from 'Music in Shakespeare' by W. H. Auden, first published in *Encounter*, 1954, and reprinted in *The Dyer's Hand*

TWENTY-NINE

Directions for *Twelfth Night*, or What You Will

AFTER the first dozen *Twelfth Night*s there are still surprises, new guises for the old masterpiece. Directors colour it golden, russet, silver or white; blue for dreams, and sometimes pink; or they allow red and even purple to dominate. They can make it sound noisy as a carnival, or eager, simple or melodious, or quarrelsome like children; it can also be strained and nervous. In 1958, Peter Hall at Stratford on Avon hung the stage with gauzes and contrived what *The Times* called a 'Watteauesque light'. And critics report that a year previously, at Stratford, Ontario, Tyrone Guthrie contrasted Feste and Malvolio in 'psychological terms', allowing the final song of the 'wind and the rain' to be 'as plaintive and wonderful as a Jewish lament'. Two years before that, at the English Stratford, Sir John Gielgud brought 'a faint chill to the air' of his production: the comics were on their best behaviour in deference to a pervasive 'charm'; the *Observer* said that the polite word for this would be 'formal', and the exact word 'mechanical'; it seemed as if, during rehearsals of the last scene, Sir John had stopped the actors and commanded, 'Be beautiful; be beautiful'.

This play might have been designed for an age when each director must make his name and register his mark. Yet there is one difficulty: in most productions there is some element that escapes direction. In Sir John's elegant *Twelfth Night*, Malvolio yielded Sir Laurence Olivier a role in which to exploit his impudent and plebeian comedy, and his last line – 'I'll be revenged on the whole pack of you' – an opportunity for the cry of a man unmade. The grey and urban setting of the Old Vic's production in 1950 was enlivened by an untrained ballet of sailors and riffraff, but Peggy Ashcroft's clear, white voice was an unechoed reminder of other directions the comedy can be given. More commonly, without such trained stars to cross the director's intentions, robust comics usurp more attention than their part in the last act is allowed to satisfy, or an intelligent Sebastian will deny his own words, a too gentle Orsino devalue Viola's ardour. There is need for vigilance: Margaret Webster, who sees *Twelfth Night* as 'filled with impermanence, fragile, imponderable', has found that:

The director will have to balance and combine his ingredients in carefully graded proportions, compensating for weaknesses, keeping a moderating hand on excessive strength. This play, above all, he must treat with a light touch and a flexible mind, keeping the final goal clearly in sight.

What happened, one wonders, before there were directors to give directions?

For if we refer back, from the theatre to the text of the play, we shall observe a similar lack of simplicity and uniformity. Malvolio can be a 'turkey cock', a common 'geck and gull' who is told to 'shake his ears'; or a fantastic who asks what 'an alphabetical position portends' and speaks repeatedly 'out of his welkin'. Yet Olivier's petty, ambitious vulgarian is also true to the text when he addresses his mistress with 'Sweet lady, ho, ho!' and with tags from popular ballads. Even Michael Hordern's tortured Malvolio at the Old Vic in 1954, 'dried up, emaciated, elongated . . . [as] an El Greco' – his hands, reaching out of the pit in the scene where Feste visits him as Sir Topas, the curate, suggested to one critic 'the damned in the *Inferno*' – has allowance in Feste's disguise, in his own first words of 'the pangs of death' and 'infirmity', in his account of how 'imagination' jades him, and in his physical and psychological isolation at the end. And yet again, Olivia's high regard for Malvolio – she 'would not lose him for half her dowry' – justifies Eric Porter's performance at Stratford on Avon in 1960, as a solid, efficient steward waking with practical good sense to worlds unrealized.

Actors seeking to express their originality will find that 'new' interpretations rise unbidden from a straightforward study of the text. Sir Toby is usually a domesticated Falstaff, but at the Old Vic in 1958, with tumultuous 'gulps and shouts', he was seen as a plain 'boor'; and for this there is plenty of support in his name,

Belch, and in his talk of 'boarding and assailing', making water and cutting 'mutton'. And the same year, at Stratford on Avon, Patrick Wymark made him young and spry, with a sense of style; for this, 'she's a beagle, true-bred' was most appropriate language, and his easy confidence in 'consanguinity' and expertise in sword-play were natural accomplishments. One might conceive, too, of a melancholy Sir Toby, tried in true service and knowing from experience that 'care's an enemy to life': his tricks upon Sir Andrew would then be a compensation for his own retirement, his wooing – off-stage and presumably brief – of Maria, a just and difficult tribute; for him, lethargy comes with drunkenness and he 'hates a drunken rogue'; he needs company, even that of a fool, an ass, and a servant. Olivia is another role which can be seen to be of different ages – either mature years or extreme youth; and she can be melancholy or gay. Maxine Audley at Stratford on Avon in 1955 presented a gracious lady, truly grieving for the death of her brother and strong enough to recognize an absurd passion for a boy; this Olivia had the 'smooth, discreet and stable bearing', the majesty, to which Sebastian and Orsino testify. And three years later, at the same theatre, Geraldine McEwen presented her as kittenish and cute, saved from triviality by fine timing of movement and verse-speaking, the dignity of 'style'. And yet another Olivia may be suggested by the text: a very young girl, at first afraid of meeting the world and therefore living in a fantasy of seven-year mourning; then a girl solemnly repeating old saws with a new understanding of their truth:

Even so quickly may one catch the plague. . . . I do I know not what, and fear to find Mine eye too great a flatterer for my mind. . . . What is decreed must be . . . how apt the poor are to be proud . . . youth is bought more oft than begg'd or borrowed . . .

and forgetting her 'discreet' bearing in breathless eagerness:

How does he love me? . . . Why, what would you? . . . not too fast: soft, soft! . . . Well, let it be. . . . That's a degree to love. . . . Yet come again. . . . I have sent after him: he says he'll come. . . . What do you say? . . . Most wonderful!

Feste, the fool, can be melancholy, or bitter, or professional, or amorous and silent, or self-contained and philosophical, or bawdy and impotent; Sir Andrew Aguecheek can be patient, sunny, feckless, gormless, animated or neurotic. (In 1958 Richard Johnson gave an assured performance of this knight as a 'paranoid manic-depressive, strongly reminiscent at times of Lucky in *Waiting for Godot*'.) Orsino can be mature or very young; and poetic or weak, or strong but deceived, or regal and distant. The text can suggest a Viola who is pert, sentimental, lyrical, practical, courageous or helpless. Shakespeare's words can support all these interpretations, and others; there are few plays which give comparable scope for enterprise and originality; the characters, the situations and the speeches are protean.

This is fully evident in the way in which a director can alter the trend of his production, even in the very last moments, to achieve what Miss Webster has called his 'balance', to arrive at his chosen 'final goal'. If sentiment needs reinforcing, Viola (as Cesario) can be given a down-stage position and a preparatory pause as the arrangements for her duel with Sir Andrew grow to a comic climax, and thus her 'I do assure you, 'tis against my will' can be, not the usual laugh-line, but a reminder of full-hearted involvement in other strifes of will; this momentary seriousness, the more impressive for its incongruous setting, has been managed with great grace by Dorothy Tutin at Stratford, in Peter Hall's production of 1958 and 1960. Still later in the play, there is another opportunity for the strong re-emphasis of Viola's depth of feeling: Peggy Ashcroft mastered this in 1950, and J. C. Trewin has well described its effect in performance:

At the end, as Sebastian faces his sister, he cries: 'What countryman? What name? What parentage?' There is a long pause now before Viola, in almost a whisper (but one of infinite rapture and astonishment), answers: 'Of Messaline'. Practically for the first time in my experience a Viola has forced me to believe in her past. . . .

More simply and without affecting any established characterization, the balance of a production can be altered by the Priest's lines in the last scene, with their special idiom and assured syntax and timing:

TWELFTH NIGHT

> A contract of eternal bond of love,
> Confirm'd by mutual joinder of your hands,
> Attested by the holy close of lips,
> Strengthen'd by interchangement of your rings;
> And all the ceremony of this compact
> Seal'd in my function, by my testimony:
> Since when, my watch hath told me, toward my grave
> I have travell'd but two hours.   v. i. 150–57

If these lines are spoken in a weighty and measured way, they can restore a sense of awe, of timeless references, to a dénouement which has become too headlong and hilarious for the director's taste. Or, at the last moment, Orsino can give 'guts' to an over-pretty production: the sight of Antonio permits an evocation of the 'smoke of war' and 'scathful grapple', and can legitimately bring a harsh quality to his voice which has hitherto been tuned to softer themes. When he invites Olivia to live 'the marble-breasted tyrant still' and turns to Cesario with:

> But this your minion, whom I know you love,
> And whom, by heaven I swear, I tender dearly,
> Him will I tear out of that cruel eye,
> Where he sits crowned in his master's spite.
> Come, boy, with me; my thoughts are ripe in mischief:
> I'll sacrifice the lamb that I do love,
> To spite a raven's heart within a dove ...   v. i. 119–25

the director can call for physical as well as verbal violence towards Viola. The lines imply that Orsino cares more for his seeming boy than for the lady of his dreams and fancy, and thus they may be acted fully and strongly; the release of passion shows the true object of that passion, and its power. (This reading of the under-text is authorized by Shakespeare, as by Freud or Stanislavski, for Orsino has just acknowledged that a 'savage' jealousy 'kills what it loves', not what it thinks it loves.) If the production is, at this stage of the play, too solemn rather than too sentimental or hilarious, there are opportunities in plenty for lightening the whole last act: Olivia's 'Where goes Cesario?', after Orsino's outburst, can easily be spoken to invite laughter; and so can her 'Most wonderful' as Viola and Sebastian confront each other. Nearly all Sebastian's lines can be tipped the same way, as 'I do perceive it hath offended you ... Fear'st thou that, Antonio ... [and, about the mole on the brow of Viola's father] And so had mine'. Antonio's 'An apple, cleft in two, is not more twin' can be directed so that it implies laughter rather than rapt amazement, and Orsino's final 'Cesario, come' can be a jest at the whole contrivance of the last act, or even at Viola's expense, rather than an unconscious recognition of his own long involvement in affection for his bride-to-be.

The opportunities for swinging a production round into line with a chosen mood – to make it 'what they will', to reverse roles as in a 'Twelfth Night' revel – have encouraged directors to tackle *Twelfth Night* and to experiment widely in the search for original interpretations. But a second practical consequence of the freedom of interpretation is of greater importance: this play challenges a longer and deeper study than is normally given to a text in the theatre. For we may be assured that the diverse ways of playing the characters and controlling the mood are not finally irreconcilable. The experience of seeing many independent productions and reading about many more does not create a multitude of separate memories; each new revelation reflects on earlier ones and, in the mind, a single view of the play is continually growing in complexity and range, and in understanding. Thus we are bound, against natural misgivings, to believe that a single production might, one day, represent to the full our single, developing awareness. Our knowledge of *Twelfth Night* and of human behaviour assures us that an Olivia may be both mature and immature, according to which side of her personality is in view; a Sir Toby energetic and melancholic, vulgar and well-schooled; and a Viola lyrical, practical and helpless. The world of the play may be gay, quiet, strained, solemn, dignified, elegant, easy, complicated, precarious, hearty, homely; the conclusion close to laughter, song, awe *and* simplicity. And this is an understanding which begs not to be hid, but to be realized on the stage.

Of course, in the theatre it is temping to simplify too early, in order to make a 'strong' impression. But with such a play as *Twelfth Night* we are drawn by another possibility, a more demanding course: five years' study, or a repeated return to its problems in a succession of productions under different conditions and for different audiences, might make possible, in view of the compound interest which experience may bring, a production which would be original, not by one-sidedness, but by answering more fully than before to Shakespeare's text and combining the strength of many interpretations. The time necessary to make this attempt would be an expensive investment. And it would be a risky one – for the speculator may not be capable of living up to the developing demands of his enterprise. Yet the business is a practical possibility, and must be considered; and Shakespeare's stage-cunning, human understanding and poetic imagination, which are all implicit in the text, would be fine assets. An exclusive pursuit of strength and originality leads to immature and insecure achievements, in theatres as in other fields of activity; a play like *Twelfth Night* offers, therefore, an opportunity and a challenge which would be salutary merely to envisage, instructive and exciting to attempt. . . .

> from 'Directions for *Twelfth Night*, or What You Will' by John Russell Brown, *Tulane Drama Review*, Summer 1961, and to appear in Mr Brown's forthcoming book, *Shakespeare's Plays in Performance*

Suggestions for Further Reading

C. L. BARBER: 'Testing Courtesy and Humanity in *Twelfth Night*' (*Shakespeare's Festive Comedy*, Chapter X). Malvolio represents the anti-holiday spirit; and 'in the long run, in the 1640s, he *was* revenged on the whole pack of them'.

M. C. BRADBROOK: *Shakespeare and Elizabethan Poetry*, XII. 3. Points out those 'Elizabethan' elements that Miss Bradbrook feels the modern reader misunderstands – for instance the practice on Malvolio. 'The jest of Sir Toby was not half as unpleasant for the victim as the majority of jests which were practised in London taverns'.

A. C. BRADLEY: 'Feste the Jester' (*A Miscellany*). Treats Feste as an individual character in the way we have learned to reject; but is worth reading for its charm, and the love of Shakespeare that Bradley so splendidly reveals.

WILLIAM EMPSON: *Seven Types of Ambiguity*, pages 98–9 (Chatto & Windus). On II. 4. 80. Explores an ambiguity of syntax that has little general significance for the play, but does give a fascinating glimpse of Shakespeare's grasshopper mind at work.

BERTRAND EVANS: '*Twelfth Night*' (*Shakespeare's Comedies*). This essay describes the highly complicated deceptions that form the action of the play, and points out that the audience enjoys some advantage in awareness over every single character. And Mr Evans briefly forsakes his analysis of 'practising' to say 'Perhaps Shakespeare never achieved a richer love … than with these voices reverberating over the chasm between the speakers' awarenesses'.

G. K. HUNTER: *Shakespeare: The Late Comedies* (British Council pamphlet, 'Writers and Their Work').

HAROLD JENKINS: *Twelfth Night* (Rice Institute pamphlet, 1959).

JANET SPENS: *An Essay on Shakespeare's Relation to Tradition*, I. 3. On the folk elements behind the play: Toby as Lord of Misrule.

MARK VAN DOREN: *Shakespeare*. Compares the play with *The Merchant of Venice*. Malvolio is the outsider threatening this world, as Shylock threatens that. We can see the case of both, but cannot love them.

THE MERRY WIVES OF WINDSOR

THIRTY

Comic Deceit

...*As You Like It*, *Much Ado About Nothing*, *The Merry Wives of Windsor*, and *Twelfth Night* all make use of disguise, and of the ambiguities which are produced by the assumption of costume on the stage of the world. Play images spring from the fact of Rosalind's doublet and hose, from the confused identities of the masque in *Much Ado About Nothing*, from Falstaff's ludicrous garb as Herne the Hunter, and from Feste in his curate's robes. Viola's dialogue with Olivia:

OLIVIA Are you a comedian?
VIOLA No, my profound heart; and yet, by the very fangs of malice I
swear, I am not that I play ....

Twelfth Night, I. 5. 171–4

belongs to a class of play metaphor common throughout Elizabethan and Jacobean drama, a class to which Jessica 'in the lovely garnish of a boy' (*The Merchant of Venice*, II. 6. 45), Julia as Sebastian, and the disguises of *The Taming of the Shrew* had contributed in Shakespeare's earlier comedies.

The theatrical nature of comic deceit is by no means dependent, however, upon disguise. In the false security of his arbour, Benedick supposes himself to be in the superior position of audience overlooking the converse of Claudio, Leonato, and Don Pedro. In reality, he is the unwitting central character of their play. A little later, Beatrice is forced into a similar position through the machinations of Hero, Ursula, and Margaret. As they discuss with each other the way in which Beatrice is to be snared, once she has been lured into the orchard, Hero and her waiting gentlewoman adopt, quite naturally, the language of the theatre. Hero impresses upon Ursula that

Our talk must only be of Benedick.
When I do name him, let it be thy part
To praise him more than ever man did merit ....
Much Ado About Nothing, III. 1. 17–19

The only disguise involved here is verbal, but the nature of the situation lends a specifically theatrical colouring to the familiar 'play the part' idiom, a colouring made more vivid by Ursula's reply: 'Fear you not my part of the dialogue' (III. 1. 31). A little later, Claudio says quite directly that 'Hero and Margaret have by this played their parts with Beatrice; and then the two bears will not bite one another when they meet' (III. 2. 67–70). Don Pedro, the deception of Benedick triumphantly accomplished, looks forward to the even more delicious comedy to come, the meeting of the two who are its unwitting players. 'That's the scene that I would see, which will be merely a dumb show' (II. 3. 198–9).

In *The Merry Wives of Windsor*, Falstaff becomes the victim of three separate illusions. Mistress Ford declares that she will 'consent to act any villainy against him' (II. 1. 86) that is not incompatible with her honesty and, as so often in Shakespeare, this word 'act' quickly declares itself to be the possessor of a latent theatrical meaning. As they play the first of their deceptions, Mistress Ford and Mistress Page invoke the idea of the play.

MRS FORD Mistress Page, remember you your cue.
MRS PAGE I warrant thee; if I do not act it, hiss me.
The Merry Wives of Windsor, III. 3. 30–33

It is the little scene which, for Falstaff himself, ends so unpleasantly in the cold waters of the Thames. Ironically enough, when he comes to describe the episode to the supposed Brook, Falstaff employs a rather airy play image of his own. He and Mistress Ford had, in his account, embraced, kissed, and, 'as it were, spoke the prologue of our comedy' (III. 5. 66) when the raging husband made his appearance. Thus, like Mistress Ford herself, Falstaff regards the encounter in terms of a play. Unfortunately for him, however, he is not in control of the production.

In the second of the three little dramas in which his lust and greed involve him, Falstaff is forced to adopt a disguise. He escapes the vigilance of Ford on this occasion only by 'counterfeiting the action of an old woman' (IV. 5. 111). The third play, the comedy of Herne the hunter which unfolds in the wintry darkness of Windsor Park, also necessitates a costume, not only for Falstaff but for all the other actors as well. It is a carefully prepared and executed fantasy in which 'Fat Falstaff | Hath a great scene' (IV. 6. 16–17). He himself, of course, is as unaware of his role, or even of the fact that a play is afoot, as Beatrice or Christopher Sly. A good deal of careful planning goes into the performance; we are permitted details of the costumes, the rehearsals and the properties, together with a brief but enchanting picture of Parson Evans, disguised as a satyr, marshalling an obedient troupe of small children and muttering, 'Trib, trib, fairies; come; and remember your parts' (V. 4. 1–2).

The little comedy itself is considerably more complicated, as well as more formal, than the two which have preceded it. Like the play scenes in *Love's Labour's Lost* and *A Midsummer Night's Dream*, the Herne the Hunter interlude represents another of Shakespeare's experiments with the relationship of illusion and reality. This time, however, it is the illusion which triumphs, holding reality momentarily helpless in its toils. Like Bottom and his friends, or the Worthies of *Love's Labour's Lost*, the actors who participate in the interlude are amateurs, and they are also, many of them, comic figures. Yet their performance is strikingly successful. Falstaff is deceived as planned, and so, in a curious sense, is the theatre audience. Despite all the preparations that have gone before, and the knowledge of how this scene must end, it is hard to watch it and not forget – unless the actors deliberately distort their lines – that the Fairy Queen is only Mistress Anne Page, and Hobgoblin Pistol. The Queen's invocation to

> You moonshine revellers, and shades of night,
> You orphan heirs of fixed destiny ...   V. 5. 36–7

the sense of the park and its huge leafless oak, the dark meadows and the castle near by are so magical and strange that Falstaff's confusion of the play with reality becomes all too understandable. Up to the point when Falstaff's recognition of 'that Welsh fairy' (V. 5. 79) brings the scene swiftly back to earth, the spectators are actually encouraged, 'in despite of the teeth of all rhyme and reason' (v. 5. 121–2), to share his delusion.

Released from their proper confines, allowed to masquerade as reality, the elements of the play are not to be treated altogether lightly. They are likely to behave in incalculable ways and, like some ungrateful jinn delivered from his prison, deceive their masters. Falstaff is gulled as expected, but so, to their own amazement, are four of the contrivers of the Herne the Hunter comedy, Page and his wife, Caius, and Slender. It is Master Fenton after all who steals away the Fairy Queen. Like *Hamlet*, to which it is close in date, *The Merry Wives of Windsor* is filled with affirmations of the power of illusion. It reminds the theatre audience that life is constantly discovering within itself bewildering conjunctions with the drama, that at times the world cannot easily be distinguished from the stage.

from Chapter VI of *Shakespeare and the Idea of the Play* by Anne Righter, 1962

ON COMEDY: AND ON
SHAKESPEARIAN COMEDY

In this last section, we move from the particular to the general. Once we leave behind the immediate impact of a work of art, and begin to reflect and generalize, it is hard for it to remain isolated: criticism will almost invariably give it a context. Of course there are many contexts – that of the author's other works, or his emotional life, or the literary tradition, or the time and place – or, as here, a context of theory. By understanding and classifying the effect of comedies, we arrive at a theory of Comedy: this in turn acts on our opinions about the plays themselves.

Admitting that no classification is anything but a poor and clumsy distortion, we can classify discussions of comedy into two: those that relate it back to comic tradition, and those that relate it outwards to the human condition. In discussing – or writing – a comedy, we can look at the comedies that have been written in the past, and theories that have been held about the nature of comedy. Or we can look at life itself – the amorphous, intellectually insidious, inescapable swamp from which all art climbs – and relate the play to our experience.

There is no shortage of modern scholars who have done the first: M. C. Bradbrook, Lily B. Campbell, Hardin Craig, Nevill Coghill, E. E. Stoll, and many others, varying in judgement and subtlety, but alike in their respect for what medieval and Renaissance critics said about literature. Such studies are obviously very valuable for understanding the Elizabethans, though we can always suspect that the poets themselves paid less attention to the theories, and more to the plays, than our modern professors. I have not included any of these studies, for it seemed better to go to the horse's mouth, and let the Renaissance speak for itself. Ben Jonson is, with Shakespeare, our greatest comic dramatist: and he was learned enough for any professor – so that by comparing his theory with his practice, we can learn a great deal about how the Elizabethans thought. But the comparison is frustrating: the theory states many of the traditional commonplaces, yet it suggests nothing of Jonson's comic masterpieces: any run-of-the-mill critic could surely have written like this of plot and diction (they did: and Jonson is partly translating them); but who else could have lingered at street-corners and in taverns, and then written *Bartholomew Fair*?

Of course *Timber* relates art to the human condition as well, though stiffly. Meredith, Lesser and Frye do this with the skill of the best modern minds; and in ways that contrast vividly with one another. It is difficult for a critic to write about life direct: such direct response is the stuff of literature itself, and criticism which uses it will tend to hover dangerously on the edge of creation, will often, in fact, be the work of creative writers – like Meredith. His essay has many of the faults, and as many of the virtues, of the creator taking time off to criticize: relaxed, stylish, unlearned, widely-read, personal, irresponsible, intelligent, charming.

The other two critics set their views of particular plays against the insight provided by another discipline – psychology (more or less Freudian) in the case of Mr Lesser, and anthropology (rather freely used) in that of Mr Frye. They also illustrate another contrast. There have tended to be two main attitudes towards comedy among those who theorize about it. There is that which takes tragedy to be the highest form of aesthetic experience, and regards comedy as less profound, less honest, something for those moments when we cannot bear tragedy. This is Mr Lesser's view: he sees comedy as psychologically necessary, but in a sense superficial. The extract is taken from the last chapter of his book, in which he discusses the nature of the aesthetic experience, and it follows after his even more brilliant discussion of tragedy as an open conflict between id and superego in the unevasive presence of the ego.

On the other hand, there are those critics who see comedy as going beyond tragedy to achieve some finer, deeper vision. Often such criticism has a religious basis: 'from the point of view of Christianity,' Mr Frye points out, 'tragedy is an episode in that larger scheme of redemption and ressurection to which Dante gave the name of *commedia*'. Mr Frye, with his scintillatingly complex scheme, is not a clear example of this school, but I know of no one else who writes with the constant brilliance that irradiates his personal blend of anthropology and logic: looking for analogies in ritual and social custom, and classifying plays into types with breath-taking dogmatism. When you most violently disagree with Mr Frye, you still find he has opened doors where you had thought the wall was solid.

THIRTY-ONE

An Elizabethan View of Comedy

WHAT IS A POET?

A POET, poeta, is that which by the Greeks is called a maker, or a feigner: his art, an art of imitation or feigning; expressing the life of man in fit measure, numbers and harmony; according to Aristotle from the word *poesis*, which signifies to make or feign. Hence he is called a poet, not he which writeth in measure only, but that feigneth and formeth a fable, and writes things like the truth. For the fable and fiction is, as it were, the form and soul of any poetical work or poem.

BUT HOW DIFFERS A POEM FROM WHAT WE CALL POESY?

A poem, as I have told you, is the work of the poet; the end and fruit of his labours and study. Poesy, poesis, is his skill or craft of making; the very fiction itself, the reason or form of the work. And these three voices differ, as the thing done, the doing, and the doer; the thing feigned, the feigning, and the feigner; so the poem, the poesy, and the poet. Now the poesy is the habit or the art; nay, rather the queen of the arts, artium regina, which had her original from heaven, received thence from the Hebrews, and had in prime estimation with the Greeks, transmitted to the Latins and all nations that professed civility. The study of it, if we will trust Aristotle, offers to mankind a certain rule and pattern of living well and happily, disposing us to all civil offices of society. If we will believe Tully, it nourisheth and instructeth our youth, delights our age, adorns our prosperity, comforts our adversity, entertains us at home, keeps us company abroad, travels with us, watches, divides the times of our earnest and sports, shares in our country recesses and recreations; insomuch as the wisest and best learned have thought her the absolute mistress of manners and nearest of kin to virtue. And whereas they entitle philosophy to be a rigid and austere poesy, they have, on the contrary, styled poesy a dulcet and gentle philosophy, which leads on and guides us by the hand to action with a ravishing delight and incredible sweetness. . . .

The poet is the nearest borderer upon the orator, and expresseth all his virtues, though he be tied more to numbers, is his equal in ornament, and above him in his strengths. And of the kind the comic comes nearest; because in moving the minds of men, and stirring of affections, in which oratory shows, and especially approves her eminence, he chiefly excels. What figure of a body was Lysippus ever able to form with his graver, or Apelles to paint with his pencil, as the comedy to life expresseth so many and various affections of the mind? There shall the spectator see some insulting with joy, others fretting with melancholy, raging with anger, mad with love, boiling with avarice, undone with riot, tortured with expectation, consumed with fear: no perturbation in common life but the orator finds an example of it in the scene. . . .

I am not of that opinion to conclude a poet's liberty within the narrow limits of laws which either the grammarians or philosophers prescribe. For before they found out those laws there were many excellent poets that fulfilled them, amongst whom none more perfect than Sophocles, who lived a little before Aristotle. Which of the Greeklings durst ever give precepts to Demosthenes? or to Pericles, whom the age surnamed Heavenly, because he seemed to thunder and lighten with his language? or to Alcibiades, who had rather Nature for his guide than Art for his master? But whatsoever nature at any time dictated to the most happy, or long exercise to the most laborious, that the wisdom and learning of Aristotle hath brought into an art, because he understood the causes of things; and what other men did by chance or custom he doth by reason; and not only found out the way not to err, but the short way we should take not to err. . . .

THE PARTS OF A COMEDY AND TRAGEDY

The parts of a comedy are the same with a tragedy, and the end is partly the same, for they both delight and teach; the comics are called *didaskaloi* (teachers) of the Greeks no less than the tragics. Nor is the moving of laughter always the end of comedy; that is rather a fowling for the people's delight, or their fooling. For, as Aristotle says rightly, the moving of laughter is a fault in comedy, a kind of turpitude that depraves some part of man's nature without a disease. As a wry face without pain moves laughter, or a deformed vizard, or a rude clown dressed in a lady's habit, and using her actions; we dislike and scorn such representations which made the ancient philosopher ever think laughter unfitting in a wise man. And this induced Plato to esteem of Homer as a sacrilegious person, because he presented the gods sometimes laughing. As also it is divinely said of Aristotle, that to seem ridiculous is a part of dishonesty, and foolish. So that what either in the words or sense of an author, or in the language or actions of men, is awry or depraved doth strangely stir mean affections, and provoke for the most part to laughter. And therefore it was clear that all insolent and obscene speeches, jests upon the best men, injuries to particular persons, perverse and sinister sayings, and the rather unexpected, in the old comedy did move laughter, especially where it did imitate any dishonesty; and scurrility came forth in the place of wit, which, who understands the nature and genius of laughter cannot but perfectly know.

Of which Aristophanes affords an ample harvest, having not only outgone Plautus or any other in that kind, but expressed all the moods and figures of what is ridiculous oddly. In short, as vinegar is not accounted good until the wine be corrupted, so jests that are true and natural seldom raise laughter with the beast, the multitude. They love nothing that is right and proper. The farther it runs from reason or possibility with them the better it is. What could have made them laugh, like to see Socrates presented, that example of all good life, honesty, and virtue, to have him hoisted up with a pulley, and there play the philosopher in a basket; measure how many foot a flea could skip geometrically, by a just scale, and edify the people from the engine. This was theatrical wit, right stage jesting, and relishing a play-house, invented for scorn and laughter; whereas, if it had savoured of equity, truth, perspicuity, and candour, to have tasten a wise or a learned palate, – spit it out presently! this is bitter and profitable: this instructs and would inform us! what need we know any thing, that are nobly born, more than a horse-race, or a hunting-match, our day to break with citizens, and such innate mysteries? This is truly leaping from the stage to the tumbril again, reducing all wit to the original dung-cart.

OF THE MAGNITUDE AND COMPASS OF
ANY FABLE, EPIC OR DRAMATIC

What the Measure of a Fable is. – The Fable or Plot of a Poem Defined. – The Epic Fable, Differing from the Dramatic

To the resolving of this question we must first agree in the definition of the fable. The fable is called the imitation of one entire and perfect action, whose parts are so joined and knit together, as nothing in the structure can be changed, or taken away, without impairing or troubling the whole, of which there is a proportionable magnitude in the members. As for example: if a man would build a house, he would first appoint a place to build it in, which he would define within certain bounds. So in the constitution of a poem, the action is aimed at by the poet, which answers place in a building, and that action hath his largeness, compass, and proportion. But as a court or king's palace requires other dimensions than a private house, so the epic asks a magnitude from other poems, since what is place in the one is action in the other; the difference is in space. So that by this definition we conclude the fable to be the imitation of one perfect and entire action, as one perfect and entire place is required to a building. By perfect, we understand that to which nothing is wanting, as place to the building that is raised, and action to the fable that is formed. It is perfect, perhaps not for a court or king's palace, which requires a greater ground, but for the structure we would raise; so the space of the action may not prove large enough for the epic fable, yet be perfect for the dramatic, and whole.

WHAT WE UNDERSTAND BY WHOLE

Whole we call that, and perfect, which hath a beginning, a midst, and an end. So the place of any building may be whole and entire for that work, though too little for a palace. As to a tragedy or a comedy, the action may be convenient and perfect that would not fit an epic poem in magnitude. So a lion is a perfect creature in himself, though it be less than that of a buffalo or a rhinocerote. They differ but in specie: either in the kind is absolute; both have their parts, and either the whole. Therefore, as in every body so in every action, which is the subject of a just work, there is required a certain proportionable greatness, neither too vast nor too minute. For that which happens to the eyes when we behold a body, the same happens to the memory when we contemplate an action. I look upon a monstrous giant, as Tityus, whose body covered nine acres of land, and mine eye sticks upon every part; the whole that consists of those parts will never be taken in at one entire view. So in a fable, if the action be too great, we can never comprehend the whole together in our imagination. Again, if it be too little, there ariseth no pleasure out of the object; it affords the view no stay; it is beheld, and vanisheth at once. As if we should look upon an ant or pismire, the parts fly the sight, and the whole considered is almost nothing. The same happens in action, which is the object of memory, as the body is of sight. Too vast oppresseth the eyes, and exceeds the memory; too little scarce admits either.

WHAT THE UTMOST BOUND OF A FABLE

Now in every action it behoves the poet to know which is his utmost bound, how far with fitness and a necessary proportion he may produce and determine it; that is, till either good fortune change into the worse, or the worse into the better. For as a body without proportion cannot be goodly, no more can the action, either in comedy or tragedy, without his fit bounds. And every bound, for the nature of the subject, is esteemed the best that is largest, till it can increase no more; so it behoves the action in tragedy or comedy to be let grow till the necessity ask a conclusion;

wherein two things are to be considered: first, that it exceeds not the compass of one day; next, that there be place left for digression and art. For the episodes and digressions in a fable are the same that household stuff and other furniture are in a house, And so far form the measure and extent of a fable dramatic.

WHAT IS MEANT BY ONE AND ENTIRE

Now that it should be one and entire. One is considerable two ways; either as it is only separate, and by itself, or as being composed of many parts, it begins to be one as those parts grow or are wrought together. That it should be one the first way alone, and by itself, no man that hath tasted letters ever would say, especially having required before a just magnitude and equal proportion of the parts in themselves. Neither of which can possibly be, if the action be single and separate, not composed of parts, which laid together in themselves, with an equal and fitting proportion, tend to the same end; which thing out of antiquity itself hath deceived many, and more this day it doth deceive.

So many there be of old that have thought the action of one man to be one, as of Hercules, Theseus, Achilles, Ulysses, and other heroes; which is both foolish and false, since by one and the same person many things may be severally done which cannot fitly be referred or joined to the same end: which not only the excellent tragic poets, but the best masters of the epic, Homer and Virgil, saw. For though the argument of an epic poem be far more diffused and poured out than that of tragedy, yet Virgil, writing of Aeneas, hath pretermitted many things. He neither tells how he was born, how brought up, how he fought with Achilles, how he was snatched out of the battle by Venus; but that one thing, how he came into Italy, he prosecutes in twelve books. The rest of his journey, his error by sea, the sack of Troy, are put not as the argument of the work, but episodes of the argument. So Homer laid by many things of Ulysses, and handled no more than he saw tended to one and the same end.

Contrary to which, and foolishly, those poets did, whom the philosopher taxeth, of whom one gathered all the actions of Theseus, another put all the labours of Hercules in one work. So did he whom Juvenal mentions in the beginning, 'hoarse Codrus', that recited a volume compiled, which he called his *Theseid*, not yet finished, to the great trouble both of his hearers and himself; amongst which there were many parts had no coherence nor kindred one with other, so far they were from being one action, one fable. For as a house, consisting of divers materials, becomes one structure and one dwelling, so an action, composed of divers parts, may become one fable, epic or dramatic. For example, in a tragedy, look upon Sophocles his *Ajax*: Ajax, deprived of Achilles's armour, which he hoped from the suffrage of the Greeks, disdains, and, growing impatient of the injury, rageth, and turns mad. In that humour he doth many senseless things, and at last falls upon the Grecian flock and kills a great ram for Ulysses: returning to his sense, he grows ashamed of the scorn, and kills himself; and is by the chiefs of the Greeks forbidden burial. These things agree and hang together, not as they were done, but as seeming to be done, which made the action whole, entire, and absolute.

> from *Timber, or Discoveries* by Ben Jonson, first published after Jonson's death, in 1641

The critical vocabulary of the Elizabethans was so different from ours that we must wonder whether our discussions of literature would even have been comprehensible to them. Of course it is the modern critics who ask the questions that interest us, and answer them in terms that fit our thinking; but when we are considering Elizabethan drama, it can surely do no harm to take a look at an Elizabethan asking the questions that interested him, and answering them in his own terms.

Ben Jonson is, with Shakespeare, the great master of Elizabethan comedy, and also the most articulate, self-conscious and learned critic of his time, so it is right that he should speak to us for his contemporaries. True, his comedies are quite unlike Shakespeare's. They belong to a different tradition of comedy, the realistic-satiric, of which they are the crowning achievements in English, as Shakespeare's are the crown of the romantic tradition. In *Timber*, however, Jonson does not distinguish the two: it is the aim of all poetry to 'dispose us to all civil offices of society'. It is an aim more obviously present in *Every Man in his Humour* or in *Volpone*, than in *Twelfth Night*, where it will be detected only by the scholar wearing his Renaissance spectacles – by Mr Paul A. Olson, say.

Just as Jonson's plays differ from Shakespeare's in a way he does not mention in his theorizing, so there are greater differences between many works of Elizabethan literature than the critical theory of the time would lead us to expect. This is perhaps the most striking thing about Elizabethan criticism, and the reason why it seems to offer us so little today. It sets up an orthodox conception of the purpose of literature, and regards every poem as an example of that, rather than growing out of the rich particularity of our varied responses. So if we feel that Jonson's remarks tell us little that explains Shakespeare's magic, we can remember that they tell us almost as little about his own sinewy brilliance.

Perhaps the section on laughter shows as clearly as anything that Jonson had an official self and a creative self. If the moving of laughter is a fault in comedy, if it is leaping from the stage to the tumbril again, then Jonson is as bad an offender as Shakespeare, for *The Alchemist* is quite as funny as – say – *Twelfth Night*, though neither is merely funny.

Jonson's criticism is Aristotelian: many of his points repeat or expand those made in the *Poetics*. This too is an Elizabethan but not a modern habit. The Renaissance did not want a critic to devise his own theories or generalize from his personal reactions: they wanted him to repeat and apply the principles which the ancients had already established. True, Jonson insists that the ancients are to be our guides, not commanders, that their writings are to be examined and not slavishly followed; but in the discussion of Aristotle above we can see how little this means. Those who lived before Aristotle are not to be rebuked for their ignorance of his laws; but now that Aristotle has written it hardly occurs to Jonson that he may have been wrong. He 'understood the causes of things'.

Aristotle is much better on plot than on anything else, and I have included all Jonson's discussion of plot (the Elizabethans called it 'fable'), which follows the *Poetics* closely. It is, as a matter of fact, not completely Jonson's own discussion: much of it is a translation of a Latin discussion of tragedy by one Heinsius, published in 1611; but no Elizabethan would have felt that such regard for one's predecessors was anything but natural. The Jonson–Heinsius point that unity must be a unity of action, not a mere biographical unity, is of course Aristotelian:

Jonson not only repeats it in his criticism, he applies it magnificently in his plays, and *The Alchemist* and *Volpone* have perhaps the most perfectly constructed plots in English drama. It would be fascinating to know what Jonson thought of Shakespeare's plots. Did he distinguish the more from the less tightly constructed, and judge the plays accordingly? Did he like *The Comedy of Errors* best? In the Induction to *Bartholomew Fair* he has a sneer at 'tales, tempests and such-like drolleries', at the 'servant-monster' of *The Tempest* and the 'nest of antiques' of (no doubt) *The Winter's Tale* – blaming Shakespeare for his romantic subject-matter, and not distinguishing between *The Winter's Tale*, whose plot covers sixteen years and two countries, and *The Tempest* which does at least preserve the unities of time and place.

I have not included Jonson's discussions of language, which come earlier in *Timber*. Here too he repeats Renaissance commonplaces; speech is the image of the mind, the language of a dramatic personage must fit his character (the doctrine of decorum). Many of these commonplaces fail to do justice to Elizabethan practice: decorum is often taken to mean no more than

grave old men should instruct, young men should show the imperfections of youth, strumpets should be lascivious, boys unhappy, and clowns should speak disorderly.　　　　George Whetstone: Dedication to *Promos and Cassandra*

This does not suggest a sensibility that appreciated Falstaff or Feste (or Mosca or Morose); but the theories that lie behind *Timber* are almost as mechanical:

Quintilian warns us that in no kind of translation, or metaphor, or allegory, we make a turn from what we began; as, if we fetch the original of our metaphor from sea and billows, we end not in flames and ashes; it is a most foul inconsequence.　　　　*Timber*, from § cxx

Shakespeare broke this precept often enough to discredit it – and so did Jonson:

> I fear I shall begin to grow in love
> With my dear self, and my most prosperous parts,
> They do so spring and burgeon; I can feel
> A whimsy in my blood: I know not how,
> Success hath made me wanton. I could skip
> Out of my skin now, like a subtle snake. . . .

Volpone, III. I. 1–6

There are parts of *Timber*, however, where the suppleness of Jonson the poet seems to be creeping into the language of Jonson the critic, where what he is actually saying is much finer than the view he is ostensibly setting forth. I conclude with a specimen of this:

Some men are tall and big, so some language is high and great. Then the words are chosen, their sound ample, the composition full, the absolution plenteous, and poured out, all grave, sinewy, and strong. Some are little and dwarfs; so of speech, it is humble and low, the words poor and flat, the members, and periods thin and weak, without knitting or number. The middle are of a just stature. There the language is plain and pleasing: even without stopping, round without swelling; all well-turned, composed, elegant, and accurate. The vicious language is vast and gaping, swelling irregular; when it contends to be high, full of rock, mountain, and pointedness: as it affects to be low, it is abject, and creeps, full of bogs and holes.   *Timber*, from § CXXII

THIRTY-TWO

An Essay on Comedy

... M. Saint-Marc Girardin, the excellent French essayist and master of critical style, tells of a conversation he had once with an Arab gentleman on the topic of the different management of these difficult creatures [women] in Orient and in Occident; and the Arab spoke in praise of many good results of the greater freedom enjoyed by Western ladies, and the charm of conversing with them. He was questioned why his countrymen took no measures to grant them something of that kind of liberty. He jumped out of his individuality in a twinkling, and entered into the sentiments of his race, replying, from the pinnacle of a splendid conceit, with affected humility of manner: '*You* can look on them without perturbation – but *we*!' ... And after this profoundly comic interjection, he added, in deep tones, 'The very face of a woman!' Our representative of temperate notions demurely consented that the Arab's pride of inflammability should insist on the prudery of the veil as the civilizing medium of his race.

There has been fun in Bagdad. But there never will be civilization where Comedy is not possible; and that comes of some degree of social equality of the sexes. I am not quoting the Arab to exhort and disturb the somnolent East; rather for cultivated women to recognize that the Comic Muse is one of their best friends. They are blind to their interests in swelling the ranks of the sentimentalists. Let them look with their clearest vision abroad and at home. They will see that where they have no social freedom, Comedy is absent: where they are household drudges, the form of Comedy is primitive: where they are tolerably independent, but uncultivated, exciting melodrama takes its place and a sentimental version of them. Yet the Comic will out, as they would know if they listened to some of the private conversations of men whose minds are undirected by the Comic Muse: as the sentimental man, to his astonishment, would know likewise, if he in similar fashion could receive a lesson. But where women are on the road to an equal footing with men, in attainments and in liberty – in what they have won for themselves, and what has been granted them by a fair civilization – there, and only waiting to be transplanted from life to the stage, or the novel, or the poem, pure Comedy flourishes, and is, as it would help them to be, the sweetest of diversions, the wisest of delightful companions.

Now, to look about us in the present time, I think it will be acknowledged that in neglecting the cultivation of the Comic idea, we are losing the aid of a powerful auxiliar. You see Folly perpetually sliding into new shapes in a society possessed of wealth and leisure, with many whims, many strange ailments and strange doctors. Plenty of common-sense is in the world to thrust her back when she pretends to empire. But the first-born of common-sense, the vigilant Comic, which is the genius of thoughtful laughter, which would readily extinguish her at the outset, is not serving as a public advocate.

You will have noticed the disposition of common-sense, under pressure of some pertinacious piece of light-headedness, to grow impatient and angry. That is a sign of the absence, or at least of the dormancy, of the Comic idea. For Folly is the natural prey of the Comic, known to it in all her transformations, in every disguise; and it is with the springing delight of hawk over heron, hound after fox, that it gives her chase, never fretting, never tiring, sure of having her, allowing her no rest.

Contempt is a sentiment that cannot be entertained by comic intelligence. What is it but an excuse to be idly minded, or personally lofty, or comfortably narrow, not perfectly humane? If we do not feign when we say that we despise Folly, we shut the brain. There is a disdainful attitude in the presence of Folly, partaking of the foolishness to Comic perception: and anger is not much less foolish than disdain. The struggle we have to conduct is essence against essence. Let no one doubt of the sequel when this emanation of what is firmest in us is launched to strike down the daughter of Unreason and Sentimentalism: such being Folly's parentage, when it is respectable.

Our modern system of combating her is too long defensive, and carried on too ploddingly with concrete engines of war in the attack. She has time to get behind entrenchments. She is ready to stand a siege, before the heavily armed man of science and the writer of the leading article or elaborate essay have primed their big guns. It should be remembered that she has charms for the multitude; and an English multitude seeing her make a gallant fight of it will be half in love with her, certainly willing to lend her a cheer. Benevolent subscriptions assist her to hire her own man of science, her own organ in the Press. If ultimately she is cast out and overthrown, she can stretch a finger at gaps in our ranks. She can say that she commanded an army and seduced men, whom we thought sober men and safe, to act as her lieutenants. We learn rather gloomily, after she has flashed her lantern, that we have in our midst able men and men with minds for whom there is no pole-star in intellectual navigation. Comedy, or the Comic element, is the specific for the poison of delusion while Folly is passing from the state of vapour to substantial form.

O for a breath of Aristophanes, Rabelais, Voltaire, Cervantes, Fielding, Molière! These are spirits that, if you know them well, will come when you do call. You will find the very invocation of them act on you like a renovating air – the South-west coming off the sea, or a cry in the Alps.

No one would presume to say that we are deficient in jokers. They abound, and the organization directing their machinery to shoot them in the wake of the leading article and the popular sentiment is good.

But the Comic differs from them in addressing the wits for laughter; and the sluggish wits want some training to respond to it, whether in public life or private, and particularly when the feelings are excited.

The sense of the Comic is much blunted by habits of punning and of using humoristic phrase: the trick of employing Johnsonian polysyllables to treat of the infinitely little. And it really may be humorous, of a kind, yet it will miss the point by going too much round about it.

A certain French Duke Pasquier died, some years back, at a very advanced age. He had been the venerable Duke Pasquier in his later years up to the period of his death. There was a report of Duke Pasquier that he was a man of profound egoism. Hence an argument arose, and was warmly sustained, upon the excessive selfishness of those who, in a world of troubles, and calls to action, and innumerable duties, husband their strength for the sake of living on. Can it be possible, the argument ran, for a truly generous heart to continue beating up to the age of a hundred? Duke Pasquier was not without his defenders, who likened him to the oak of the forest — a venerable comparison.

The argument was conducted on both sides with spirit and earnestness, lightened here and there by frisky touches of the polysyllabic playful, reminding one of the serious pursuit of their fun by truant boys, that are assured they are out of the eye of their master, and now and then indulge in an imitation of him. And well might it be supposed that the Comic idea was asleep, not overlooking them! It resolved at last to this, that either Duke Pasquier was a scandal on our humanity in clinging to life so long, or that he honoured it by so sturdy a resistance to the enemy. As one who has entangled himself in a labyrinth is glad to get out again at the entrance, the argument ran about to conclude with its commencement.

Now, imagine a master of the Comic treating this theme, and particularly the argument on it. Imagine an Aristophanic comedy of THE CENTENARIAN, with choric praises of heroical early death, and the same of a stubborn vitality, and the poet laughing at the chorus; and the grand question for contention in dialogue, as to the exact age when a man should die, to the identical minute, that he may preserve the respect of his fellows, followed by a systematic attempt to make an accurate measurement in parallel lines, with a tough rope-yarn by one party, and a string of yawns by the other, of the veteran's power of enduring life, and our capacity for enduring *him*, with tremendous pulling on both sides.

Would not the Comic view of the discussion illumine it and the disputants like very lightning? There are questions, as well as persons, that only the Comic can fitly touch. . . .

. . . You may estimate your capacity for Comic perception by being able to detect the ridicule of them you love, without loving them less: and more by being able to see yourself somewhat ridiculous in dear eyes, and accepting the correction their image of you proposes.

Each one of an affectionate couple may be willing, as we say, to die for the other, yet unwilling to utter the agreeable word at the right moment; but if the wits were sufficiently quick for them to perceive that they are in a comic situation, as affectionate couples must be when they quarrel, they would not wait for the moon or the almanac, or a Dorine, to bring back the flood-tide of tender feelings, that they should join hands and lips.

If you detect the ridicule, and your kindliness is chilled by it, you are slipping into the grasp of Satire.

If instead of falling foul of the ridiculous person with a satiric rod, to make him writhe and shriek aloud, you prefer to sting him under a semi-caress, by which he shall in his anguish be rendered dubious whether indeed anything has hurt him, you are an engine of Irony.

If you laugh all round him, tumble him, roll him about, deal him a smack, and drop a tear on him, own his likeness to you and yours to your neighbour, spare him as little as you shun, pity him as much as you expose, it is a spirit of Humour that is moving you.

The Comic, which is the perceptive, is the governing spirit, awakening and giving aim to these powers of laughter, but it is not to be confounded with them: it enfolds a thinner form of them, differing from satire, in not sharply driving into the quivering sensibilities, and from humour, in not comforting them and tucking them up, or indicating a broader than the range of this bustling world to them. . . .

. . . The Comic poet is in the narrow field, or enclosed square, of the society he depicts; and he addresses the still narrower enclosure of men's intellects, with reference to the operation of the social world upon their characters. He is not concerned with beginnings or endings or surroundings, but with what you are now weaving. To understand his work and value it, you must have a sober liking of your kind and a sober estimate of our civilized qualities. The aim and business of the Comic poet are misunderstood, his meaning is not seized nor his point of view taken, when he is accused of dishonouring our nature and being hostile to sentiment, tending to spitefulness and making an unfair use of laughter. Those who detect irony in Comedy do so because they choose to see it in life. Poverty, says the satirist, has nothing harder in itself than that it makes men ridiculous. But poverty is never ridiculous to Comic perception until it attempts to make its rags conceal its bareness in a forlorn attempt at decency, or foolishly to rival ostentation. Caleb Balderstone, in his endeavour to keep up the honour of a noble household in a state of beggary, is an exquisitely comic character. In the case of 'poor relatives', on the other hand, it is the rich, whom they perplex, that are really comic; and to laugh at the former, not seeing the comedy of the latter, is to betray dullness of vision. Humorist and Satirist frequently hunt together as Ironists in pursuit of the grotesque, to the exclusion of the Comic. That was an affecting moment in the history of the Prince Regent, when the First Gentleman of Europe burst into tears at a sarcastic remark of Beau Brummell's on the cut of his coat. Humour, Satire, Irony, pounce on it altogether as their common prey. The Comic spirit eyes but does not touch it. Put into action, it would be farcical. It is too gross for Comedy.

Incidents of a kind casting ridicule on our unfortunate nature instead of our conventional life, provoke derisive laughter, which thwarts the Comic idea. But derision is foiled by the play of the intellect. Most of doubtful causes in contest are open to Comic interpretation, and any intellectual pleading of a doubtful cause contains germs of an Idea of Comedy.

The laughter of satire is a blow in the back or the face. The laughter of Comedy is impersonal and of unrivalled politeness, nearer a smile; often no more than a smile. It laughs through the mind, for the mind directs it; and it might be called the humour of the mind.

One excellent test of the civilization of a country, as I have said, I take to be the flourishing of the Comic idea and Comedy; and the test of true Comedy is that it shall awaken thoughtful laughter. . . .

. . . You must, as I have said, believe that our state of society is founded in common-sense, otherwise you will not be struck by the contrasts the Comic Spirit perceives, or have it to look to for your consolation. You will, in fact, be standing in that peculiar oblique beam of light, yourself illuminated to the general eye as the very object of chase and doomed quarry of the thing obscure to you. But to feel its presence and to see it is your assurance that many sane and solid minds are with you in what you are experiencing: and this of itself spares you the pain of satirical heat, and the bitter craving to strike heavy blows. You share the sublime of wrath, that would not have hurt the foolish, but merely demonstrate their foolishness. Molière was contented to revenge himself on the critics of the *École des femmes*, by writing the *Critique de l'école des femmes*, one of the wisest as well as the playfullest of studies in criticism. A perception of the comic spirit gives high fellowship. You become a citizen of the selecter world, the highest we know of in connexion with our old world, which is not supermundane. Look there for your unchallengeable upper class! You feel that you are one of this our civilized community, that you cannot escape from it, and would not if you could. Good hope sustains you; weariness does not over-whelm you; in isolation you see no charms for vanity; personal pride is greatly moderated. Nor shall your title of citizenship exclude you from worlds of imagination or of devotion. The Comic spirit is not hostile to the sweetest songfully poetic. Chaucer bubbles with it: Shakespeare overflows: there is a mild moon's ray of it (pale with super-refinement through distance from our flesh and blood planet) in *Comus*. Pope has it, and it is the daylight side of the night half obscuring Cowper. It is only hostile to the priestly element, when that, by baleful swelling, transcends and overlaps the bounds of its office: and then, in extreme cases, it is too true to itself to speak and veils the lamp: as, for example, the spectacle of Bossuet over the dead body of Molière: at which the dark angels may, but men do not laugh.

We have had comic pulpits, for a sign that the laughter-moving and the worshipful may be in alliance: I know not how far comic, or how much assisted in seeming so by the unexpectedness and the relief of its appearance: at least they are popular, they are said to win the ear. Laughter is open to perversion, like other good things: the scornful and the brutal sorts are not unknown to us; but the laughter directed by the Comic spirit is a harmless wine, conducing to sobriety in the degree that it enlivens. It enters you like fresh air into a study; as when one of the sudden contrasts of the comic idea floods the brain like reassuring daylight. You are cognizant of the true kind by feeling that you take it in, savour it, and have what flowers live on, natural air for food. That which you give out – the joyful roar – is not the better part; let that go to good fellowship and the benefit of the lungs. Aristophanes promises his auditors that if they will retain the ideas of the comic poet carefully, as they keep dried fruits in boxes, their garments shall smell odoriferous of wisdom throughout the year. The boast will not be thought an empty one by those who have choice friends that have stocked themselves according to his directions. Such treasuries of sparkling laughter are wells in our desert. Sensitiveness to the comic laugh is a step in civilization. To shrink from being an object of it is a step in cultivation. We know the degree of refinement in men by the matter they will laugh at, and the ring of the laugh; but we know likewise that the larger natures are distinguished by the great breadth of their power of laughter, and no one really loving Molière is refined by that love to despise or be dense to Aristophanes, though it may be that the lover of Aristophanes will not have risen to the height of Molière. Embrace them both, and you have the whole scale of laughter in your breast. Nothing in the world surpasses in stormy fun the scene in *The Frogs*, when Bacchus and Xanthias receive their thrashings from the hands of businesslike Oeacus, to discover which is the divinity of the two, by his imperviousness to the mortal condition of pain, and each, under the obligation of not crying out, makes believe that his horrible bellow – the god's *iou iou* being the lustier – means only the stopping of a sneeze, or horseman sighted, or the prelude to an invocation to some deity: and the slave contrives that the god shall get the bigger lot of blows. Passages of Rabelais, one or two in *Don Quixote*, and the Supper in the Manner of the Ancients, in *Peregrine Pickle*, are of a similar cataract of laughter. But it is not illuminating; it is not the laughter of the mind. Molière's laughter, in his purest comedies, is ethereal, as light to our nature, as colour to our thoughts. The

Misanthrope and the *Tartuffe* have no audible laughter; but the characters are steeped in the comic spirit. They quicken the mind through laughter, from coming out of the mind; and the mind accepts them because they are clear interpretations of certain chapters of the Book lying open before us all. Between these two stand Shakespeare and Cervantes, with the richer laugh of heart and mind in one; with much of the Aristophanic robustness, something of Molière's delicacy.

The laughter heard in circles not pervaded by the Comic idea, will sound harsh and soulless, like versified prose, if you step into them with a sense of the distinction. You will fancy you have changed your habitation to a planet remoter from the sun. You may be among powerful brains too. You will not find poets – or but a stray one, over-worshipped. You will find learned men, undoubtedly, professors, reputed philosophers, and illustrious dilettanti. They have in them, perhaps, every element composing light, except the Comic. They read verse, they discourse of art; but their eminent faculties are not under that vigilant sense of a collective supervision, spiritual and present, which we have taken note of. They build a temple of arrogance; they speak much in the voice of oracles; their hilarity, if it does not dip in grossness, is usually a form of pugnacity.

> from *On the Idea of Comedy and of the Uses of the Comic Spirit* by George Meredith, 1877

Meredith's *Essay on Comedy* is much too long to include in full, and perhaps abridgement does it no great harm. The above extracts reproduce about one sixth of the whole. This seems drastic cutting, but is not as bad as it first appears, for I have left out all the detailed criticism, the discussions of Molière, Congreve, Aristophanes and others, that are sometimes interesting but by no means essential to Meredith's argument. I have also left out the praise of France at the expense of Germany and England, and a good deal of the more airy and elegant froth.

Meredith's prose has a faded, precious charm that attracts us less than it did his contemporaries, and we can perhaps do without the personification of the Comic Spirit who 'has the sage's brows, and the sunny malice of a faun lurks at the corners of the half-closed lips drawn in an idle wariness of half-tension'.

What remains after these cuts is some very clear-headed literary theory, with its wise and lucid distinctions between comedy, humour, satire and irony; some shrewd social commentary (was Meredith the first to say, what Shakespeare clearly assumed, that comedy must assume some degree of equality between the sexes?); and a style that in its more restrained elegances is sheer delight. The glimpse of Bossuet 'over the dead body of Molière' is brilliant because briefer and sharper than the more elaborate effects.

Meredith is not writing about Shakespeare, and the comedy he discusses is not Shakespearian comedy: Shakespeare has the comic spirit, but he has humour too, and blends them constantly. This Meredith realizes and almost says: who but Shakespeare can have been in his mind in one splendid sentence, that has got squeezed out of this abridgement:

The stroke of the great humorist is world-wide, with lights of Tragedy in his laughter.

THIRTY-THREE

The Argument of Comedy

THE Greeks produced two kinds of comedy, Old Comedy, represented by the eleven extant plays of Aristophanes, and New Comedy, of which the best known exponent is Menander. About two dozen New Comedies survive in the work of Plautus and Terence. Old Comedy, however, was out of date before Aristophanes himself was dead; and today, when we speak of comedy, we normally think of something that derives from the Menandrine tradition.

New Comedy unfolds from what may be described as a comic Oedipus situation. Its main theme is the successful effort of a young man to outwit an opponent and possess the girl of his choice. The opponent is usually the father (*senex*), and the psychological descent of the heroine from the mother is also sometimes hinted at. The father frequently wants the same girl, and is cheated out of her by the son, the mother thus becoming the son's ally. The girl is usually a slave or courtesan, and the plot turns on a *cognitio* or discovery of birth which makes her marriageable. Thus it turns out that she is not under an insuperable taboo after all but is an accessible object of desire, so that the plot follows the regular wish-fulfilment pattern. Often the central Oedipus situation is thinly concealed by surrogates or doubles of the main characters, as when the heroine is discovered to be the hero's sister, and has to be married off to his best friend. In Congreve's *Love for Love*, to take a modern instance well within the Menandrine tradition, there are two Oedipus themes in counterpoint: the hero cheats his father out of the heroine, and his best friend violates the wife of an impotent old man who is the heroine's guardian. Whether this analysis is sound or not, New Comedy is certainly concerned with the manoeuvring of a young man towards a young woman, and marriage is the tonic chord on which it ends. The normal comic resolution is the surrender of the *senex* to the hero, never the reverse. Shakespeare tried to reverse the pattern in *All's Well That Ends Well*, where the king of France forces Bertram to marry Helena, and the critics have not yet stopped making faces over it.

New Comedy has the blessing of Aristotle, who greatly preferred it to its predecessor, and it exhibits the general pattern of Aristotelian causation. It has a material cause in the young man's sexual desire, and a formal cause in the social order represented by the *senex*, with which the hero comes to terms when he gratifies his desire. It has an efficient cause in the character who brings about the final situation. In classical times this character is a tricky slave; Renaissance dramatists often use some adaptation of the medieval 'vice'; modern writers generally like to pretend that nature, or at least the natural course of events, is the efficient cause. The final cause is the audience, which is expected by its applause to take part in the comic resolution. All this takes place on a single order of existence. The action of New Comedy tends to become probable rather than fantastic, and it moves towards realism and away from myth and romance. The one romantic (originally mythical) feature in it, the fact that the hero or heroine turns out to be freeborn or someone's heir, is precisely the feature that trained New Comedy audiences tire of most quickly.

The conventions of New Comedy are the conventions of Jonson and Molière, and *a fortiori* of the English Restoration and the French rococo. When Ibsen started giving ironic twists to the same formulas, his startled hearers took them for portents of a social revolution. Even the old chestnut about the heroine's being really the hero's sister turns up in *Ghosts* and *Little Eyolf*. The average movie of today is a rigidly conventionalized New Comedy proceeding towards an act which, like death in Greek tragedy, takes place off stage, and is symbolized by the final embrace.

In all good New Comedy there is a social as well as an individual theme which must be sought in the general atmosphere of reconciliation that makes the final marriage possible. As the hero gets closer to the heroine and opposition is overcome, all the right-thinking people come over to his side. Thus a new social unit is formed on the stage, and the moment that this social unit crystallizes is the moment of the comic resolution. In the last scene, when the drama-tist usually tries to get all his characters on the stage at once, the audience witnesses the birth of a renewed sense of social integration. In comedy as in life the regular expression of this is a festival, whether a marriage, a dance, or a feast. Old Comedy has, besides a marriage, a *komos*, the processional dance from which comedy derives its name; and the masque, which is a by-form of comedy, also ends in a dance.

This new social integration may be called, first, a kind of moral norm and, second, the pattern of a free society. We can see this more clearly if we look at the sort of characters who impede the progress of the comedy towards the hero's victory. These are always people who are in some kind of mental bondage, who are helplessly driven by ruling passions, neurotic compulsions, social rituals, and selfishness. The miser, the hypochondriac, the hypocrite, the pedant, the snob: these are humours, people who do not fully know what they are doing, who are slaves to a predictable self-imposed pattern of behaviour. What we call the moral norm is, then, not morality but deliverance from moral bondage. Comedy is designed not to condemn evil, but to ridicule a lack of self-knowledge. It finds the virtues of Malvolio and Angelo as comic as the vices of Shylock.

The essential comic resolution, therefore, is an individual release which is also a social reconciliation. The normal individual is freed from the bonds of a humorous society, and a normal society is freed from the bonds imposed on it by humorous individuals. The Oedipus pattern we noted in New Comedy belongs to the indi-vidual side of this, and the sense of the ridiculousness of the humour to the social side. But all real comedy is based on the principle that these two forms of release are ultimately the same: this principle may be seen at its most concentrated in *The Tempest*. The rule holds whether the resolution is expressed in social terms, as in *The Merchant of Venice*, or in individual terms, as in Ibsen's *An Enemy of the People*.

The freer the society, the greater the variety of individuals it can tolerate, and the natural tendency of comedy is to include as many as possible in its final festival. The motto of comedy is Terence's 'Nothing human is alien to me'. This may be one reason for the traditional comic importance of the parasite, who has no business to be at the festival but is nevertheless there. The spirit of reconciliation which pervades the comedies of Shakespeare is not to be ascribed to a personal attitude of his own, about which we know nothing whatever, but to his impersonal concentration on the laws of comic form.

Hence the moral quality of the society presented is not the point of the comic resolution. In Jonson's *Volpone* the final assertion of the moral norm takes the form of a social revenge on Volpone, and the play ends with a great bustle of sentences to penal servitude and the galleys. One feels perhaps that the audience's sense of the moral norm does not need so much hard labour. In *The Alchemist*, when Lovewit returns to his house, the virtuous characters have proved so weak and the rascals so ingenious that the action dissolves in laughter. Whichever is morally the better ending, that of *The Alchemist* is more concentrated comedy. *Volpone* is starting to move towards tragedy, towards the vision of a greatness which develops *hybris* and catastrophe.

The same principle is even clearer in Aristophanes. Aristophanes is the most personal of writers: his opinions on every subject are written all over his plays, and we have no doubt of his moral attitude. We know that he wanted peace with Sparta and that he hated Cleon, and when his comedy depicts the attaining of peace and the defeat of Cleon we know that he approved and wanted his audience to approve. But in *Ecclesiazusae* a band of women in disguise railroad a communistic scheme through the Assembly, which is a horrid parody of Plato's *Republic*, and proceed to inaugurate Plato's sexual communism with some astonishing improvements. Presumably Aristophanes did not applaud this, yet the comedy follows the same pattern and the same resolution. In *The Birds* the Peisthetairos who defies Zeus and blocks out Olympus with his Cloud-Cuckoo-Land is accorded the same triumph that is given to the Trygaeus of the *Peace* who flies to heaven and brings a golden age back to Athens.

Comedy, then, may show virtue her own feature and scorn her own image – for Hamlet's famous definition of drama was originally a definition of comedy. It may emphasize the birth of an ideal society as you like it, or the tawdriness of the sham society which is the way of the world. There is an important parallel here with tragedy. Tragedy, we are told, is expected to raise but not ultimately to accept the emotions of pity and terror. These I take to be the sense of moral good and evil, respectively, which we attach to the tragic hero. He may be as good as Caesar, and so appeal to our pity, or as bad as Macbeth, and so appeal to terror, but the particular thing called tragedy that happens to him does not depend on his moral status. The tragic catharsis passes beyond moral judgement, and while it is quite possible to construct a moral tragedy, what tragedy gains in morality it loses in cathartic power. The same is true of the comic catharsis, which raises sympathy and ridicule on a moral basis, but passes beyond both.

Many things are involved in the tragic catharsis, but one of them is a mental or imaginative form of the sacrificial ritual out of which tragedy arose. This is the ritual of the struggle, death, and rebirth of a God-Man, which is linked to the yearly triumph of spring over winter. The tragic hero is not really killed, and the audience no longer eats his body and drinks his blood, but the corresponding thing in art still takes place. The audience enters into communion with the body of the hero, becoming thereby a single body itself. Comedy grows out of the same ritual, for in the ritual the tragic story has a comic sequel. Divine men do not die: they die and rise again. The ritual pattern behind the catharsis of comedy is the resurrection that follows the death, the epiphany or manifestation of the risen hero. This is clear enough in Aristophanes, where the hero is treated as a risen God-Man led in triumph with the divine honours of the Olympic victor, rejuvenated, or hailed as a new Zeus. In New Comedy the new human body is, as we have seen, both a hero and a social group. Aristophanes is not only closer to the ritual pattern, but contemporary with Plato; and his comedy, unlike Menander's, is Platonic and dialectic: it seeks not the entelechy of the soul but the Form of the Good, and finds it in the resurrection of the soul from the world of the cave to the sunlight. The audience gains a vision of that resurrection whether the conclusion is joyful or ironic, just as in tragedy it gains a vision of a heroic death whether the hero is morally innocent or guilty.

Two things follow from this: first, that tragedy is really implicit or uncompleted comedy; second, that comedy contains a potential tragedy within itself. With regard to the latter, Aristophanes is full of traces of the original death of the hero which precedes his resurrection in the ritual. Even in New Comedy the dramatist usually tries to bring his action as close to a tragic overthrow of the hero as he can get it, and reverses this movement as suddenly as possible. In Plautus the tricky slave is often forgiven or even freed after having been threatened with all the brutalities that a very brutal dramatist can think of, including crucifixion. Thus the resolution of New Comedy seems to be a realistic foreshortening of a death-and-resurrection pattern, in which the struggle and rebirth of a divine hero has shrunk into a marriage, the freeing of a slave, and the triumph of a young man over an older one.

As for the conception of tragedy as implicit comedy, we may notice how often tragedy closes on the major chord of comedy: the Aeschylean trilogy, for instance, proceeds to what is really a comic resolution, and so do many tragedies of Euripides. From the point of view of Christianity, too, tragedy is an episode in that larger scheme of redemption and resurrection to which Dante gave the name of *commedia*. This conception of *commedia* enters drama with the miracle-play cycles, where such tragedies as the Fall and the Crucifixion are episodes of a dramatic scheme in which the divine comedy has the last word. The sense of tragedy as a prelude to comedy is hardly separable from anything explicitly Christian. The serenity of the final double chorus in the *St Matthew Passion* would hardly be attainable if composer and audience did not know that there was more to the story. Nor would the death of Samson lead to 'calm of mind all passion spent' if Samson were not a prototype of the rising Christ.

New Comedy is thus contained, so to speak, within the symbolic structure of Old Comedy, which in its turn is contained within the Christian conception of *commedia*. This sounds like a logically exhaustive classification, but we have still not caught Shakespeare in it.

It is only in Jonson and the Restoration writers that English comedy can be called a form of New Comedy. The earlier tradition established by Peele and developed by Lyly, Greene, and the masque writers, which uses themes from romance and folk-lore and avoids the comedy of manners, is the one followed by Shakespeare. These themes are largely medieval in origin, and derive, not from the Mysteries or the Moralities or the interludes, but from a fourth dramatic tradition. This is the drama of folk ritual, of the St George play and the mummers' play, of the feast of the ass and the Boy Bishop, and of all the dramatic activity that punctuated the Christian calendar with the rituals of an immemorial paganism. We may call this the drama of the green world, and its theme is once again the triumph of life over the waste land, the death and revival of the year impersonated by figures still human and once divine as well.

When Shakespeare began to study Plautus and Terence, his dramatic instinct, stimulated by his predecessors, divined that there was a profounder pattern in the argument of comedy than appears in either of them. At once – for the process is beginning in *The Comedy of Errors* – he started groping towards that profounder pattern, the ritual of death and revival that also underlies Aristophanes, of which an exact equivalent lay ready to hand in the drama of the green world. This parallelism largely accounts for the resemblances to Greek ritual which Colin Still has pointed out in *The Tempest*.

The Two Gentlemen of Verona is an orthodox New Comedy except for one thing. The hero Valentine becomes captain of a band of outlaws in a forest, and all the other characters are gathered into this forest and become converted. Thus the action of the comedy begins in a world represented as a normal world, moves into the green world, goes into a metamorphosis there in which the comic resolution is achieved, and returns to the normal world. The forest in this play is the embryonic form of the fairy world of *A Midsummer Night's Dream*, the Forest of Arden in *As You Like It*, Windsor Forest in *The Merry Wives of Windsor*, and the pastoral world of the mythical sea-coasted Bohemia in *The Winter's Tale*. In all these comedies there is the same rhythmic movement from normal world to green world and back again. Nor is this second world confined to the forest comedies. In *The Merchant of Venice* the two worlds are a little harder to see, yet Venice is clearly not the same world as that of Portia's mysterious house in Belmont, where there are caskets teaching that gold and silver are corruptible goods, and from whence proceed the wonderful cosmological harmonies of the fifth act. In *The Tempest* the entire action takes place in the second world, and the same may be said of *Twelfth Night*, which, as its title implies, presents a carnival society, not so much a green world as an evergreen one. The second world is absent from the so-called problem comedies, which is one of the things that makes them problem comedies.

The green world charges the comedies with a symbolism in which the comic resolution contains a suggestion of the old ritual pattern of the victory of summer over winter. This is explicit in *Love's Labour's Lost*. In this very masque-like play, the comic contest takes the form of the medieval debate of winter and spring. In *The Merry Wives of Windsor* there is an elaborate ritual of the defeat of winter, known to folk-lorists as 'carrying out Death', of which Falstaff is the victim; and Falstaff must have felt that, after being thrown into the water, dressed up as a witch and beaten out of a house with curses, and finally supplied with a beast's head and singed with candles while he said, 'Divide me like a brib'd buck, each a haunch,' he had done about all that could reasonably be asked of any fertility spirit.

The association of this symbolism with the death and revival of human beings is more elusive, but still perceptible. The fact that the heroine often brings about the comic resolution by disguising herself as a boy is familiar enough. In the Hero of *Much Ado About Nothing* and the Helena of *All's Well That Ends Well*, this theme of the withdrawal and return of the heroine comes as close to a death and revival as Elizabethan conventions will allow. The Thaisa of *Pericles* and the Fidele of *Cymbeline* are beginning to crack the conventions, and with the disappearance and revival of Hermione in *The Winter's Tale*, who actually returns once as a ghost in a dream, the original nature-myth of Demeter and Proserpine is openly established. The fact that the dying and reviving character is usually female strengthens the feeling that there is something maternal about the green world, in which the new order of the comic resolution is nourished and brought to birth. However a similar theme which is very like the rejuvenation of the *senex* so frequent in Aristophanes occurs in the folk-lore motif of the healing of the impotent king on which *All's Well That Ends Well* is based, and this theme is probably involved in the symbolism of Prospero.

The conception of a second world bursts the boundaries of Menandrine comedy, yet it is clear that the world of Puck is no world of eternal forms or divine revelation. Shakespeare's comedy is not Aristotelian and realistic like Menander's, nor Platonic and dialectic like Aristophanes's, nor Thomist and sacramental like Dante's, but a fourth kind. It is an Elizabethan kind, and is not confined either to Shakespeare or to the drama. Spenser's epic is a wonderful contrapuntal intermingling of two orders of existence, one the red and white world of English history, the other the green world of the Faerie Queene. The latter is a world of crusading virtues proceeding from the Faerie Queene's court and designed to return to that court when the destiny of the other world is fulfilled. The fact that the Faerie Queene's knights are sent out during the twelve days of the Christmas festival suggests our next point.

Shakespeare too has his green world of comedy and his red and white world of history. The story of the latter is at one point interrupted by an invasion from the comic world, when Falstaff *senex et parasitus* throws his gigantic shadow over Prince Henry, assuming on one occasion the role of his father. Clearly, if the Prince is ever to conquer France he must re-assert the moral norm. The moral norm is duly re-asserted, but the rejection of Falstaff is not a comic resolution. In comedy the moral norm is not morality but deliverance, and we certainly do not feel delivered from Falstaff as we feel delivered from Shylock with his absurd and vicious bond. The moral norm does not carry with it the vision of a free society: Falstaff will always keep a bit of that in his tavern.

Falstaff is a mock king, a lord of misrule, and his tavern is a Saturnalia. Yet we are reminded of the original meaning of the Saturnalia, as a rite intended to recall the golden age of Saturn. Falstaff's world is not a golden world, but as long as we remember it we cannot forget that the world of *Henry V* is an iron one. We are reminded too of another traditional denizen of the green world, Robin Hood, the outlaw who manages to suggest a better kind of society than those who make him an outlaw can produce. The outlaws in *The Two Gentlemen of Verona* compare themselves, in spite of the Italian setting, to Robin Hood, and in *As You Like It* Charles the wrestler says of Duke Senior's followers: 'There they live like the old Robin Hood of England: they say many young gentlemen flock to him every day, and fleet the time carelessly, as they did in the golden world.'

In the histories, therefore, the comic Saturnalia is a temporary reversal of normal standards, comic 'relief' as it is called, which subsides and allows the history to continue. In the comedies, the green world suggests an original golden age which the normal world has usurped and which makes us wonder if it is not the normal world that is the real Saturnalia. In *Cymbeline* the green world finally triumphs over a historical theme, the reason being perhaps that in that play the incarnation of Christ, which is contemporary with Cymbeline, takes place off-stage, and accounts for the halcyon peace with which the play concludes. From then on in Shakespeare's plays, the green world has it all its own way, and both in *Cymbeline* and in *Henry VIII* there may be suggestions that Shakespeare, like Spenser, is moving towards a synthesis of the two worlds, a wedding of Prince Arthur and the Faerie Queene.

This world of fairies, dreams, disembodied souls, and pastoral lovers may not be a 'real' world, but, if not, there is something equally illusory in the stumbling and blinded follies of the 'normal' world of Theseus's Athens with its idiotic marriage law, of Duke Frederick and his melancholy tyranny, of Leontes and his mad jealousy, of the Court Party with their plots and intrigues. The famous speech of Prospero about the dream nature of reality applies equally to Milan and the enchanted island. We spend our lives partly in a waking world we call normal and partly in a dream world which we create out of our own desires. Shakespeare endows both worlds with equal imaginative power, brings them opposite one another, and makes each world seem unreal when seen by the light of the other. He uses freely both the heroic triumph of New Comedy and the ritual resurrection of its predecessor, but his distinctive comic resolution is different from either; it is a detach-ment of the spirit born of this reciprocal reflection of two illusory realities. We need not ask whether this brings us into a higher order of existence or not, for the question of existence is not relevant to poetry.

We have spoken of New Comedy as Aristotelian, Old Comedy as Platonic and Dante's *commedia* as Thomist, but it is difficult to suggest a philosophical spokesman for the form of Shakespeare's comedy. For Shakespeare, the subject-matter of poetry is not life, or nature, or reality, or revelation, or anything else that the philosopher builds on, but poetry itself, a verbal universe. That is one reason why he is both the most elusive and the most substantial of poets.

'The Argument of Comedy' by Northrop Frye, *English Institute Essays*, 1948

THIRTY-FOUR

The Aesthetic Experience: Comedy

WHILE immersed in the world of tragedy, we accept tragedy's high seriousness without question; we may temporarily forget that there are many other ways of looking at things. A single evening with tragedy's easy-going sister, comedy, will quickly remind us that the tragic attitude is in fact a quite special one – and perhaps make us feel that it is unnaturally and undesirably rigid.

The contrast between the tragic and the comic approach to life could scarcely be more sharp. Tragedy raises – more technically it over-cathects – everything it touches. It depicts characters of heroic mould, involves them in large events, compels them to choose between extreme alternatives. It invites us to face and work through the aspects of our own nature and the human predicament which are most likely to arouse anxiety. In contrast, comedy tries to spare us anxiety and to dissipate whatever anxiety we may already feel. It minimizes and belittles. It tells us that everyone and everything, ourself included, is less important than we think. It focuses our attention upon characters who are either not large enough or not serious enough to commit the kind of offences which shatter the lives of the protagonists of tragedy. To eat and drink well, have as much fun as possible and keep one's skin intact – these are the only goals to which most comic characters are likely to be firmly committed. Unlike the heroes of tragedy, they are usually quite willing to compromise.

To be sure, comic characters have their faults; some of them seem to be composed largely of faults. Comic characters may be indolent, unreliable, vain, hypocritical, frivolous, acquisitive or lascivious – and sometimes a single character has almost this entire roster of failings. But while such failings may arouse scorn, they do not excite fear. Particularly since they are usually buttressed by such qualities as cunning and resilience, they do not threaten to involve the characters in anything worse than the kind of scrapes from which, after a little squirming, we feel sure they will be able to extricate themselves. And the prospect of their having to suffer a certain amount of trouble is positively pleasing. Unlike other forms of fiction, comedy keeps us dissociated from its characters so that even when they are amiable we do not feel that we are debarred from having a certain amount of fun at their expense. We watch their antics in very much the same spirit in which we might observe the foolish behaviour of small children, and while our mood would change instantly if they did something which put them in serious danger, so long as they do not we are unashamedly amused. When the characters are reprobates, comedy invites the kind of laughter which has some malice in it. Since we are not identified with the characters, nothing prevents us from laughing *at* them – from feeling scorn or some other emotion in which there is an element, sometimes a large element, of hostility. The emphasis on their weaknesses puts us in a good psychological position to entertain such feelings, for it causes our own weaknesses to sit more lightly upon us.

However, the pleasure we take in the misadventures of comic characters is not fully explained by the nature of their weaknesses, even when allowance is made for our comforting sense of dissociation. Objectively considered, in fact, those weaknesses are often not as insignificant as comedy pretends; and, because they are our own weaknesses, if treated in the wrong way they would arouse anxiety and guilt, so that we would feel obliged to take a disapproving attitude towards them as a way of asserting our innocence. Here, as in tragedy, attitude is of coordinate importance with substance. By one means or another comedy compels us to regard the weaknesses as of small consequence, and to judge them more leniently than we ordinarily do. It sets the tone for the response of its audience. The attitude of most comedies is that of an urbane and tolerant friend, amused rather than censorious about that blonde he saw us out with the night before. In a world where such an attitude prevails, we sense that it would be unseemly and foolish to let ourselves become exercised by the spectacle of human frailty. Other comedies are caustic and the reverse of indulgent, but they suggest a scale of values against which the shortcomings and misdeeds of the characters seem trivial – less important, in many cases, than the characters would like to think them. Human beings are errant knaves all, these more astringent comedies remind us, and, granted that the little people it sets before us are far from admirable, they, and by inference we ourselves, are no worse than anyone else.

Comedy also minimizes the seriousness of the situations in which its characters become involved. In most cases the characters co-operate: they do not take their affairs too seriously themselves. They quite cheerfully compromise, or even reverse their position, when that seems expedient. They do not permit themselves to get into extreme predicaments in which their very life may hang in the balance. When they stumble into trouble, and this they tend to do, they resort to any device which suggests itself, not excluding subterfuges which would be beneath the dignity of the tragic hero, in order to get out of it. Because they are flexible and resourceful, there always seem to be many possibilities open to them. For reasons we shall consider in a minute, even when comic characters are of a different stamp, and beset by innumerable troubles, they never give the impression of being trapped, isolated like a tragic hero whose doom is imminent in a small and contracting square of space. The world of comedy adjoins the one we know and is as spacious as that world appears when we are young.

When comedy deals with characters who take life seriously – and some of its characters, especially if they are youthful, may be guilty of this heresy – it is careful not to let the reader follow suit. Some comedies mercilessly expose the triviality and meretriciousness of the things to which the characters attach importance; they ask us to laugh at their scale of values as we laugh at everything else. Shakespeare and certain other writers feel too much affection for their characters to employ such an approach, but they also contrive to depreciate the importance of the matters which seem so momentous to the characters. They do this so caressingly that the very enthusiasm of the characters cause us to love them the more. Nevertheless, another attitude emerges, and prevails against theirs. Whereas tragedy may suggest that if necessary one should gladly risk life itself to win the woman one desires, and certain zealous comic characters espouse the same doctrine, comedy is likely to treat love as an engaging but irrational prejudice – 'the delusion', in the words of H. L. Mencken's aphorism, 'that one woman differs from another'. The characterization typical of the kind of comedies of which I am speaking supports this attitude. Neither its Lysanders and Demetriuses, nor its Hermias and Helenas, are sharply enough differentiated to permit a bystander to suppose that it is a matter of world-shaking significance who mates with whom.

Not that comedy is unaccommodating. It is willing, and even desirous, that every Jack shall have his Jill. But it wants to tease Jack a bit first for our pleasure. It knows that in the end he will prize his Jill the more, and we will enjoy their union the more, if it is not brought about straightaway. The danger of this course is that we may also have to share the anxiety the characters experience during the more discouraging phases of their affairs. To prevent this from happening, comedy nearly always finds some means of letting the reader know that everything will work out well in the end. It may make us privy at once to the explanation of difficulties which perplex the characters. Shakespeare employs this device, for example, in *The Comedy of Errors* and *A Midsummer Night's Dream*.

In good time – when we have been sufficiently stimulated and before the characters are too discouraged – comedy begins to unravel the apparently hopeless snarl it has created. The task is never so difficult as it appears. Frequently the complications depend upon nothing more substantial than mistaken notions about what one or another of the characters has done or mix-ups of identity. The more hardened characters of comedy have manifest skill, and we would surmise experience, in extricating themselves from embarrassing predicaments; the more ingenuous ones at least have the virtue of persisting until matters can be straightened out. And comedy shows how good-natured it really is by the kind of help it now begins to furnish the artful and the innocent alike. Whereas tragedy appears to get more rigorous and deterministic as it proceeds, comedy usually becomes increasingly slack and haphazard. It utilizes whatever means seem handiest for setting matters straight, not shunning accidents, coincidences or supernatural intervention, and not troubling its carefree soul too greatly about plausibility; Voltaire unhesitatingly resurrects characters when that suits his purpose. The concluding phases of some comedies remind one of the kind of scurried tidying-up which may go on when a family has only a minute or two to prepare for the arrival of unexpected guests.

It is evident that comedy seeks to spare us anxiety and reduce feelings of guilt. Even when it is frenzied, and all but shouts with laughter about the foibles of humanity, it whispers its real message: 'You foolish reader, with your small vanities and small vices, which you struggle so desperately to conceal and deny – relax, you're not so bad!' Comedy is by no means immoral. Implicitly if not explicitly it extols certain of the fundamental virtues, above all humaneness and honesty. But it suggests that to err is human, and – certain comedies such as *Gulliver's Travels* excepted – it minimizes the importance of our lapses from grace. Whether critical or compassionate, it views the foibles of human beings in somewhat the same perspective in which adults observe the shortcomings of children. It invites us to take weaknesses which are a source of shame and apprehension more lightly than we ordinarily do. The reduction of guilt and anxiety which ensues when we accept its invitation always produces a feeling of exhilaration, and when it is sudden and considerable may precipitate that outward sign of pleasure, laughter.

It could be urged that there is something irresponsible and even dishonest about the attitude of comedy. Its book-keeping is often lax. The weaknesses it exposes sometimes involve us in difficulties which leave permanent scars. But there is something else to be said; if there were not, we would be unable to explain our respect for comedy, our feeling that it makes some contribution without which life would be infinitely more onerous. The respect is not adequately explained, in my opinion, by the common notion that what comedy supplies is escape, that it transports us to a pleasurable artificial world which has no relevance for our everyday existence. We value comedy, I believe, because it supplies us with an attitude which is important, perhaps indispensable, for our survival in the world in which we live and err and suffer, the only world we shall ever know.

Without occasional recourse to that attitude, a creature like man, aspiring and god-like but also frail and fallible, might find it impossible to come to terms with himself. *Inter urinas et faeces nascimur*. If our standards are too high, how shall we find it possible to forgive ourselves for the compromises which we, no less than the characters of comedy, must continually make not only to succeed but to survive in a predatory and sinful world? The code of comedy is perhaps not literally defensible, but it is a necessary corrective to man's tendency to judge himself too pitilessly.

Apart from its utility, furthermore, there is something admirable about comedy. Even serious comedies do not confront the ugly and painful aspects of human life as unblinkingly as tragedy, but in their own way they not only deal with them, they attempt to wring pleasure out of them. It would be a serious mistake to equate comedy with the things it depicts. These, as we know, are often mean and paltry. What is wonderful about comedy is the way it treats even potentially depressing material, its equanimity and buoyance, the zest which manifests itself in pace and tone and style. Comedy's very resilience suggests that there is more to man than the rather soiled side of our nature it sometimes exposes. There is something tonic and redemptive about our ability to laugh at ourselves and perceive what a ridiculous figure we sometimes cut in a universe little impressed by our posturing or our accomplishments. An observation Freud made about humour applies without alteration to any masterpiece of comedy, such as *Candide*: 'what is fine about [humour] is the triumph of narcissism, the ego's victorious assertion of its own invulnerability. It refuses to be hurt by the arrows of reality or to be compelled to suffer. It insists that it is impervious to wounds dealt by the outside world, in fact, that these are merely occasions for affording it pleasure. . . . Humour is not resigned; it is rebellious. It signifies the triumph not only of the ego, but also of the pleasure principle, which is strong enough to assert itself here in the face of the adverse real circumstances.'

from Chapter XI of *Fiction and the Unconscious* by Simon O. Lesser, 1957

THIRTY-FIVE

Shakespearian Comedy: the Consummation

... On a purely and superficially formal consideration, it is remarkable that these mature plays seem to exhibit little progress in such external things as plotcraft and dramatic illusiveness when set beside Shakespeare's earlier experiments in comedy. *Much Ado* is so informal that it makes its sub-plot much more significant than its nominally main plot. *Twelfth Night* builds itself formally on circumstances like those of *The Comedy of Errors* and even increases the theatrical improbability of all plays of mistaken identity by adding sex-disguise to make stage-illusion still more difficult. *As You Like It* gratuitously imports lions into the forest of Arden; it trades as extensively as *Twelfth Night* in sex-disguise, and it rounds off its action with a hastier and even less suitable marriage than is that of Olivia and Sebastian. But the appearance of casualness in plotcraft is delusory. These plays are held together, not by the nexus of external circumstance, but by the coherence of their spiritual substance. Their apparent diversity is moulded into unity by what Coleridge would have called an esemplastic power. They are the unified shape of an embodied idea, the representation of a created world which has become an organic universe because its every operation manifests that universality of its own proper laws.

To see these plays as a form of comedy, it is perhaps easiest to begin by realizing that in kind they are essentially and obviously different from traditional classical comedy. Their main characters arouse admiration; they excite neither scorn nor contempt. They inspire us to be happy with them; they do not merely cajole us into laughing at them. Therein lies the fundamental difference between classical and Shakespearian comedy. Classical comedy is conservative. It implies a world which has reached stability sufficient for itself. Its members are assumed to be fully aware of the habits and the morals which preserve an already attained state of general well-being. The main interest is the exposure of offenders against common practice and against unquestioned propriety in the established fitness of things. Hence, its manner is satire, and its standpoint is public common sense. But Shakespearian comedy is a more venturesome and a more imaginative undertaking. It does not assume that the conditions and the requisites of man's welfare have been certainly established, and are therefore a sanctity only to be safeguarded. It speculates imaginatively on modes, not of preserving a good already reached, but of enlarging and extending the possibilities of this and other kinds of good. Its heroes (or heroines, to give them the dues of their sex) are voyagers in pursuit of a happiness not yet attained, a brave new world wherein man's life may be fuller, his sensations more exquisite and his joys more widespread, more lasting, and so more humane. But as the discoverer reaches this higher bliss, he (or rather she) is making his conquests in these realms of the spirit accessible not only to himself but to all others in whom he has inspired the same way of apprehending existence. He has not merely preserved the good which was; he has refined, varied, and widely extended it. Hence Shakespearian comedy is not finally satiric; it is poetic. It is not conservative; it is creative. The way of it is that of the imagination rather than that of pure reason. It is an artist's vision, not a critic's exposition.

But though the ultimate world of Shakespeare's comedy is romantic, poetic, and imaginative, it is by no means unsubstantial and fantastic. The Forest of Arden is no conventional Arcadia. Its inhabitants are not exempt from the penalty of Adam. Winter, rough weather, the season's differences, the icy fang and churlish chiding of the winter's wind invade Arden as often as they invade this hemisphere of ours. Nor does manna fall to it from heaven. One may come by a sufficient sustenance of flesh, if one has the weapons and the impulse to make a breach in the conventionality of idyllic Nature by killing its own creatures, the deer, to whom the forest is the assigned and native dwelling-place. Arden, too, is not ignorant of the earthly landlordism which cramps the labourers' life with harshness:

> My master is of churlish disposition
> And little recks to find the way to heaven
> By doing deeds of hospitality.
>
> *As You Like It*, ii. 4. 75–7

And, after all, pastoral life in Arden is merely episodic in the round of man's fuller existence: 'when I was at home, I was in a better place.' Rosalind and Orlando will return to live their adult life in the society of man and in a civilization which will impose on them the duties of extended social responsibilities. Only by hearsay is life in Arden reputed to be a fleeting the time carelessly as they did in the golden age; even young Orlando knows that it may be a losing and a neglecting of the creeping hours. Arden, indeed, may properly excite the witticisms of Touchstone by its rusticities; it may arouse the twisted sentimentalism of Jaques by its Darwinian illustrations of the cruel struggle for survival.

But Arden survives. It survives as an immeasurable enlargement of the universe of comedy. No longer is the comic spirit confined to the city and to the market-place. And not only is there Arden. There is Illyria. There are the vast expanses of a less known world; romantic countries on whose coasts all the strange and stirring episodes that man has dreamed may come true: shipwreck, piracy, warfare, marvellous escapes from imminent death, hazards boldly and even recklessly encountered. Or, may be, lands of *dolce far niente*, where music is the food of love, where corporeal and material exigencies offer no impediment to man's grasp at the opulence of a merely sentimental existence. In such a climate, a duke may wallow orientally in the luxuriance of sheer sensuous excitement; but, in the same air, the witchcraft of adventure will strike from a simple ship's captain a nobility of benevolence which will sacrifice all for another's good.

'This is the air, this is the glorious sun.' But it is not only in its geographical atmosphere that the world of these comedies is so vastly larger than that of classical comedy, so much more radiant than that of Shakespeare's earlier romantic comedies, and so much more rich than that of Falstaff's Eastcheap. In its own turn, the world of the spirit has been equally extended. As one obvious sign of it, man has become more exquisitely conscious of music. Of course, there has always been a human impulse for caterwauling; and, in their cups, men have commonly felt themselves to be such dogs at a catch that they could rouse the night-owl and make the welkin dance. But it is in these great plays that men are suddenly brought up against the stupendous and apparently incredibly foolish circumstance that sheep's guts are potent to hale the souls out of their bodies.

There had, of course, always been music in Elizabethan plays. It was hallowed by their earliest tradition. In daily life, too, an Elizabethan, whether nobleman or peasant, had found music as much an habitual part of his occupation as was eating or drinking or working.

> O, fellow, come, the song we had last night.
> Mark it, Cesario, it is old and plain;
> The spinsters and the knitters in the sun
> And the free maids that weave their thread with bones
> Do use to chant it.   *Twelfth Night*, II. 4. 41–5

It is not only that song and music irradiate these plays – the very clown of one of them has almost lost his clownage to qualify as a singer – the important point is that the men and women of the play, and Shakespeare and his audience, are becoming conscious of what the spell of music implies. 'That strain again'; these old and antique songs were apt to arouse amorousness in Orsino and yet 'to relieve him of his passion much'. To recognize the palpable effect of music was the first step: to become aware of its implications was another. In men's secular lives, music ministered most powerfully to their passion of love. 'If music be the food of love, play on.' And so they found themselves at the very heart of the mystery, the recognition that, however strange, sheep's guts did in fact hale their souls out of their bodies. They were feelingly aware that the soul is susceptible to strange and unaccountable impulses, and that, responding to them, it enters a rich and novel spiritual kingdom.

What this means for the purposes of Shakespearian comedy is this. Man had discovered that he was a much less rational and a much more complex creature than he had taken himself to be. His instincts and his intuitions, his emotions and his moods were as real and as distinctive a part of him as his reason and his plain common-sense. They were, in fact, a much more incalculable yet often a much more exciting and satisfying part of his nature than was his sober intellect. Man was rediscovering the validity of his intuitions and of his emotions; he was, in particular, and for the express purpose of comedy, becoming intellectually aware that the tumultuous condition of his being which followed his falling in love and urged him on to woo was in fact no mean and mainly physical manifestation of his personality; it was, in fact, the awakening in him of the fuller capacities of his spirit.

So, amongst the themes of Elizabethan comedy, love had now justified its primacy. It had willy-nilly always been the major interest. But, as the earlier comedies have shown, its usurpations had been hazardous for the spirit of comedy. It had hitherto forced itself into a Pyrrhic triumph as an alien invader backed only by the forces of popular preference. It could now rightly take its place in Elizabethan comedy as the recognized presiding genius. It was the touchstone by which fine spirits were struck to their finest issues. It was also, of course, a test by which weaker mortals revealed their weakness, grosser ones their grossness, and foolish ones their folly. It is noteworthy, however, that though these three great comedies are even more exclusively the plays of lovers and their wooing than are the earlier ones, seldom does Shakespeare allow their wooing to express itself through the full gamut of its lyric modulations. Its utterance is adapted to a dramatic, and, indeed, to a comic scene: depth of affection is displayed rather by hints and by deeds than by the conventional phrase of the love poet. The homily of love from its gentle pulpiters is felt to be tedious, and is seldom allowed to weary its hearers. Often, indeed, when the wooing itself is an extended episode of the story, it is camouflaged in circumstances shaped by the wooers to cover their real passion. Beatrice and Benedick deliberately adopt a kind of inverted technique of love-making; and for them, the normal idiom of lovers is feigned by others so as to be overheard by the two who are to be the victims of the device. Rosalind, disguised as Ganymede, pretends to be herself in order to teach Orlando to woo. Viola expresses her own love only by innuendo, and finds a sort of outlet for her inhibition, as well as a gratification for her own sense of restraint, in unfolding to Olivia the passion of the Duke's love, as if hallooing her name to the reverberate hills to make the babbling gossip of the air cry out 'Olivia'. But having done this, Viola will find it easier to be her natural self. 'I took great pains to study it, and 'tis poetical.' In the throes of her own love, she will revert to sanity.

Indeed, deeply as these heroines fall in love, no person in the plays is more aware of the follies into which love may delude its victims. It is Rosalind who reproves the foolish shepherd Silvius for following Phebe like foggy south puffing with wind and rain:

> 'tis such fools as you
> That make the world full of ill-favoured children.
> *As You Like It*, III. 5. 52–3

But she will advise silly giddy-brained Phebe to go down on her knees and thank heaven fasting for a good man's love. Lunacy and love are yet not entirely different diseases. 'Love is merely a madness, and, I tell you, deserves as well a dark house and a whip as madmen do: and the reason why they are not so punished and cured is, that the lunacy is so ordinary that the whippers are in love too.' Madness, but inevitable madness: and a madness in which the visions are a mingling of revelation and of hallucination. Who shall know which is which? Who better than the one who knows most of the frequency of hallucination? Rosalind is well aware of what may be falsely claimed for love, so well aware that she can make mock of the possibilities: 'the poor world is almost six thousand years old, and in all this time there was not any man died in his own person, videlicet, in a love cause. Troilus had his brains dashed out with a Grecian club; yet he did what he could to die before, and he is one of the patterns of love. Leander, he would have lived many a fair year, though Hero had turned nun, if it had not been for a hot midsummer night; for, good youth, he went but forth to wash him in the Hellespont and being taken with the cramp was drowned: and the foolish chroniclers of that age found it was "Hero of Sestos". But these are all lies: men have died from time to time and worms have eaten them, but not for love.' Yet there is no wrestling with Rosalind's affections, when they take the part of the man with whom she has fallen desperately and suddenly in love.

Rosalind, Viola, and, to a less extent, Beatrice, are Shakespeare's images of the best way of love. They, and the men in whom they inspire love, are Shakespeare's representation of the office of love to lift mankind to a richer life. So, by the entry into it of love, not only has the world of these comedies become a bigger world: the men and women who inhabit it have become finer and richer representatives of human nature. They have entered into the possession of spiritual endowments which, if hitherto suspected to exist at all, had either been distrusted as dangerous or had become moribund through desuetude. They have claimed the intuitive, the subconscious, and the emotional as instruments by which personality may bring itself into a fuller consciousness of and a completer harmony with the realities of existence. They have left Theseus far behind; they have also outgrown Falstaff.

But if the new world of these mature comedies is one of which Falstaff could never have attained the mastery, there is yet room in it for much even of the corporeal and for all of the immortal parts of him. He is relegated, however, to his proper place therein. Perhaps Sir Toby is as much of him as will survive a final approbation. To both Toby and Falstaff, care is the chief enemy of life; its main sustenance is capons and canary. Their values are much the same: Falstaff's deepest contempt is for a brewer's horse; Sir Toby's symbol of a world without life is an unfilled can. Both live by their wits, deluding the gullible into disbursing. 'Let's to bed, knight; thou hadst need send for money.' But if Toby never attains the plenitude of Falstaff's dominion, at least he escapes rejection, and achieves ultimately a more settled survival. He lives on under the leading or misleading strings of Maria: and, characteristically, this is a kindly fate into which he was inveigled by his admiration for the devilry of Maria's wit. It is Toby, too, who puts into words the most pertinent principle which can be propounded in defence of the Falstaffian life, a principle which goes beyond the mere assertion of high spirits and acclaims the cordial law of tolerance: 'because thou art virtuous, shall there be no more cakes and ale?'

But the acceptance of Toby as an integral part of the ideal world of romantic comedy does not fully indicate how much of the essential virtue of Falstaff Shakespeare, after the antipathy of his dark comedies, endeavoured to find permanently serviceable to humanity. For Toby has not the full measure of Falstaff's wit. Perhaps Beatrice of *Much Ado* is Shakespeare's completest picture of the way in which sheer wit may serve the cause of human sanity in human society and thereby extend the scope of its possible happiness. But whereas it is only Falstaff's wit which prompts him sportingly to plead instinct as a final protection, it is the complete surrender of wit and the actual resort to instinct which makes Beatrice the instrument of happiness in the crucial moment of the plot of *Much Ado*. Still, it may well be that in the make-up of Beatrice, allying the exercise of wit with the innate geniality of a disposition born under a star which laughed, Shakespeare was giving such intellectual agility as was Falstaff's its opportunity to display how much of real human good it was capable of effecting. But even Beatrice — and we take her to have been grafted by Shakespeare on to an earlier play of his own which thus became *Much Ado* — even Beatrice has not grown into the full liberality of Rosalind's and Viola's humanity, close as her birth must have been to theirs. She is the direct counterpart of Helena, and perhaps her next successor: and she in turn was followed almost at once by Rosalind and Viola.

Technically, the most remarkable achievement of Beatrice is that, with hardly anything at all to do in what is nominally the main plot, she nevertheless becomes the chief figure of the piece, and the primary instigator of the sentiment which leads to the happy solution of the story. She is a lively symbol of the new state of affairs in the domain of comedy. The hero has been dethroned, losing not only his rank but something also of personality; he has been replaced by the heroine. It is a commonplace that the main men of these comedies are but pygmies compared in stature with the heroines. Moreover, these ladies are not only the heroines in the material and formal sense that they have most of the scenes of the play. They are heroines in the sense that they provide the efficient force which resolves the dilemma of the play into happiness.

That happiness is palpably a state of affairs which, in so far as it springs from human effort, is specifically an outcome of their making.

Nor is it difficult to see the virtue by which they are the bringers of so much joy. Shakespeare's enthronement of woman as queen of comedy is no mere accident, and no mere gesture of conventional gallantry. Because they are women, these heroines have attributes of personality fitting them more certainly than men to shape the world towards happiness. His menfolk, a Hamlet or a Macbeth or an Othello, may have a subtler intellect, a more penetrating imagination, or a more irresistible passion. But what they have more largely in one kind of personal endowment, they own only at the expense of other properties no less essential to the encountering of such varied circumstances as are presented by the act of living. These heroes, in effect, are out of harmony with themselves, and so are fraught with the certainty of tragic doom. Their personality is a mass of mighty forces out of equipoise: they lack the balance of a durable spiritual organism. It was in women that Shakespeare found this equipoise, this balance which makes personality in action a sort of ordered interplay of the major components of human nature. In his women, hand and heart and brain are fused in a vital and practicable union, each contributing to the other, no one of them permanently pressing demands to the detriment of the other, yet each asserting itself periodically to exercise its vitality, even if the immediate effect be a temporary disturbance of equilibrium, for not otherwise will they be potent to exercise their proper function when the whole of their owner's spiritual nature is struck into activity. Perhaps it was primarily because Shakespeare found women more sensitive to intuition and more responsive to emotion that he first promoted them to dominion in the realm of comedy. He found, moreover, in their instincts a kind of finely developed mother-wit, a variety of humanized common-sense which, because it was impregnated with humane feeling, was more apt to lay hold of the essential realities of existence than was the more rarified and isolated intellect of man. But, though it was what to this extent may be called their essential feminity which gave his heroines their first claims to rulership in comedy, Shakespeare insisted in his maturest comedies that all the qualities which his heroines owed to the promptings of intuition and instinct were only certainly beneficent in human affairs when instinct and intuition were guided by a mind in which a sublimated common-sense had established itself as the habitual director of action and behaviour.

It is unnecessary here to attempt to describe these heroines one by one, or even to name in detail all their generic traits. It will be enough to indicate one or two of their characteristic virtues. They have all the gift of inspiring and of returning affection. They have the good-will of all who know them. They are simply human and patently natural in their response to emotional crises like that of falling in love. Rosalind's excitement when she first meets Orlando is as palpable as are her transparent endeavours to hide it. Their own passion still further sharpens the affection through which they seek the good of others. Once they are conscious of their own desire they are master-hands in reaching it. Rosalind is the main plotter of the flight to Arden; it is she who devises the means of ensuring Orlando's frequent company. Viola resolves at once to remedy her lot by taking service with the Duke; and immediately becomes his confidant and his private minister. She overcomes all the ceremonial obstacles which bar access to Olivia, using, when need be, the bluster and the rudeness which she learns from her opponents. She seizes a situation on the instant; and even when the outcome is not clearly to be foreseen, she acts in a manner which will save unnecessary suffering to others: 'she took the ring of me,' is her lie to Malvolio, guessing at once how the distraught Olivia had tried to hide her device from her steward and messenger. In crises, all of them, Rosalind, Viola, and Beatrice, are guided by intuitive insight. Beatrice acclaims Hero's innocence in the face of damning evidence. Viola judges her ship's captain by the same inner vision, and she confides in him implicitly. Yet the instinct and the intuition are always open-eyed and cautiously safeguarded against mere casual vagary or whimsical sentimentality. When Viola judges the captain's worth by his fair and outward character, she remembers that nature with a beauteous wall doth oft close in pollution. Rosalind and Celia are equally immune from this widespread romantic fallacy. They know that there is no certain and predictable relation between

341

beauty and honesty in mankind: they would have laughingly recommended all the Tennysonian moralists of their day, who thought beauty to be either truth or virtue, to stroll through the equivalent of their West End after the theatres were shut and when the restaurants were coming to the end of their cabarets. Yet, with all the efficiency and savoir faire of which these heroines prove themselves to be possessed, they are amazingly modest. It is this modesty which prevents them from endeavouring to compass what is beyond mortal reach. Fortune, they know, is but a blind worker; and she doth most mistake in her gifts to woman. Viola undoubtedly is confident, but not over-confident: she will do what she can, but

> O time! thou must untangle this, not I;
> It is too hard a knot for me to untie.
>
> *Twelfth Night*, II. 2. 38–9

And Rosalind never forgets how full of briers is this work-a-day world. But in the end, they triumph; and they triumph because they are just what they are, the peculiar embodiment in personality of those traits of human nature which render human beings most lovable, most loving, and most serviceable to the general good.

But these ladies are not only doers and inspirers of action. Merely by their presence in the play, they serve as standards whereby degrees of worth and worthlessness in other characters are made manifest. Hence the rich variety of theme, of episode, and of person in these plays is knit together and holds as a coherent structure. The beneficence of emotion and of intuition is no wise belittled by the revelation of the follies which spring from feeling in less stable creatures than are the heroines. So, *Twelfth Night* is largely occupied with the disclosure of unbalanced sentiment. There is the enervating sentimentality of Orsino, there is the unrestrained emotionalism of Olivia. *As You Like It* handles an allied theme by its exposure of merely conventional pastoralism. Indeed, once the positive construction of their larger world has been effected by the heroines, there is no place, not only for their own safeguards for it, such as this perpetual alertness to expose the dangers of unbalanced sentiment, there is also place for the sort of direct satire and the forthright comicality which were the manner of the older classical tradition. Just as Sir Toby finds his station in *Twelfth Night*, so do Andrew and even Malvolio; there, in Andrew's case, simply to display his own foolish inanity as do the witless in all sorts of comedy; and in Malvolio's, to enter almost as Jonson gave his characters entry, for a more subtle but still classical kind of discomfiture. As Malvolio in *Twelfth Night*, so Jaques in *As You Like It*, another of the few attempts of Shakespeare to project malcontentism for comic purposes. Besides these, traditional clowns may now also play their part, whether the English Shakespearian ones of the tribe of Bottom, such as Dogberry and Verges, or the more technical ones, Feste and Touchstone, grown now by contact with natural Costards into something more substantial and more homely than the mere traditional corrupters of words, and therefore playing not the part of an added funny interlude, but an essential role in the orientation of the idea of comedy. 'Since the little wit that fools have was silenced, the little foolery that wise men have makes a great show.' The true fool's return is restorative. A fool of his sort will use his folly like a stalking-horse, and under the presentation of that, will shoot his wit. Yet his range will necessarily be limited now. Only the crassest folly falls to such arrows, for those who have become expert in human traffickings can assume an easy indifference to simple and direct hits:

> He that a fool doth very wisely hit
> Doth very foolishly, although he smart,
> Not to seem senseless of the bob; if not,
> The wise man's folly is anatomized
> Even by the squandering glances of the fool.
> *As You Like It*, II. 7. 53–7

Thus the motley of romantic comedies is subtler than the slap-dash skittle-knocking of the satire in classical comedy. Their reformatory way, too, is fundamentally different from the simple exposure of ludicrous abnormality which had been the approved manner of older comedy. They entice to a richer wisdom by alluring the imagination into desire for larger delights. They are not mainly concerned to whip offenders into conventional propriety by scorn and by mockery. They persuade one to the better state by presenting it in all its attractiveness: they depict a land of heart's desire, and, doing that, reveal the way of human and natural magic by which it is to be attained.

from *Shakespearian Comedy* by H. B. Charlton, 1938

Suggestions for Further Reading

C. L. Barber: *Shakespeare's Festive Comedy*. As well as its treatment of particular plays, this book is invaluable for the general view of festive comedy which it advances. Barber explores the relationship between comedy and holiday. Starting from evidence of festive customs in sixteenth-century England, he moves through Nashe (*Summer's Last Will and Testament*) to Shakespeare. Holiday is a social custom in which normal responsibilities are replaced by misrule; comedy, in the hands of a serious dramatist, both expresses such release, and explores its relation to reality.

J. R. Brown: *Shakespeare and his Comedies*. Traces a number of themes through the comedies under the headings of 'Love's Wealth', 'Love's Truth', 'Love's Order'.

Nevill Coghill: 'The Basis of Shakespearean Comedy' (*Essays and Studies*, 1950, reprinted in *Shakespeare Criticism 1935–1960*, World's Classics). Treats Shakespeare and Jonson as the culmination of two comic traditions, the romantic, or medieval, and the satiric, or Renaissance.

Barbara Everett: '*Much Ado About Nothing*' (*Critical Quarterly*, Winter 1961). Much of this essay deals with Shakespeare's comedies as a whole, suggesting that 'the expression of humane principle, of generous and constant feeling, comes principally from the women'.

Cyrus Hoy: *The Hyacinth Room: An Investigation into the Nature of Comedy, Tragedy, and Tragicomedy*. Emphasizes the resemblances between comedy and tragedy. Hoy belongs with those critics who feel comedy to be the more profound.

Sir Barry Jackson: 'Producing the Comedies', in *Shakespeare Survey* 8. A delightful description of changing styles in Shakespearean theatre since the 1890s, with accounts of actual productions, some seen, others directed, by the author.

T. M. Parrott: *Shakespearean Comedy*. Scholarly, balanced, uneccentric.

Janet Spens: *An Essay on Shakespeare's Relation to Tradition*. The 'tradition' is folk-tradition, and the essay belongs to the school that goes back immediately to Gilbert Murray, and ultimately to *The Golden Bough* – and forward to the much more subtle work of Northrop Frye and C. L. Barber.

D. L. Stevenson: *The Love Game Comedy*. Tries to distinguish the frankly romantic (even escapist) comedies – *The Merchant of Venice, Twelfth Night* – from the love-game comedies that play antagonistic attitudes to love against each other, that analyse what romantic comedy accepts. The love-game comedies appeal to the ironic thinker, and 'they appeal because they suggest that there is an essentially comic unity to be found in inherent opposites, that the basic incongruity between what is possible in love and what is desired is amusing and therefore can be endured'.

J. DOVER WILSON: *Shakespeare's Happy Comedies*. An easy-going work of criticism at the end of a long scholarly career.

MORE ABOUT PENGUINS

If you have enjoyed reading this book you may wish to know that *Penguin Book News* appears every month. It is an attractively illustrated magazine containing a complete list of books published by Penguins and still in print, together with details of the month's new books. A specimen copy will be sent free on request.

Penguin Book News is obtainable from most bookshops; but you may prefer to become a regular subscriber at 3s. for twelve issues. Just write to Dept EP, Penguin Books Ltd, Harmondsworth, Middlesex, enclosing a cheque or postal order, and you will be put on the mailing list.

Some other books published by Penguins are described on the following pages.

Note: *Penguin Book News* is not
available in the U.S.A., Canada or Australia.

The first volume in the new *Penguin Shakespeare Library*

SHAKESPEARE AND THE IDEA
OF THE PLAY

ANNE RIGHTER

What was Shakespeare's attitude towards the theatre? How far did he share contemporary assumptions about the stage, and in what respects was he an experimental dramatist?

In this book Anne Righter discusses Shakespeare's plays in relation to sixteenth century dramatic ideas, and considers how the relationship between actors and audience changed after the Medieval plays. Shakespeare's plays are covered chronologically under such topics as the play metaphor and its proliferation into figures of shadows and dreams; the player king; the plot devices of deceit and disguise; and the use of the actor image in the major tragedies. Mrs Righter argues that Shakespeare finally developed a strong revulsion from the theatre which is reflected in the imagery of his last plays.

'I have never before read a book (is there one?) which invited me to consider Shakespeare's achievement from this point of view. The result is one of those extremely rare critical works that change one's attitude towards the subject' – John Wain in the *Observer*

LIFE IN SHAKESPEARE'S ENGLAND

JOHN DOVER WILSON

Many people who have learned to enjoy Shakespeare feel they would like to know more about his life and times, and this authoritive book, reprinted again in Pelicans, is the answer. It is not a biographical study, but an anthology collected from many contemporary sources so as to illuminate the conditions, the appearance, the habits, pastimes, and beliefs of Shakespeare's time. Professor Dover Wilson's method of assembling this panorama of the period is to pin-point the clues provided by scores of passages in the plays and follow them up by relevant supporting evidence from what we nowadays call the 'documentary' writers of the time. Thus we are able to see city and countryside, school and university, court and theatre, as the man of Shakespeare's day saw them with his own eyes. We observe at close quarters his sports, his superstitions, his daily life at home or abroad, his experiences in childhood and age. Actor, sailor, courtier, traveller, and beggar relate, in their own words, what living was like in the great days of sixteenth-century England.

THE LIFE OF SHAKESPEARE

F. E. HALLIDAY

On 26 April 1564 'Gulielmus filius Johannes Shakspere' was christened at Holy Trinity Church at Stratford-upon-Avon, and on 25 April 1616 'Will Shakspere, gent' was buried at the same church. In between lived the man we know as William Shakespeare.

Modern scholarship has enormously enriched our understanding of Shakespeare's plays and of the world in which he moved and wrote, yet it is now ten years since the last full-scale biography of Shakespeare was written. Mr Halliday, using recent research – in particular the work of Leslie Hotson and T. W. Baldwin – steers a lively course between the meagre dust of contemporary records and the higher fancies of Shakespeare's 'lost years'.

'A quick-moving and workmanlike biography...admirably compact and comprehensive . . . we are given as much information as others have provided in twice the length' – Ivor Brown in the *Observer*

The companion to this book

SHAKESPEARE'S TRAGEDIES

LAURENCE LERNER

Shakespeare's tragedies have always been fertile acres for comment and criticism. The same dramas which inspired a Keats to write poetry appealed to A. C. Bradley – or to Ernest Jones, the psycho-analyst – as studies of character; and where the New Criticism has been principally interested in language and imagery, other critics in America have seen the plays as superb examples of plot and structure. Most of Aristotle's elements of tragedy have found their backers, and – as the editor points out in his introduction – these varying approaches to Shakespeare are by no means incompatible.

In what *The Times Literary Supplement* described as an 'excellent collection' Laurence Lerner has assembled the best examples of the modern schools of criticism and arranged them according to the plays they deal with. With its 'Suggestions for Further Reading' and the general sections on tragedy, this is a book which will stimulate the serious reader and do much to illuminate Shakespearian drama.